二语写作

Chinese Journal of Second Language Writing

主编　王俊菊

第七辑

外语教学与研究出版社
FOREIGN LANGUAGE TEACHING AND RESEARCH PRESS
北京 BEIJING

2023

图书在版编目（CIP）数据

二语写作. 第七辑. 2023 / 王俊菊主编. -- 北京 ：外语教学与研究出版社，2024. 6. -- ISBN 978-7-5213-5316-7

I. H05-53

中国国家版本馆 CIP 数据核字第 2024KU6563 号

《二语写作》第七辑（2023）

ERYU XIEZUO

出 版 人　王　芳
责任编辑　陈　阳
责任校对　周　娜
封面设计　李　高　彩奇风
出版发行　外语教学与研究出版社
社　　址　北京市西三环北路 19 号（100089）
网　　址　https://www.fltrp.com
印　　刷　北京九州迅驰传媒文化有限公司
开　　本　787×1092　1/16
印　　张　9.5
字　　数　212 千字
版　　次　2024 年 6 月第 1 版
印　　次　2024 年 6 月第 1 次印刷
书　　号　ISBN 978-7-5213-5316-7
定　　价　40.00 元

如有图书采购需求，图书内容或印刷装订等问题，侵权、盗版书籍等线索，请拨打以下电话或关注官方服务号：
客服电话：400 898 7008
官方服务号：微信搜索并关注公众号“外研社官方服务号”
外研社购书网址：https://fltrp.tmall.com

物料号：353160001

记载人类文明
沟通世界文化
www.fltrp.com

《二语写作》第七辑

（2023 年 12 月）

目录

Contents

卷首语

人工智能的迅猛发展对写作领域产生了深刻影响，技术赋能下的二语写作教学与研究受到学界越来越多的关注。在此背景下，国内外学者不断探索新理论、新方法、新实践，在二语写作超语实践、二语写作情绪、二语写作教学技术、二语写作教学模式、二语写作与思辨能力等诸多领域积极开拓，取得丰硕的研究成果。《二语写作》第七辑重点关注上述话题，并在“研究述评”“写作教学”“写作研究”和“新作评介”等栏目中展示多位学者的最新研究成果。

本期的“研究述评”栏目重点关注多模态写作、超语写作和写作情绪等话题。Emily Di ZHANG、Chunhong LIU和Shulin YU采用范围综述法，梳理数字多模态二语写作的研究焦点，对当前研究主题和方法进行讨论，指出未来研究的发展趋势，以期促进数字化多模态二语写作在教学中的应用。Li ZHANG、Yachao SUN和Ruiyun SUN探讨了二语写作中超语实践的概念，阐述超语实践的积极影响及其面临的挑战，呼吁通过进一步实证研究评估其有效性，促进写作教学实践的包容性。胡萍萍和王雨钦基于2013—2022年中国知网中的相关文献，借助CiteSpace软件，利用文献计量分析法梳理了国内二语写作焦虑研究的现状与趋势。

“写作教学”栏目重点关注二语写作教学策略、教学模式和实践场景等话题。杨熙以“后方法”教学理论为理论框架，探索“混合教学”背景下教师教学策略的发展与变化，对写作教学发展提供启示。陈宁阳从双语体裁视角出发，考察新手作者汉英学术写作的实践场景、体裁知识储备及其双语写作实践中体裁知识的应用情况。吴琼基于对学术英语的规约性、社会性、情境性、动态性和开放性的认知，开展思辨性博士生学术英语写作教学，发现该教学模式对博士生学术英语写作具有明显的促进作用。

“写作研究”栏目重点关注写作支持、协同写作等话题。Jing ZHANG和Fan FANG通过混合研究法调查中国一所师范类高校学生对英语写作支持的自感需求、求助行为以及对英语写作中心的使用和感受，为中国高校个性化写作支持的发展提出相关建议。杨晋将协作学习引入职场英语写作的课堂教学，发现协作学习对不同写作水平的学生均产生积极影响。

“新作评介”栏目重点关注二语写作中的技术运用这一崭新话题。杜宇通过评价《二语写作中的技术运用：撰写、翻译、教学与数据驱动学习的进展》一书，梳理了机器翻译、在线反馈及多模态写作等多元技术手段与二语写作的结合，重点讨论了当前二语写作领域中主流技术手段的应用及其效果，对技术手段在写作教学与研究中的应用具有重要启示。

作为本刊特色，本辑整理出2023年国内出版和发表的二语写作相关书籍和期刊文章，便于读者把握该领域的最新发展动态。

以上栏目各具特色，视角多元，立足学术前沿，运用量化、混合、质性等方法，解决二语写作教学中的实际问题，探究二语写作研究热点和未来发展方向。

热切期待国内外学者踊跃投稿，为二语写作研究与教学提供学术支持。本刊也将一如既往地为广大学者和一线教师提供学术平台，鼓励学术交流，展示学术成果，助力中国二语写作研究的蓬勃发展。

Digital Multimodal Composing in a Second Language Context: A Scoping Review of Research

Emily Di Zhang[1] Chunhong Liu[2] Shulin Yu[3]

[1] Shanghai Jiao Tong University, China
[2] Simon Fraser University, Canada
[3] University of Macau, China

Abstract: Given that digital multimodal composing (DMC) has received increasing attention from researchers and teaching practitioners in second language (L2) learning contexts, this study employed the scoping review method and explored the overall landscape of the current scholarship on L2 DMC. Following a constant comparison approach, we found three themes from the literature: (1) the "learning" of DMC; (2) the "teaching" of DMC; (3) the "assessing" of DMC. Discussion on the thematical and methodological issues in the current DMC research was presented, and directions for future research were discussed. This review could deepen our understanding of L2 DMC by sketching out what and how current research has found about DMC, and it also illustrates the learning and teaching affordances embedded in DMC practices.

Keywords: digital multimodal composing; scoping review; educational technology; research synthesis; writing instruction

DOI: 10.20081/j.cnki.cjslw.2023.07.001

1. Introduction

In the digital age, the ubiquitous use of technology has challenged the conception of writing and writing pedagogies (Hafner 2013; Yi et al. 2017). The traditional language- or text-based monomodal approach to literacy now appears narrow because of the wide range of semiotic modes involved in meaning making in the contemporary communicative landscape (Nelson & Kern 2012). Given this, much attention has been directed at DMC, a meaning-making process that involves the use of digital tools to facilitate communication and combines multiple semiotic modes like words, images, sounds, and gestures (Bezemer & Kress 2008; Jiang 2017). The multimodal products can take the form of academic posters, picture books, brochures, graphic novels, PowerPoint slides, video documentaries, or webpages (Hafner & Ho 2020; Jiang 2017). According to Hafner (2013), DMC is characterized by: (1) new forms of meaning representation such as hypertext and multimedia; (2) collaboration and remix; and (3) accessibility to wide, authentic online audiences. Regarding its pedagogical values, DMC is believed to facilitate success for students in the digital, global world (Kress 2003; New London Group 1996) and has been widely employed in L2 learning classrooms. As observed by Lotherington and Jenson (2011), DMC enables a new way of approaching L2 literacy as a multidimensional construct that acknowledges learners' agency and ownership in mobilizing their semiotic resources in their L1 and/or L2. Empirical studies have suggested that DMC could afford L2 learner/writer development in various aspects, for example, semiotic awareness (Nelson 2006), identity construction (Honcyford 2014), authorial voice (Hafner 2014; Hepple et al. 2014), learning and writing motivation (Hafner & Miller 2011; Jiang & Luk 2016), and genre or audience awareness (Cimasko & Shin 2017). Hence, it is of great necessity to equip learners with adequate DMC skills.

While there is a proliferation of studies on DMC in L2 contexts, its overall research landscape is largely unknown due to a limited number of relevant synthesis studies. Li and Akoto (2021) reviewed studies concerning the DMC practices of L2 learners. After a comprehensive examination of contexts and participants, technologies and tasks, and major findings of L2 DMC studies, they identified three major strands of research: students' composing process, their perceptions of DMC, and the influences of DMC. Their review revealed the current practices and research of DMC in L2 contexts, thus providing more supporting evidence for its facilitative role in enhancing writing literacy, identity formation, and L2 competence. However, this review mainly approached DMC from students' perspective, and how teachers would perceive, implement, and assess DMC projects was not fully discussed. Smith et al. (2021) recently reviewed research on secondary school emergent bilingual students' DMC practices, and they identified five major themes, i.e., identity expression and agency, reshaping classroom spaces, developing as multimodal designers, expanding linguistic repertoires, and multimodal composing-to-learn. Their review presented a holistic picture regarding the benefits of DMC for emergent bilingual students at a lower grade. However, it should be noted that DMC is also incorporated into writing instruction in higher education (e.g., Cimasko & Shin 2017; Hafner 2014; Jiang 2017). A similar review study was conducted by Zhang et al. (2023), but focused on post-secondary L2 settings.

Albeit the three illuminating research syntheses, it remains unknown regarding the extent and nature of current research on DMC in L2 contexts. Given this, this present study employs a scoping review method and synthesizes the methodological considerations and research topics pertaining to the field of L2 DMC. A scoping review is a research synthesis approach that could "examine the extent, range, and nature of research activity in a topic area; determine the value and potential scope and cost of undertaking a full systematic review; summarize and disseminate research findings; and identify research gaps in the existing literature" (Pham et al. 2014: 371-372). It is particularly valuable when a research field (in this case, DMC in L2 contexts) witnesses an emergence of extensive, complex, and heterogeneous findings (Peters et al. 2015). This review could provide a comprehensive picture of L2 DMC research and identify potential researchable gaps that warrant further exploration.

Following Arksey and O'Malley's (2005) methodological framework, the present review was conducted in five stages: identifying research questions, retrieving relevant studies, selecting studies for review, charting the data, and collating, summarizing, and reporting the results. First, as the scoping review aims to map the breadth of evidence in scholarship (Arksey & O'Malley 2005), a broad question was proposed to guide the review: What has been researched in the existing literature on DMC in an L2 context? Ambitious as it is, this question could help the researchers to reduce the possibility of missing some relevant works and to form a comprehensive understanding of the current research landscape of DMC in L2. Figure 1 presents the overall process for searching, screening, evaluating, and including relevant articles for the review. To retrieve relevant articles, three major electronic databases were used: Scopus, Web of Science, and the Educational Resources Information Centre (ERIC). Search results were limited to English-medium peer-reviewed journal articles focusing on DMC. Keywords used for the search included: "digital multimodal composing", "multiliteracies", "multimodality", "multimodal writing", "multimodal compositions", "digital writing", and "new literacy". To ensure a sufficient pool of articles, no restriction was placed on the time span except the cutoff date in April 2023 when the sampling started. The retrieved articles were then screened and assessed through a close reading of their titles and abstracts. Duplicates and articles not relevant to L2 DMC were excluded. The full text of the remaining articles was collected and examined to ensure their eligibility to be included in the review.

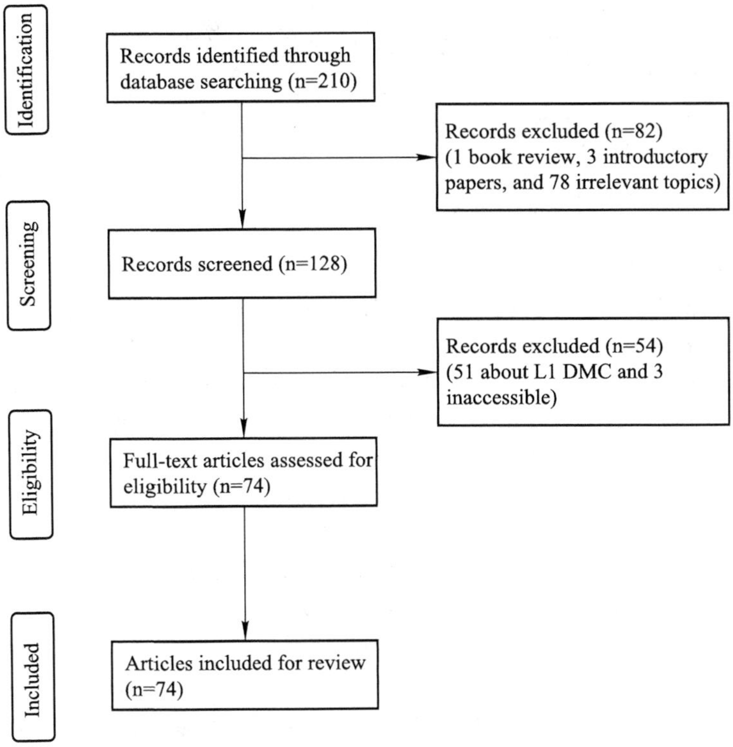

Figure 1. The flowchart of data screening

Finally, 74 articles were included in the final sample for the review. To ensure that the "'outcome' is contextualized and more understandable to readers" (Arksey & O'Malley 2005: 26), the finalized set of articles was then charted with their key bibliographic and methodological information (author, publication date, research context, participants, methods, and data sources) recorded in a spreadsheet. The analysis of the articles followed open coding and axial coding. Free nodes were first used to describe the major themes of these studies, and multiple codes were allowed where a study concerned more than one research theme. For example, the research by Jiang and Luk (2016) was found to involve two research topics, the "learning" and the "teaching" of DMC. The follow-up axial coding employed a consistent comparison approach through which the coding of the selected articles was constantly compared and modified, a process by which a refined categorization was identified regarding the prevalent research topics in the current scholarship of DMC.

2. Thematic Interpretation of Extant DMC Research

This section illustrates the three major themes in the current landscape of L2 DMC research. They are the "learning", "teaching", and "assessing" of DMC. The statistics of each research strand are provided in Table 1.

Table 1. Three major lines of research on DMC

Category	***n***	**%**
The "learning" of DMC	48	64.9%
The "teaching" of DMC	15	20.3%
The "assessing" of DMC	11	14.9%

2.1 The "learning" of DMC

The "learning" of DMC concerns its affordances for L2 learners, as well as possible challenges. The reviewed studies have found advantages of DMC pedagogy related to its educational, social, and technological affordances. However, it was also found that DMC might elicit negative feelings among students due to its possible incompatibility with the exam-oriented learning context.

Regarding educational affordance, earlier studies have found that DMC could improve L2 students' linguistic skills, such as vocabulary learning (Goulah 2007; Hava 2021; Lee et al. 2021; Yeh 2018), listening skill (Verdugo & Belmonte 2007), speaking skill (Hava 2021; Hwang et al. 2016; Somdee & Suppasetseree 2007), reading skill, and writing skill (Castañeda 2013; Dzekoe 2017; Hava 2021; Lee 2014; Smythe & Neufeld 2010; Timucin & Irgin 2015; Vandommele et al. 2017; Vorobel & Kim 2017). DMC facilitated L2 students' writing skills by helping them achieve greater clarity and advanced argumentation (Zhang & O'Halloran 2019), enhancing genre or audience awareness (Castañeda 2013; Cimasko & Shin 2017; Dzekoe 2017; Jiang & Luk 2016; Kim 2017; Smythe & Neufeld 2010; Zhang & Yu 2023a), expressivity (Kim & Li 2021; Lam 2000; Lee et al. 2021; Timucin & Irgin 2015; Yang &

Wu 2012), and authorial voice (Dzekoe 2017; Hafner 2015; Lee et al. 2021; Nelson 2006; Yang 2016).

DMC projects conduced to some psychological aspects of L2 learning: DMC reduced low-proficiency L2 students' learning anxiety (Kang & Kim 2019; Kim & Belcher 2020; Ono 2014), raised L2 students' learning motivation (Hafner & Miller 2011; Hava 2021; Jiang 2017; Jiang & Luk 2016; Kim & Belcher 2020; Lee 2014; Li 2020; Pardo 2014; Torres et al. 2012; Yoon 2013; Vorobel & Kim 2017; Zhang & Yu 2023a), self-efficacy (Yang & Wu 2012), learner autonomy (Hafner & Miller 2011; Jiang & Luk 2016; Jiang 2017; Kim 2014; Lee et al. 2021), and increased their enjoyment in L2 learning (Goulah 2007; Hava 2021; Kim & Belcher 2020). DMC also enhanced L2 students' classroom performance by enabling student active class participation (Jiang 2017; Lee 2014; Yoon 2013), engaging students with authentic learning tasks (Castañeda 2013; Jiang 2017), connecting their in-class and out-of-class literacy practices (Burke & Hardware 2015), realizing effective learning of the course content (Jiang 2017; Li 2020), and increasing their investment in L2 learning (Jiang & Luk 2016; Jiang et al. 2020). It also improved students' high-order skills, such as critical thinking ability (Ono 2014; Yang & Wu 2012), multiliteracies (Dogan & Robin 2009; Goulah 2007; Jiang 2017; Vinogradova et al. 2011; Yeh 2018), and creativity (Goulah 2007; Kim & Li 2021; Smythe & Neufeld 2010).

In terms of the social affordance of DMC, early literature found that DMC could foster peer interaction and collaboration (Hafner & Miller 2011; Jiang 2017; Jiang & Luk 2016; Li 2020; Ono 2014; Vorobel & Kim 2017), student-teacher interaction (Elola & Oskoz 2017; Jiang 2017; Jiang & Luk 2016), critical multimodal literacy to address sociopolitical issues (Janks 2010; Kendrick et al. 2006; Stein 2004), and civic participation (Jiang 2017; Jiang & Gu 2023). What's more, DMC was found to develop students' digital empathy (Jiang & Gao 2020) and prepare students for literate lives in the digital world (Hafner 2015). In addition, DMC could help students construct desirable identities, such as accomplished creators and readers of English texts (Black 2009), affinity identities within native communities, biliterate and bicultural identities (Cummins et al. 2015; Honeyford 2014), positive ethnic identities (Jiang & Ren 2020), disciplinary identities (Tardy 2005), and fantasy identities of "expert scientist", "reporter", and "traveler" (Hafner 2014). It was also reported that in DMC, students showcased the identities of agentive authors (Hull & Katz 2006), competent designers (Bailey 2009), outspoken and confident English-speaking college students (Cimasko & Shin 2017), thoughtful and creative authors (Lee 2014), renewed and projective identities (Goulah 2007), teacher identities (Kim & Li 2021), and secret agent identities (Hafner 2015).

The DMC project had technological affordances for L2 learners as well, such as displaying or exhibiting the work to people across time and distance, translating meaning from one mode to another (Jiang 2017), and helping students gain digital and multimedia skills while making videos (Hava 2021; Li 2020; Yeh 2018).

Despite the widely perceived affordances of DMC, L2 students also faced challenges in the DMC project. Kang and Kim (2019) found that some students were skeptical about

DMC and preferred monomodal writing to develop their ideas and think critically. Hava (2021) reported that some students viewed DMC to be time-consuming and difficult, which called for a basic level of English proficiency. In Vorobel and Kim's (2017) study, some students had concerns about hurting peers' feelings in the DMC projects and found it difficult to incorporate peer feedback and make revisions. In Jiang (2017), one focal case student failed to invest in the DMC project due to his feeling that DMC was a distraction from his goal of passing high-stakes English exams.

Thematically, the review showed that this line of studies takes up the majority of the studies on DMC (n=48, 64.9%), and the affordances of DMC focus on the educational and social affordances (n=44), while few studies have reported the technological affordances (n=4). The educational affordances cover monomodal linguistic skills, such as reading, listening, speaking, and writing skills, psychological aspects of L2 learning (e.g., motivation, anxiety, and enjoyment), classroom performance (e.g., class participation, content learning, and investment), and high-order thinking capacities (e.g., critical thinking and creativity). The social affordances include issues like learner identity construction, peer collaboration, digital activism, and so forth. That said, students also pronounced concerns and challenges about DMC, which warrants attention from teachers and researchers.

Methodologically, most studies are qualitative (n=37) with data collected from interviews, questionnaires, reflections, and documents, while quantitative studies (n=4) and mixed-methods studies (n=7) are rare. Of the qualitative studies, some adopted the case study approach (n=22) or ethnography (n=5), and others (n=10) did not specify the approaches, indicating a lack of methodological diversity in the current DMC scholarship. While the qualitative research paradigm can afford rich and thick data (Lotherington et al. 2001), it is limited in providing generalizable information. Hence, more quantitative research is needed. A mixed-methods approach is also recommendable, which draws on insights from both qualitative and quantitative paradigms and minimizes both of their limitations, thus adding to the scientific rigor of DMC research. In addition, while most studies have reported the short-term affordances of DMC (e.g., over one semester), longitudinal studies that last more than one year have been rarely undertaken to explore whether DMC projects can have long-term affordances for students.

2.2 The "teaching" of DMC

The second line of studies focuses on teachers' perceptions towards the implementation of DMC in L2 classrooms (e.g., Hafner & Ho 2020; Jiang & Luk 2016; Jiang et al. 2020; Jiang et al. 2021; Kim & Belcher 2020; Thang et al. 2014; Yi & Choi 2015). It was found that teachers tended to acknowledge the value of DMC: It could motivate and engage students (Rance-Roney 2010; Ryan et al. 2010; Yi & Choi 2015), raise struggling students' confidence (Yi & Choi 2015), allow students to learn independently and critically (Rance-Roney 2010), and enable low-proficiency students to express themselves better and shackle the incompetent learner identity (Yi & Choi 2015). DMC also helped teachers learn about students' capabilities (Yi & Choi 2015), deepen their understanding of the teaching content (Rance-Roney 2010), and help them invest in using DMC as an instructional activity and construct new language teacher identities such as a guide, a change agent, and a peer mentor (Jiang et al. 2020).

However, concerns were also voiced by L2 teachers: The emphasis on non-linguistic semiotic modes might sidetrack students from the systematic learning of English vocabulary and grammar (Jiang & Ren 2020). Teachers were also worried that while students were enthusiastic about new technologies, students might merely address superficial aspects of the technology like speed and color, which is less likely to lead to significant learning (Ryan et al. 2010). Some teachers had growing anxiety as DMC added a burden to their jobs, and they needed to deal with a variety of technologies and available software and countless possibilities within them (Ryan et al. 2010). Teachers also encountered obstacles in implementing DMC projects, such as unreliable internet connection in the classroom (Almusharraf & Engemann 2020), resistance to technology (Thang et al. 2014), lack of systematic pedagogical training and insufficient preparation, materials, and resources (Farias & Veliz 2019), time constraints (Farias & Veliz 2019; Yi & Choi 2015), pressure of rigid curriculum and language-dominant standardized tests (Jiang et al. 2021; Yi & Angay-Crowder 2016; Yi & Choi 2015), concerns of DMC being not academic (Yi & Choi 2015), difficulties of assessing DMC projects (Hafner & Ho 2020; Yi & Choi 2015), and difficulties of establishing relevance of DMC to curriculum-mediated instruction, being digital novices, meeting students' diverse needs in composing, and high workload (Jiang et al. 2022).

Thematically, the review indicated that studies on the "teaching" of DMC mainly focus on teachers' perceptions of DMC, including the pedagogical benefits of DMC for learning and teaching, as well as the concerns and constraints of implementing DMC projects. However, merely 15 studies were conducted to address the "teaching" of DMC. As the implementers of DMC projects, teachers play an indispensable role in realizing the learning potential of DMC. As teachers' voices of launching DMC projects are compelling for teacher educators to come up with suggestions and solutions for the successful implementation of DMC, there is a pressing need to undertake more studies on teachers' views and experiences in DMC projects. What's more, few studies have examined the factors that might account for the differences in teachers' perceptions of DMC. Additionally, little is explored in terms of the DMC-related training for teachers in teacher education programs.

Methodologically, most of this strand of studies have adopted qualitative research methods (n=12), and few have tried out quantitative (n=1) and mixed-methods research designs (n=2). Of the studies with qualitative research methods, most did not specify the approaches they adopted. Plus, most studies were conducted over a semester, which is a relatively short term, as teachers' perceptions of DMC are not static and might undergo changes as time goes by.

2.3 The "assessing" of DMC

The last strand of DMC studies concerns the assessment of L2 students' DMC performance. Researchers have endeavored to clarify what and how to assess in DMC projects. Hung et al. (2012) developed a theory-based rubric to assess EFL junior university students' multimodal compositions in Taiwan, China. This rubric highlighted the *cohesion of modes* as its core, which ranges from level 5 (excellent cohesion) to level 1 (poor cohesion). However, only assessing cohesion may fail to provide a comprehensive picture of students' DMC performance. Hafner and Ho (2020) probed into teachers' practice of teaching and assessing DMC and found that their teacher participants highlighted *creativity and originality*, *organization*, *language*, *delivery*, *modal interaction*, *variety*, *and genre* in evaluating DMC products. Jiang et al. (2022) developed a genre-based rating scale to assess DMC performance, which entailed *purpose*, *base units* (i.e., multiple modes), *layout* (i.e., placement of multiple modes), *navigation* (i.e., structures), and *rhetoric* (i.e., meaning). Cheung (2023) adapted Jiang et al.'s (2022) genre-based model for DMC and proposed product- and process-oriented formative assessment rubrics to guide L2 students' self- and peer-assessment tools in a blog writing activity. The rubrics included *base units* (the accuracy and diversity of word choices, the clarity and creativity of the visual input, and the relevance of the video input), *layout* (the hierarchical structures and typographical/visual configurations of the base units), *navigation* (reader expectations, communicative purpose, and writer-reader relationships with student stance and reader engagement), and *rhetoric* (relations of meaning between and within the base units). The process orientation of the rubrics centered around equality (whether students collectively discuss and make decisions in anchoring the directions of writing and whether they make equal contributions to the project) and mutuality (whether students address each other's ideas, handle task-related problems, and encourage each other during the process of DMC). Judging the quality of student writings and their discussion, the product-oriented assessment rubric was reported to lead to significant improvement in *layout*, *navigation*, and *rhetoric*, and the process-oriented rubric also enhanced the equality and mutuality of the collaborative process.

Zhang and Yu (2023b) explored DMC competence from the perspective of L2 students who had first-hand participatory experiences in designing DMC works, and they discovered that the students tapped into the *utilization of multiple modes*, *genre awareness* (with a subdimension *audience awareness*), *digital skills*, *creativity*, *delivery*, *cohesion of modes*, *identity expression*, *language use* (with a subdimension *linguistic choices*), and *organization* in the DMC designing processes. Zhang and Yu (2023c) went further to develop and validate a self-assessment DMC competence scale, which comprises *digital skills*, *genre awareness*, *language use*, and *cohesion of modes*. This scale paints a more comprehensive picture of L2 DMC competence and displays great value in implementing formative assessment for DMC projects.

Other researchers adopted various rubrics in their studies on DMC. For example, the DMC rubric in Lee et al. (2021) encompassed *language use* in terms of fluency, accuracy, and style suitable for audiences' needs, *text-image composition* regarding the complementarity between texts and images, and *authenticity and uniqueness* concerning whether new meaning was made using self-selected modes or reshaping the available modes. Li (2020) created a rubric to assess students' DMC performance, which included *content*, *technology*, *graphic design*, *language and mechanics*, and *creativity*. Li and Pham (2022) employed a rubric capturing *content/organization*, *multimedia/visual effects*, and *language use* to assess students' performance in the DMC project on infographics. Kim et al.'s (2022) rubric comprised *task fulfillment*, *content*, *organization*, *language & mechanics*, and *effectiveness of using multi-modes*. Ryu et al. (2022) developed a rubric to assess L2 students' DMC performance in the meme project, which consisted of *multimodality*, *cultural aspects*, *linguistic components*, and *task/functions*.

By and large, research on L2 DMC assessment is still limited (n=11). Assessing DMC is one of the most urgent issues to be addressed in DMC research, and most L2 teachers struggle to assess student DMC projects (Belcher 2017; Li & Li 2022; Zhang et al. 2023). As such, more studies are warranted to address assessment issues in DMC projects. Of the existing DMC assessment studies, one pinpointed problem is that the criteria in these rubrics differed from one study to another, calling for a more comprehensive model of *what to assess* in DMC projects. Another problem is that most teachers designed or adopted rubrics to summatively assess the end products of student DMC projects in a one-shot manner, and few have utilized rubrics as Assessment as Learning (AaL) tools for the purpose of fostering student learning of DMC competence (Earl 2013) by providing rubric-referenced feedback, which has been reported to be effective to student learning (e.g., Andrade & Boulay 2003; Andrade & Du 2007; Andrade et al. 2008; Cohen et al. 2002; Hawe & Dixon 2014; Timperley & Parr 2009). While Cheung (2023) and Zhang and Yu (2023c) have constructed formative assessment rubrics for DMC, little has been done to examine the application of these rubrics in the formative assessment of DMC projects.

3. Directions for Future Research

In terms of the "learning" of DMC, while a vast majority of the studies focused on the affordances of DMC, research on possible challenges and difficulties related to L2 DMC pedagogy is sparse and calls for scholarly attention. As the research on DMC affordances has heavily relied on qualitative methods, especially interviews, students might be under the pressure of "social desirability" and only articulated the bright side of DMC to please the teacher and researcher. What's more, qualitative studies on DMC had a small sample size, and students' perceptions might not represent the majority and be less generalizable. As such, more quantitative or mixed-methods research is needed to collect large-scale data about students and teachers' views of DMC, such as distributing questionnaires using random sampling to elicit a large population's perceptions of DMC. Although many studies reported that DMC could benefit students' monomodal writing skills, more quantitative studies are warranted to examine the effect of DMC on the specific linguistic areas of writing ability, for example, accuracy, fluency, and lexical and syntactic complexity measured by Coh-metrics or L2SCA, and the quantitative method (e.g., *t*-test) can be utilized to examine whether the gains are statistically significant. Furthermore, there is a paucity of studies on the "how" and "why" dimensions of DMC affordances, calling for future studies to delve into the mechanisms of DMC affordances. For example, it remains to be explored how DMC projects enhance students' motivation, anxiety, and enjoyment in L2 learning, how they evolve in the DMC projects, what factors influence the evolvement of student motivation, anxiety, and enjoyment, and how the DMC projects help L2 students construct new identities and what factors mediate such influence. Methodologically, other approaches to qualitative studies are needed, such as ethnography, phenomenology, narrative inquiry, and grounded theory (Yin 2002). For example, narrative inquiry can be adopted to examine L2 students' lived experiences and stories of participating in the DMC projects to shed light on students' DMC beliefs and practices. The grounded theory approach can be used to conceptualize DMC competence so as to clarify the construct of DMC competence and provide a basis for DMC assessment. Ethnography can be employed to examine the longitudinal development of L2 students' DMC competence and the long-term impact of DMC on L2 students.

As for the "teaching" of DMC, the review indicates the need to give more attention to teachers' sense-making of DMC pedagogies, such as their experiences of initializing DMC projects, especially their challenges and struggles, teacher professional development in implementing DMC projects, teachers' action research on DMC implementation, teachers' beliefs and practices of DMC, and teachers' assessment practices of DMC with more qualitative approaches, such as ethnography, phenomenology, narrative inquiry, and grounded theory (Yin 2002). The research on the teaching materials of DMC competence calls for attention from curriculum designers, textbook developers, and teacher educators. Courses and textbooks about DMC competence might be developed for L2 students so as to more systematically nurture L2 students' DMC competence. Methodologically, more quantitative and mixed-methods research is needed to collect large-scale data about teachers' perceptions and practices of DMC, the factors that influence teachers' perceptions of DMC, and the effect of teacher training on teachers' implementation of DMC projects. More longitudinal studies over a longer stretch of time are needed to examine the dynamics of teachers' perceptions of DMC.

Regarding the research on DMC assessment, limited research has been conducted as well. As developing student DMC competence and modifying teacher DMC instruction inevitably require assessment, how teachers undertake assessment is of vital importance. As the DMC assessment criteria are less consistent, more work is needed to conceptualize the construct of DMC competence for L2 learners, and the grounded theory approach might be welcome in this respect. In addition, the existing rubrics are mostly designed by teachers based on their knowledge and intuition without rigorously following the steps of rubric development and validation. Thus, future studies might involve more collaboration between teachers and researchers to take theory-based, intuition-based, or data-based approaches to designing rubrics for L2 students and then validating them by drawing on the argument-based validation framework (e.g., Chapelle 2008; Kane 2006) or the sociocognitive validation framework (e.g., Chalhoub-Deville & O'Sullivan 2020; Weir 2005) to systematically examine the validity of the DMC rubrics. Furthermore, more research is needed on the learning-oriented assessment of DMC, such as peer- and self-assessment. In addition, it is worthwhile to probe into students' peer- and self-assessment literacy in the DMC projects, the interplay between different sources of feedback, and teachers' assessment literacy.

Overall, the "learning", "teaching", and "assessing" of L2 DMC have not been harmoniously weaved together. To maximize the learning and teaching potential of DMC, future studies are encouraged to connect these three dimensions in their research: for example, connecting learning goals with instructional activities and assessment criteria to make the DMC pedagogy more ecologically valid. AaL (Earl 2013; Lee 2017) or learning-oriented assessment (Turner & Purpura 2016) might be useful approaches to address this issue.

References

Almusharraf, N. M. & J. F. Engemann. 2020. Postsecondary instructors' perspectives on teaching English as a Foreign Language by means of a multimodal digital literacy approach [J]. *International Journal of Emerging Technologies in Learning* 15(18): 86-107.

Andrade, H. & B. Boulay. 2003. The role of rubric-referenced self-assessment in learning to write [J]. *Journal of Educational Research* 97(1): 21-34.

Andrade, H. & Y. Du. 2007. Student responses to criteria-referenced self-assessment [J]. *Assessment & Evaluation in Higher Education* 32: 159-181.

Andrade, H., Y. Du & X. Wang. 2008. Putting rubrics to the test: The effect of a model, criteria generation, and rubric-referenced self-assessment on elementary school students' writing [J]. *Educational Measurement: Issues and Practices* 27(2): 3-13.

Arksey, H. & L. O'Malley. 2005. Scoping studies: Towards a methodological framework [J]. *International Journal of Social Research Methodology* 8(1): 19-32.

Bailey, N. M. 2009. "It makes it more real": Teaching new literacies in a secondary English classroom [J]. *English Education* 41(3): 207-234.

Belcher, D. 2017. On becoming facilitators of multimodal composing and digital design [J]. *Journal of Second Language Writing* 38: 80-85.

Bezemer, J. & G. Kress. 2008. Writing in multimodal texts: A social semiotic account of designs for learning [J]. *Written Communication* 25(2): 166-195.

Black, R. W. 2009. Online fanfiction, global identities, and imagination [J]. *Research in the Teaching of English* 43(4): 397-425.

Burke, A. & S. Hardware. 2015. Honouring ESL students' lived experiences in school learning with multiliteracies pedagogy [J]. *Language, Culture and Curriculum* 28(2): 143-157.

Castañeda, M. E. 2013. "I am proud that I did it and it's a piece of me": Digital storytelling in the foreign language classroom [J]. *CALICO Journal* 20(1): 44-62.

Chalhoub-Deville, M. & B. O'Sullivan. 2020. *Validity: Theoretical Development and Integrated Arguments* [M]. Sheffield: Equinox Publishing.

Chapelle, C. A. 2008. The TOEFL validity argument [A]. In C. A. Chapelle, M. K. Enright & J. Jamieson (eds.). *Building a Validity Argument for the Test of English as a Foreign Language* [C]. London: Routledge. 319-352.

Cheung, A. (2023). Developing and evaluating a set of process and product-oriented classroom assessment rubrics for assessing digital multimodal collaborative writing in L2 classes [J]. *Assessing Writing* 56. doi: 10.1016/j.asw.2023.100723.

Cimasko, T. & D. Shin. 2017. Resemiotization and authorial agency in L2 multimodal writing [J]. *Written Communication* 34(4): 387-413.

Cohen, E., R. Lotan, B. Scarloss, S. Schultz & P. Abram. 2002. Can groups learn? [J] *Teachers College Record* 104(6): 1045-1068.

Cummins, J., S. Hu, P. Markus & M. K. Montero. 2015. Identity texts and academic achievement: Connecting the dots in multilingual school contexts [J]. *TESOL Quarterly* 49(3): 555-581.

Dogan, B. & B. Robin. 2009. Educational uses of digital storytelling: Creating digital storytelling contests for K-12 students and teachers [A]. In I. Gibson et al. (eds.). *Proceedings of Society for Information Technology & Teacher Education International Conference 2009* [C]. Waynesville, NC: AACE. 633-638.

Dzekoe, R. 2017. Computer-based multimodal composing activities, self-revision, and L2 acquisition through writing [J]. *Language Learning & Technology* 21(2): 73-95.

Earl, L. M. 2013. *Assessment as Learning: Using Classroom Assessment to Maximize Student Learning* [M]. Thousand Oaks: Corwin Press.

Elola, I. & A. Oskoz. 2017. Writing with 21st century social tools in the L2 classroom: New literacies, genres, and writing practices [J]. *Journal of Second Language Writing* 36: 52-60.

Vorobel, O. & D. Kim. 2017. Adolescent ELLs' collaborative writing practices in face-to-face and online contexts: From perception to action. *System* 65: 78-89.

Farias, M. & L. Véliz. 2019. Multimodal texts in Chilean English teaching education: Experiences from educators and pre-service teachers [J]. *Profile: Issues in Teachers' Professional Development* 21(2): 13-27.

Goulah, J. 2007. Village voices, global visions: Digital video as a transformative foreign language learning tool [J]. *Foreign Language Annals* 40(1): 62-78.

Hafner, C. A. 2013. Digital composition in a second or foreign language [J]. *TESOL Quarterly* 47(4): 830-834.

Hafner, C. A. 2014. Embedding digital literacies in English language teaching: Students' digital video projects as multimodal ensembles [J]. *TESOL Quarterly* 48: 655-685.

Hafner, C. A. 2015. Remix culture and English language teaching: The expression of learner voice in digital multimodal compositions [J]. *TESOL Quarterly* 49(3): 486-509.

Hafner, C. A. & W. Y. J. Ho. 2020. Assessing digital multimodal composing in second language writing: Towards a process-based model [J]. *Journal of Second Language Writing* 47: 100710.

Hafner, C. & L. Miller. 2011. Fostering learner autonomy in English for science: A collaborative digital video project in a technological learning environment [J]. *Language Learning & Technology* 15(3): 68-86.

Hava, K. 2021. Exploring the role of digital storytelling in student motivation and satisfaction in EFL education [J]. *Computer Assisted Language Learning* 34(7): 958-978.

Hawe, E. M. & H. R. Dixon. 2014. Building students' evaluative and productive expertise in the writing classroom [J]. *Assessing Writing* 19: 66-79.

Hepple, E., M. Sockhill, A. Tan & J. Alford. 2014. Multiliteracies pedagogy: Creating claymations with adolescent, post-beginner English language learners [J]. *Journal of Adolescent & Adult Literacy* 58(3): 219-229.

Honeyford, M. 2014. From aquí and allá: Symbolic convergence in the multimodal literacy practices of adolescent immigrant students [J]. *Journal of Literacy Research* 46(2): 194-233.

Hull, G. A. & M. L. Katz. 2006. Crafting an agentive self: Case studies of digital storytelling [J]. *Research in the Teaching of English* 41(1): 43-81.

Hung, H. T., Y.-C. J. Chiu & H.-C. Yeh. 2012. Multimodal assessment of and for learning: A theory-driven design rubric [J]. *British Journal of Educational Technology* 44(3): 400-409.

Hwang, W. Y., R. Shadiev, J. L. Hsu, Y. M. Huang, G. L. Hsu & Y. C. Lin. 2016. Effects of storytelling to facilitate EFL speaking using Web-based multimedia system [J]. *Computer Assisted Language Learning* 29(2): 215-241.

Janks, H. 2010. *Literacy and Power* [M]. London: Routledge.

Jiang, J. & M. M. Gu. 2023. Understanding youths' civic participation online: A digital multimodal composing perspective [J]. *Learning, Media and Technology* 47(4): 537-556.

Jiang, L. 2017. The affordances of digital multimodal composing for EFL learning [J]. *ELT Journal* 71(4): 413-422.

Jiang, L. & W. Ren. 2020. Digital multimodal composing in L2 learning: Ideologies and impact [J]. *Journal of Language, Identity & Education* 20(3): 167-182.

Jiang, L. & J. Gao. 2020. Fostering EFL learners' digital empathy through multimodal composing [J]. *RELC Journal* 51(1): 70-85.

Jiang, L. & J. Luk. 2016. Multimodal composing as a learning activity in English classrooms: Inquiring into the sources of its motivational capacity [J]. *System* 59: 1-11.

Jiang, L., M. Yang & S. Yu. 2020. Chinese ethnic minority students' investment in English learning empowered by digital multimodal composing [J]. *TESOL Quarterly* 54(4): 954-979.

Jiang, L., S. Yu & I. Lee. 2022. Developing a genre-based model for assessing digital multimodal composing in second language writing: Integrating theory with practice [J]. *Journal of Second Language Writing* 57: 100869.

Jiang, L., S. Yu & Y. Zhao. 2021. Teacher engagement with digital multimodal composing in a Chinese tertiary EFL curriculum [J]. *Language Teaching Research* 25(4): 613-632.

Jiang, L., S. Yu & Y. Zhao. 2022. Incorporating digital multimodal composing through collaborative action research: Challenges and coping strategies [J]. *Technology, Pedagogy and Education* 31(1): 45-61.

Kane, M. T. 2006. Validation [A]. In R. Brennan (ed.). *Educational Measurement* [C]. Westport: American Council on Education/Praeger. 17-64.

Kang, S. & Y. Kim. 2019. Learners' perceptions toward digital multimodal composing practices in an EFL high school classroom [R]. Paper presented at the Symposium on Second Language Writing, Tempe, Arizona, USA.

Kendrick, M., S. Jones, H. Mutonyi & B. Norton. 2006. Multimodality and English education in Ugandan schools [J]. *Studies in Africa* 49(1): 94-114.

Kim, D. & M. Li. 2021. Digital storytelling: Facilitating learning and identity development [J]. *Journal of Computers in Education* 8: 33-61.

Kim, S. 2014. Developing autonomous learning for oral proficiency using digital storytelling [J]. *Language Learning & Technology* 18(2): 20-35.

Kim, S. 2017. "It was kind of a given that we were all multilingual": Transnational youth identity work in digital translanguaging [J]. *Linguistics and Education* 43: 39-52.

Kim, Y. & D. Belcher. 2020. Multimodal composing and traditional essays: Linguistic performance and learner perceptions [J]. *RELC Journal* 51(1): 86-100.

Kim, Y., S. Kang, Y. Nam & S. Skalicky. 2022. Peer interaction, writing proficiency, and the quality of collaborative digital multimodal composing task: Comparing guided and unguided planning [J]. *System* 106(4): 102722.

Kress, G. 2003. *Literacy in the New Media Age* [M]. London: Routledge.

Lam, W. S. E. 2000. L2 literacy and the design of the self: A case study of a teenager writing on the Internet [J]. *TESOL Quarterly* 34(3): 457-482.

Lee, I. 2017. *Classroom Writing Assessment and Feedback in L2 School Contexts* [M]. Singapore: Springer.

Lee, L. 2014. Digital news stories: Building language learners' content knowledge and speaking skills [J]. *Foreign Language Annals* 47(2): 338-356.

Lee, S., Y. Lo & T. Chin. 2021. Practicing multiliteracies to enhance EFL learners' meaning making process and language development: A multimodal problem-based approach [J]. *Computer Assisted Language Learning* 34(1-2): 27-66.

Li, J. & M. Li. 2022. Assessing L2 writing in the digital age: Opportunities and challenges [J]. *Journal of Second Language Writing* 57(8): 100913.

Li, M. 2020. Multimodal pedagogy in TESOL teacher education: Students' perspectives [J]. *System* 94: 102337.

Li, M. & M. Akoto. 2021. Review of recent research on L2 digital multimodal composing [J]. *International Journal of Computer-Assisted Language Learning and Teaching* 11(3): 1-16.

Li, M. & Q. N. Pham. 2022. Three heads are better than one? Digital multimodal composition completed collaboratively versus individually [J]. *Language Teaching Research.* https://doi.org/10.1177/13621688221102536 (accessed 16/04/2024).

Lotherington, H. & J. Jenson. 2011. Teaching multimodal and digital literacy in L2 settings: New literacies, new basics, new pedagogies [J]. *Annual Review of Applied Linguistics* 31: 226-246.

Lotherington, H., M. L. Morbey, C. Granger & L. Doan. 2001. Tearing down the walls: New literacies and new horizons in the elementary school [A]. In B. Barrell (ed.). *Technology, Teaching and Learning: Issues in the Integration of Technology* [C]. Calgary: Detselig Enterprises. 131-161.

Nelson, E. M. & R. Kern. 2012. Language teaching and learning in the postlinguistic condition? [A] In L. Alsagoff, S. L. McKay, G. Hu & W. A. Renandya (eds.). *Principles and Practices for Teaching English as an International Language* [C]. London: Routledge. 47-66.

Nelson, M. E. 2006. Mode, meaning, and synaesthesia in multimedia L2 writing [J]. *Language, Learning, & Technology* 19(2): 56-76.

New London Group. 1996. A pedagogy of multiliteracies: Designing social futures [J]. *Harvard Educational Review* 66(1): 60-92.

Ono, Y. 2014. Motivational effects of digital storytelling on Japanese EFL learners [A]. In *Proceedings of CLaSIC: Knowledge, Skills and Competencies in Foreign Language Education* [C]. Singapore: NUS Centre for Language Studies. 414-431.

Pardo, B. S. 2014. Digital storytelling: A case study of the creation, and narration of story by EFL learners [J]. *Digital Education Review* 26: 74-84.

Peters, M. D. J., C. M. Godfrey, H. Khalil, P. McInerney, D. Parker & C. B. Soares. 2015. Guidance for conducting systematic scoping reviews [J]. *International Journal of Evidence-Based Healthcare* 13(3): 141-146.

Pham, M. T., A. Rajić, J. D. Greig, J. M. Sargeant, A. Papadopoulos & S. A. McEwen. 2014. A scoping review of scoping reviews: Advancing the approach and enhancing the consistency [J]. *Research Synthesis Methods* 5(4): 371-385.

Rance-Roney, J. 2010. Jump-starting language and schema for English-language learners: Teacher-composed digital jumpstarts for academic reading [J]. *Journal of Adolescent & Adult Literacy* 53(5): 386-395.

Ryan, J., A. Scott & M. Walsh. 2010. Pedagogy in the multimodal classroom: An analysis of the challenges and opportunities for teachers [J]. *Teachers and Teaching: Theory and Practice* 16(4): 477-489.

Ryu, J., Y. A. Kim, S. Eum, S. Park, S. Chun & S. Yang. 2022. The assessment of memes as digital multimodal composition in L2 classrooms [J]. *Journal of Second Language Writing* 57. doi: 10.1016/j.jslw.2022.100914.

Smith, B. E., M. B. Pacheco & M. Khorosheva. 2021. Emergent bilingual students and digital multimodal composition: A systematic review of research in secondary classrooms [J]. *Reading Research Quarterly* 56(1): 33-52.

Smythe, S. & P. Neufeld. 2010. Podcast time: Negotiating digital literacies and communities of learning in a middle years ELL classroom [J]. *Journal of Adolescent & Adult Literacy* 53(6): 488-496.

Somdee, M. & S. Suppasetseree. 2007. Developing English speaking skills of Thai undergraduate students by digital storytelling through websites [J]. *The Foreign Language Learning and Teaching International Conference* 2(4): 166-176.

Stein, P. 2004. Representation, rights and resources: Multimodal pedagogies in the language and literacy classroom [A]. In B. Norton & K. Toohey (eds.). *Critical Pedagogies and Language Learning* [C]. Cambridge: Cambridge University Press. 95-115.

Tardy, C. 2005. Expressions of disciplinarity and individuality in a multimodal genre [J]. *Computers and Composition* 22(3): 319-336.

Thang, S., L. Lin, N. Mahmud, K. Ismail & N. Zabidi. 2014. Technology integration in the form of digital storytelling: Mapping the concerns of four Malaysian ESL instructors [J]. *Computer Assisted Language Learning* 27(4): 311-329.

Timperley, H. S. & J. M. Parr. 2009. What is this lesson about? Instructional processes and student understandings in writing classrooms [J]. *The Curriculum Journal* 20(1): 43-60.

Timucin, M. & P. Irgin. 2015. Digital storytelling: An outlet for expression in EFL context [J].

International Journal of Languages Education and Teaching 3(1): 288-302.

Torres, A. R., E. P. Ponce, & M. D. G. Pastor 2012. Digital storytelling as a pedagogical tool within a didactic sequence in foreign language teaching [J]. *Digital Education Review* 22: 2-18.

Turner, C. E. & J. E. Purpura. 2016. Learning-oriented assessment in second and foreign language classrooms [A]. In D. Tsagari & J. Banerjee (eds.). *Handbook of Second Language Assessment* [C]. Berlin: De Gruyter. 255-274.

Vandommele, G., K. Van den Branden, K. Van Gorp & S. De Maeyer. 2017. In-school and out-of-school multimodal writing as an L2 writing resource for beginner learners of Dutch [J]. *Journal of Second Language Writing* 36: 23-36.

Verdugo, D. R. & I. A. Belmonte. 2007. Using digital stories to improve listening comprehension with Spanish young learners of English [J]. *Language Learning & Technology* 11(1): 87-101.

Vinogradova, P., H. A. Linville & B. Bickel. 2011. "Listen to my story and you will know me": Digital stories as student-centered collaborative projects [J]. *TESOL Journal* 2(2): 173-202.

Vorobel, O. & D. Kim. 2017. Adolescent ELLs' collaborative writing practices in face-to-face and online contexts: From perceptions to action [J]. *System* 65: 78-89.

Weir, C. J. 2005. *Language Testing and Validation: An Evidence-based Approach* [M]. London: Macmillan.

Yang, S. 2016. Potential phases of multilingual writers' identity work [A]. In X. You (ed.). *Transnational Writing Education: Theory, History and Practice* [C]. London: Routledge. 115-137.

Yang, Y. T. C. & W. C. I. Wu. 2012. Digital storytelling for enhancing student academic achievement, critical thinking, and learning motivation: A year-long experimental study [J]. *Computers & Education* 59(2): 339-352.

Yeh, H. C. 2018. Exploring the perceived benefits of the process of multimodal video making in developing multiliteracies [J]. *Language Learning & Technology* 22(2): 28-37.

Yi, Y. & J. Choi. 2015. Teachers' views of multimodal practices in K-12 classrooms: Voices from teachers in the United States [J]. *TESOL Quarterly* 49(4): 838-847.

Yi, Y. & T. Angay-Crowder. 2016. Multimodal pedagogies for teacher education in TESOL [J]. *TESOL Quarterly* 50: 988-998.

Yi, Y., N. King & A. Safriani. 2017. Re-conceptualizing assessment of digital multimodal literacy [J]. *TESOL Journal* 8(4): 878-885.

Yin, R. K. 2002. *Case Study Research: Design and Methods* [M]. London: SAGE.

Yoon, T. 2013. Are you digitized? Ways to provide motivation for ELLs using digital storytelling [J]. *International Journal of Research Studies in Educational Technology* 2(1): 25-34.

Zhang, E. D. & S. Yu. 2023a. Implementing digital multimodal composing in L2 writing instruction: A focus on developing L2 student writers [J]. *Innovation in Language Learning and Teaching* 17(4): 769-777.

Zhang, E. D. & S. Yu. 2023b. Conceptualizing digital multimodal composing competence in L2 classroom: A qualitative inquiry [J]. *Computer Assisted Language Learning*. https://doi.org/10.1080/09588221.2023.2177310 (accessed 16/04/2024).

Zhang, E. D. & S. Yu. 2023c. The development and validation of an L2 student digital multimodal composing competence scale [J]. *Computer Assisted Language Learning*. https://doi.org/10.1080/09

588221.2023.2201342 (accessed 16/04/2024).

Zhang, M., M. Akoto & M. Li. 2023. Digital multimodal composing in post-secondary L2 settings: A review of the empirical landscape [J]. *Computer Assisted Language Learning* 36(4): 694-721.

Zhang, Y. & K. O'Halloran. 2019. Empowering the point: Pains and gains of a writer's traversals between print-based writing and multimodal composing [J]. *Linguistics and Education* 51: 1-11.

About the Authors

Emily Di Zhang, Shanghai Jiao Tong University, Ph.D. Main research field: technology-mediated L2 writing learning and assessment.

Chunhong Liu, Simon Fraser University, Ph.D. Main research field: EFL writing, discourse analysis, and English for Academic Purposes.

Shulin Yu, University of Macau, Ph.D. Main research field: second language writing and classroom feedback and assessment in higher education. Email: shulinyu@um.edu.mo

Conversations Around Translingual Practice in EAL Writing Education*

Li ZHANG[1] Yachao SUN[2] Ruiyun SUN[3]

[1] Yushan Middle School
[2] Duke Kunshan University
[3] Northeast Forestry University

Abstract: This review explores the increasingly popular concept of translingual practice within English as an Additional Language (EAL) writing education. While translingual practice has been advocated for promoting linguistic and cultural diversity and encouraging writer agency, it also raises concerns related to theoretical understandings, ideological acceptance, and pedagogical implications. Confusion between translingual and L2 writing, resistance to dominant language norms, and potential negative impacts on students' academic success have all been highlighted as key issues. Through a critical examination of these benefits and concerns, this review emphasizes the need for further refinement of translingual pedagogies and more empirical research on their effectiveness. Recognizing these issues can contribute to a more inclusive and equitable approach to writing instruction that values the linguistic and cultural diversity of all students.

Keywords: translingual practice; EAL; writing education; benefits; concerns
DOI: 10.20081/j.cnki.cjslw.2023.07.002

1. Introduction

Translingual practice, a newly developed approach to writing research and education, positions itself against the rigidity of monolingualism and encourages the acceptance of linguistic heterogeneity as the norm. This approach empowers writers to have an active role in shaping their language use, viewing it as a tool for exploration rather than limitation (Canagarajah 2013a; Horner et al. 2011). Within the context of teaching and learning, it regards additional languages not as hurdles but as resources that enrich the use of a target language. The integration of this approach into writing practice and pedagogy has contributed to the evolution of writing education (Sun & Lan 2021b). However, some scholars have questioned the blurred boundaries between translingual practice and second language (L2) writing, leading to questions about its pedagogical implications for language learners (Atkinson et al. 2015; Ferris 2014; Gevers 2018; Matsuda 2014; Ruecker 2014; Severino 2017; Tardy 2017). These apprehensions encompass aspects like undermining the importance of language norms (Matsuda 2014; Ruecker 2014),

* This project is supported by the General Program of Philosophy and Social Science Research in Colleges and Universities of Jiangsu Province (no. 23KJSED057), Jiangsu Education Department.

overlooking the language development process of learners (Atkinson & Tardy 2018; Severino 2017), and an absence of clear guidance in students' language practices (Bou Ayash 2016; Zheng 2017). In order to alleviate these concerns, the concept of translingual practice has been reframed, not as an adversary of L2 writing but as a rhetorical model that enhances the understanding of writing (Donahue 2016; Horner 2018). In this light, it is not about replacing traditional approaches but rather about adding an alternative perspective to the pedagogical toolbox. Thus, translingual practice has also been evaluated as a potential orientation for writing practice and pedagogy, especially in the context of enhancing English as an Additional Language (EAL) writing education (Sun 2023; Sun et al. 2023; Xie & Sun 2023).

The notion of translingual practice has garnered recognition as a potent orientation to writing pedagogy in EAL writing education. Advocates of this approach, such as Sun (2023) and Sun et al. (2023), illuminate the potential advantages of incorporating translingual practices into EAL writing instruction. Through a broader, more inclusive embrace of language and its variances, translingual practice paves the way for a nuanced comprehension of language development and fosters more effective pedagogical methods. It acknowledges the dynamism of language, valuing students' linguistic heritage and experiences as resources for classroom instruction. In this sense, EAL writing educators who enact translingual practices can cultivate an inclusive, supportive learning milieu that accommodates students' linguistic needs and abilities, empowering them to hone their writing skills. Research, including studies conducted by Sun and Lan (2021a) and Sun (2022), has reviewed the empirical evidence for translingual writing practices, shedding light on their advantages and potential challenges. Yet, the review of the theoretical, ideological, and pedagogical conversations surrounding translingual practice, particularly within the context of EAL writing education, remains relatively underexplored. In response to this knowledge gap, the present study undertakes a systematic review of the ongoing conversations around this subject. The aim is to refine our understanding of translingual practice and further enrich its pedagogical applications, an endeavor of significant relevance to EAL writing education.

2. Literature Review

2.1 Historical development of translingual practice

The theoretical foundation of translingual practice is built upon extensive research in the field of writing studies that investigate language variations. This includes differences among English variants, such as Standard Written English (SWE) and African American Vernacular English (AAVE), as well as disparities between distinct languages such as English, Chinese, and Spanish (Canagarajah 2013a; Horner & Tetreault 2017; Horner et al. 2011). The groundbreaking endorsement for the acceptance of diverse English varieties in academic contexts came with the statement, Students' Right to Their Own Language (SRTOL), which was issued at the 1974 Conference on College Composition and Communication. Support for the notion of linguistic diversity also permeates the fields of

Teaching English to Speakers of Other Languages (TESOL) and L2 writing. Pioneering research in these areas (Matsuda 1999, 2006; Silva 1997; Silva et al. 1997) champions the integration of multilingual students' first language (L1) into their L2 writing processes. This body of work poses a strong challenge to monolingual norms by empowering writers to mold their language usage. Furthermore, it reframes linguistic diversity, which views it as a valuable resource instead of a deficit. These transformative perspectives serve as the foundation for the further exploration and development of translingual practice within writing education.

The challenge to monolingualism, coupled with strong advocacy for writer agency, has led scholars to explore the practical use of language resources within diverse contexts. Here, the notion of "contact zones," first proposed by Pratt (1991), plays a significant role. Frequently cited in translingual studies, this idea underscores the complex intermingling of languages and cultures during the process of meaning negotiation and construction. The goal of this perspective is to empower all language users to question and challenge prevailing norms. Contrary to the traditional view of languages as separate, discrete, and monolithic entities, Pratt (1991) contended that such a perspective does not accurately reflect the dynamic and multifaceted nature of language use in communities and societies. To address this discrepancy, she coined and defined contact zones as "social spaces where cultures meet, clash, and grapple with each other, often in contexts of highly asymmetrical relations of power, such as colonialism, slavery, or their aftermaths as they are lived out in many parts of the world today" (p. 34). This characterization emphasizes the ubiquity of heterogeneity in human interaction. Lu (1994), building on Pratt's concept of contact zones, elaborated on a multicultural approach to writing. For instance, within Lu's classroom, the phrase "can able to," used by a Malaysian Chinese student, served as an illustration of creative language use in contact zones and demonstrated a linguistic blend of Chinese and English. Lu interpreted this structure as the "ability from the perspective of external circumstances" (p. 452). In this context, the concept of contact zones accentuates the reciprocal interplay of language and cultural resources in meaning-making. It encourages the negotiation of non-standard language use, reframing it as a creative adaptation rather than an error or mistake. These investigations, emphasizing the synergistic nature of language practices, significantly contribute to the conceptualization of translingual practice.

The use of contact zones as a conceptual framework for translingual practice has sparked robust debates about English-only policies within writing studies. Notably, Horner (2001) argued that, despite its affirming title, the SRTOL statement falls short in addressing language legislation issues. He suggested that approaches that depict language learners as deficient or that categorize unconventional language structures as errors overlook the reality of language as a social practice — emergent, contingent, and intertwined with various material and social elements. Consequently, Horner (2018) advocated for a heightened awareness of the contentious issues surrounding English-only policies in writing studies. Expanding on this notion, Horner and Trimbur (2002) scrutinized the English-only debates in U.S. writing studies and criticized English monolingualism, territorialization, and the reification of languages. They posited that an English-only or monolingualist stance is ill-equipped to cater to the internationalization of writing studies and the dynamism of globalization. Horner et al. (2010) further contribute to the conceptualization of translingual practice by challenging monolingualism in writing studies. Their edited collection underscores the harmful effects of the English-only policy, which is widespread in U.S. society and higher education, and argues that it devalues the linguistic and cultural resources that multilingual students bring to the classroom and overlooks the complexity and variability of students' language use. These studies advocate for a more heterogeneous and dynamic approach to writing education and contest the prevailing paradigm of English monolingualism — these ideas have become central tenets of translingual practice.

2.2 Current understandings of translingual practice

The integration of translingual practice in writing education is fundamentally aligned with these explorations of language and language variety differences, dialogues on contact zones, and debates surrounding the English-only policy. This approach is underpinned by three core tenets: (1) acknowledging the power all language users possess to adapt language for specific ends, (2) recognizing the linguistic diversity inherent in all language users, both within and outside the U.S., and (3) proactively addressing the expectations of English monolingualism, by instructing writers to interact both with and against these expectations, rather than merely conforming to them (Horner et al. 2011). These foundational principles give shape to translingual practice within writing education, a paradigm that Canagarajah (2013a) and Lu and Horner (2013) further developed and refined. They posited language and language use as performative and emergent acts of translation, intrinsically tied to their context. These acts are not only ideological but also contingent, adding depth and complexity to translingual practice in writing education.

Translingual practice has evolved through a series of conceptual shifts, with each stage incrementally building upon its predecessor. Initially, translingual practice centered on the interplay between languages, with multilingual writers traversing between their "native" language and the realm of academic discourse. However, this framework, despite its merits, was limited, failing to encompass the intricate and dynamic facets of language use in its entirety. In response to this constraint, Lu and Horner (2013) advocated for a more nuanced, temporal-spatial approach to language difference. This perspective portrays language use as a continuously unfolding, mutually constitutive process. It recognizes that language use is contingent, interacting synergistically with various elements across diverse temporal and spatial contexts — including purposes, conversation partners, topics, and broader contexts. Consequently, it emphasizes the fluidity of language, language users, practices, conventions, and contexts with respect to time and space. In this view, diversity becomes the norm. Building on this theme, Horner and Tetreault (2016) expanded upon this notion by emphasizing the concept of "translation" as an inherent facet of all linguistic practices. They eschewed traditional views of translation as merely finding equivalent meanings between distinct, static, and unified languages. Instead, they portrayed it as a deliberate act performed by actors located within specific social and historical contexts, an act that both contributes to the establishment of convention and recontextualizes it. These scholarly contributions consolidate translingual practice, focusing on temporal-spatial and translation perspectives, thereby laying the groundwork for further principles of translingual practice.

In recent work, Canagarajah (2018) developed the concept of translingual practice by referring to spatial repertoires that highlight their synergistic and emergent characteristics. These repertoires are contextually crafted, dynamically assimilating individual life trajectories, related others, and temporal-spatial elements. Language, then, is intrinsically situated within specific time-space coordinates, intimately involved in particular activities and co-constructing meaning with other resources in various contexts. Although language possesses sedimented norms over time, these norms remain fluid, with the language open to modification as it intersects with other semiotic assemblages in the process of meaning-making. This perspective underscores the significance of spatial materials in translingual practice, while subtly reframing the roles of both language and human agency in the act of meaning-making. Collectively, these shifts in the understanding of translingual practice underscore the fluid and emergent characteristics of language use and highlight the importance of acknowledging the agency of both humans and materials in constructing meaning.

The evolution of the concept of translingual practice has fostered a more comprehensive and nuanced comprehension of language use that accentuates the creativity and context-sensitivity inherent in communication. Therefore, translingual practice has been gaining increased recognition across various disciplines, such as composition studies (Zhang-Wu 2023), applied linguistics (Canagarajah 2022), bilingual education (Gómez & Lewis 2022), TESOL (Sánchez-Martín 2022), and literacy studies (Brubacher 2022). Nonetheless, its pedagogical value within writing education continues to spark debates (Silva & Wang 2020; Williams & Condon 2016). While certain scholars (for instance, Matsuda 2014; Tardy 2017) have expressed reservations about employing translingual writing solely for its elevated status, such concerns appear to be dwindling within EAL writing education. This trend necessitates a renewed examination of these conversations to effectively guide translingual practices within the context of EAL writing education, thereby ensuring translingual practice is utilized for its intellectual merit and to foster efficient writing education. Thus, revisiting these conversations is vital to refining and enhancing the implementation of translingual practice in EAL writing education.

3. The Study

To gain a deeper understanding of the ongoing conversations around translingual practice, we employed research synthesis as our analytical method (Cooper et al. 2009; Norris & Ortega 2006). This method amalgamates findings from diverse databases to spot trends in research and offer a more holistic understanding of the subject matter. Past research syntheses in the field of L2 writing have provided invaluable insights into various facets of L2 writing research. Although recent reviews by Sun and Lan (2021a) and Sun (2022) have primarily centered on empirical studies investigating translingual writing practices and their implications for EAL writing education, they have yet to address the ongoing theoretical, ideological, and pedagogical conversations related to translingual practice. This study seeks to fill this gap, examining how these conversations influence EAL writing education. To fulfill this objective, we employed a methodology similar to that utilized by Sun and Lan (2021a) and Sun (2022) for data collection and analysis.

3.1 Study selection

This study's objective was to gain a comprehensive understanding of the conversations surrounding translingual practice in EAL writing education. To achieve this, we conducted a thorough search of a research-oriented university's online library, using a selection of 'trans-' terms such as translingual, translanguaging, translingualism, transcultural, transliteracy, and transmodality as keywords. Initially, we assessed 1,346 publications at the abstract/introduction level, from which we further screened 337 publications in their entirety. Our criteria for inclusion comprised publications that explored translingual writing practices, offered pedagogical insights, and analyzed or discussed writings by multilingual writers identified as ELLs, ESL, EFL, EAL, multilingual, and emerging bilingual students. Conversely, we excluded publications that merely touched upon translingual writing practices, focused predominantly on speaking activities, assessed non-English writing, or did not provide a comprehensive discussion of writing processes or activities. Consequently, a pool of 236 publications was assembled for closer scrutiny. These came from a variety of relevant sources, including journals such as *The Modern Language Journal*, *Applied Linguistics*, *TESOL Quarterly*, *Language Teaching*, *Language Teaching Research*, *College English*, *College Composition and Communication*, *Journal of Second Language Writing*, *Composition Studies*, and *Research in the Teaching of English*, and books such as Canagarajah (2013a), Hall and Horner (2023), Horner and Tetrault (2017), Silva and Wang (2020). To ensure we had not overlooked any pertinent studies, we also conducted a search on Google Scholar.

3.2 Data analysis

In our pursuit to review the conversations surrounding translingual practice in EAL writing education, we employed a systematic procedure encompassing several steps during the data analysis phase. Our first step involved a thorough reading and summarization of the key arguments, findings, and evidence, both supporting and critiquing translingual writing practices that were present in the selected publications. For instance, we ascribed the argument by Flores and Aneja (2017), who proposed that translingual writing practices aid students in developing a nuanced perception of language and identity to the "benefits" theme. On the other hand, Kubota's (2016) cautionary argument that translingual practices might unintentionally reinforce power imbalances and discrimination in academic writing was categorized under the "concerns" theme.

Following the preliminary categorization into these two overarching themes, we further segregated these studies into subthemes based on their theoretical, ideological, and pedagogical implications — either benefiting or expressing concern. Notably, certain studies, such as those by Arnold (2016) and Cavazos (2017), addressed both benefits and concerns, and as such, we incorporated them in both categories with corresponding emphases during the data analysis. We then amalgamated the key points from each study to provide a summarized view of the conversations surrounding translingual practice in EAL writing education. This procedure was repeated multiple times to ensure the analysis was as comprehensive as possible. We decided not to present the conversations in terms of frequencies and percentages as many studies highlighted both benefits and concerns regarding the implementation of translingual practice in EAL writing education. Our objective was to delve into the nuances of how best to approach EAL writing instruction with translingual practice. In the ensuing sections, we present a summary and discussion of these conversations, categorized by the key arguments for (benefits) and against (concerns) translingual practice in EAL writing education. In doing so, we aim to furnish a comprehensive understanding of these conversations, with the intention of enriching EAL writing education.

4. The Benefits of Translingual Practice for EAL Writing Education

As we dissect the arguments brought forth by various researchers, we first focus our attention on the benefits attributed to the application of translingual practice in EAL writing education. Such advantages encompass enhanced language proficiency, cultivation of intercultural competence, and broader flexibility and adaptability in communication. Delving into the theoretical, ideological, and pedagogical implications of translingual practice within EAL writing education, we draw from arguments present in the chosen studies. Moreover, we explore the tangible strategies and techniques educators can employ to bring translingual writing practices to life in their classrooms. Our examination of these advantages aims to provide a comprehensive understanding of the value that translingual practice can bring to EAL writing education.

From a theoretical perspective, translingual practice can bring valuable contributions to EAL writing education. EAL writing involves studying written English as a non-native language, marking it as a transdisciplinary field (Matsuda 2013a; 2021). As Matsuda (2021) explained, characterizing L2 writing as transdisciplinary is less about its academic status and more about how this field dynamically interacts with other intellectual disciplines (also see Sun & Lan 2023). This broad interpretation encourages a spectrum of theoretical approaches in EAL writing, encompassing structural linguistic, contrastive/intercultural rhetoric, process, EAP, genre, sociopolitical, sociocultural, and sociocognitive approaches. Such diversity creates a welcoming platform for relevant theories within the study of EAL writing. Translingual practice, for instance, is a theoretical approach that can be effectively applied to both study and instruction of EAL writing. Some studies have explored the potential benefits of integrating translingual practice. For instance, Smith et al. (2017) found that employing translingual practice enabled teachers to acknowledge and validate the linguistic and cultural resources students brought into the classroom, consequently enhancing the awareness of both teachers and students about the existing language and cultural diversity in learning environments. Similarly, Kiernan et al. (2017) argued that translingual practice could shed light on the unseen aspects of reading and writing, thereby fostering students' academic and cognitive growth. These studies suggest that the incorporation of translingual practice as a theoretical approach to EAL writing can yield benefits for both teachers and students. By acknowledging and appreciating the linguistic and cultural diversity of students, translingual practice can facilitate the creation of a more inclusive learning environment, encourage students to utilize their multilingual and multimodal resources for EAL writing, and boost students' metalinguistic awareness.

Ideologically speaking, translingual practice can enrich discussions surrounding language ideologies in EAL writing education. It does this by advocating for an inclusive and open stance toward unconventional language use in writing. Silva's (1997) ethical approach to ESL writers, emphasizing writer agency and challenging deficit ideology, lays the groundwork for treating multilingual writers with respect and fairness. Tardy and Whittig (2017) extended this ethical treatment, calling for active advocacy for EAL writers. To challenge the dominance of monolingual ideologies, Silva et al. (1997) suggested that adopting perspectives from L2 studies could help prevent writing studies from becoming monolingual, monocultural, and ethnocentric. Echoing this sentiment, Matsuda (1999, 2006) championed heterogeneity as a norm in writing classrooms to counter English monolingual ideologies within writing studies. Translingual practice builds on these insights, providing a holistic perspective on language ideologies in writing studies, thus fostering the growth of EAL writing education.

Recent research has analyzed various language ideologies and models that could be adopted in writing education to better serve students. Horner et al. (2011) examined three models: the monolingual, the traditional multilingual, and the translingual. While the monolingual model perceives a language as a static entity, viewing all other languages as threats, the traditional multilingual model sees individual language systems within one's mind. Conversely, translingual practice perceives all languages as resources in a unified repertoire for meaning-making. Similarly, Canagarajah (2015) differentiated translingual practice from three other bi/multilingual models (subtractive, additive, recursive), emphasizing that language acquisition is a multidirectional process, language competence is comprehensive, and language proficiency is continually evolving. These ideologies can be applied in classrooms to enhance EAL writing education. Translingual practice has been employed in EAL writing teaching and learning to help students challenge dominant language ideologies, build positive multilingual identities, and develop pedagogical strategies using their multiple language and cultural resources. For instance, Flores and Aneja (2017) discovered that translingual practice was particularly beneficial for preservice non-native English-speaking (NNES) teachers. Meanwhile, Jain (2014) and Malcolm (2017) found that it increased language and cultural awareness in writing classrooms by validating students' languages and challenging monolingual ideologies.

These studies underscore the benefits of integrating translingual practice in EAL writing education from an ideological standpoint.

Pedagogically, translingual practice carries far-reaching implications for teaching and learning. Many studies have explored how translingual pedagogies can enhance the instruction of EAL writers across a variety of contexts and research focuses. Translingual pedagogies underscore the critical role of writer agency (Pacheco et al. 2019), the utilization of languages and modalities as resources (Sun et al. 2021), the acceptance of heterogeneity as a norm (Arnold 2016), and the challenge to monolingualism (Bou Ayash 2016). These principles have been applied in writing courses through a diverse array of strategies and activities. These encompass envoicing, recontextualization, interaction, and entextualization strategies and extend to activities such as translating, multimodal composing, cross-cultural collaborating, and reflective writing. Scholars such as Beiler and Dewilde (2020), Gonzales (2015), Kiernan et al. (2017), Kulavuz-Onal and Vásquez (2018), Lee and Jenks (2016), and Smith et al. (2017) have analyzed and demonstrated the effectiveness of these pedagogical practices in enhancing the instruction of EAL writers.

Therefore, integrating translingual practice into EAL writing education can lead to the evolution of EAL writing pedagogy, one that values linguistic and cultural diversity and fosters inclusivity. Additionally, translingual pedagogies introduce promising strategies for EAL writing education. By engaging students in writing activities that involve translation (Beiler & Dewilde 2020; Kiernan et al. 2017), multimodal composition (Pacheco & Smith 2015; Smith et al. 2017), cross-cultural collaboration (Kulavuz-Onal & Vásquez 2018; Lee & Jenks 2016), and reflective writing (Hartse et al. 2018; Wang 2017), teachers can empower students with the agency to utilize diverse language and cultural resources for EAL writing. Translingual practice also encourages students to challenge dominant norms and ideologies. It presents writing as a synergistic, emergent, and contingent process and heightens students' awareness of language and cultural diversity in various contexts. While these studies highlight the theoretical, ideological, and pedagogical benefits of translingual practice for EAL writing education, they also bring attention to concerns about adopting translingual writing practices.

5. The Concerns About Translingual Practice in EAL Writing Education

The rising interest in applying translingual practice within EAL writing education has given rise to certain concerns. These include the potential misinterpretation of sociolinguistic and L2 study concepts (Matsuda 2013b; Severino 2017), the risk of overlooking language similarities and differences (Gilyard 2016; Matsuda 2014), the neglect of discussions around marginality, inequality, and language imperialism (Flores 2013; Kubota 2016), and the scarcity of comprehensive pedagogical implications for language learners (Atkinson & Tardy 2018; Ferris 2014). Given these concerns, this section presents a summary and analysis of the theoretical, ideological, and pedagogical issues that arise when considering the adoption of translingual practice in EAL writing education. Addressing these concerns is of paramount importance for the further evolution of EAL writing education. It enables educators to effectively integrate translingual practice into their curriculum in a manner that is beneficial for EAL writing students while being mindful of their unique linguistic and cultural backgrounds.

The embrace and application of translingual practice as a theoretical construct in EAL writing education are met with challenges due to varying theoretical interpretations of translingual writing and its overlapping ideas with L2 writing. Though some scholars utilize the term "translingual writing" to understand writing from a translingual perspective, the precise definition remains disputed. Tannenbaum (2014), for instance, defined translingual writing as "writing in a language different from one's mother tongue" (p. 99), which aligns with a typical definition of L2 writing. Matsuda (2014) viewed translingual writing as a loosely related set of ideas, while Atkinson et al. (2015) saw it as "a particular orientation to how language is conceptualized and implicated in the study and teaching of writing" (p. 384). Canagarajah (2016), on the other hand, interpreted it as "a form of situated literate practice where writers negotiate their semiotic resources in relation to the dominant conventions of language and rhetoric" (p. 266). These varying theoretical definitions indicate the overlap of certain ideas between translingual writing and L2 writing, such as the endorsement of writer agency, the challenge to monolingualism, and the recognition of heterogeneity as the norm.

The blurred boundary between translingual writing and L2 writing has triggered discussions regarding their conflation (Canagarajah 2013b). Scholars such as Atkinson et al. (2015) have responded to this issue, delineating the difference between the two. Certain translingual scholars (e.g., Donahue 2016; Horner 2018; Lu & Horner 2016) argue that "translingual" serves as a rhetorical model or theoretical orientation for understanding, learning, and teaching writing rather than a distinct form of writing like codemeshing; therefore, translingual practice could potentially benefit EAL writing. Nonetheless, confusion between the two approaches persists, and their ability to coexist or cooperate with other approaches to enrich and enhance EAL writing education warrants further exploration. This, in turn, introduces the next concern associated with implementing translingual practice in EAL writing education: the ideological conversation over the utility of language norms that L2 writing scholars and instructors strive to impart to students. These norms have become targets of resistance in translingual studies.

The ideological concerns surrounding the application of translingual practice hinge upon the appraisal of prevailing language norms. While numerous studies underscore the utilization of translingual practice in challenging these norms, a deeper conversation is needed regarding the role of language norms as resources. Scholars have probed into how EAL writing students leverage their L1s or heritage languages to contest dominant language norms, as seen in the use of unconventional constructs such as "can able to" (Lu 1994) or the blended use of AAVE and SWE (Young 2004). However, this ideology of resistance raises concerns about the ability of translingual practice to support EAL writing students in achieving academic and social success, as pointed out by some scholars (e.g., Atkinson & Tardy 2018; Ferris 2014; Gevers 2018, Matsuda 2014; Severino 2017;

Tardy 2017). Criticisms label this concern as "ghettoizing" (Canagarajah 2013b) and "isolationist" (Canagarajah 2015), thereby triggering further queries about the potential benefits for language learners in resisting dominant language norms. Matsuda (2014) issued a warning that translingual ideologies fostering resistance to dominant language norms may result in "linguistic tourism" within EAL writing education — a phenomenon characterized by an infatuation with the unfamiliar and the adoption of appealing yet unrepresentative linguistic features. Similarly, Ruecker (2014), studying the transitions of Latina/Latino students from high school to higher education, proposed that EAL writers require learning a standardized variety of English for academic success, and translingual ideologies might hinder this acquisition, consequently negatively impacting students' academic performance. These ideological conversations inevitably trigger further concerns about the pedagogical implications of translingual practice within EAL writing.

The pedagogical implications of translingual practice are intricate and necessitate careful deliberation. A primary concern centers on the potential adverse consequences for students' language progression and academic success. While translingual practice can equip multilingual writers to challenge prevailing language norms, an overemphasis on resistance might cause educators to prioritize distinctive linguistic features over fundamental language proficiencies. This concern becomes particularly salient in the context of academic writing, where adhering to standard language rules is often critical for success. Scholars such as Atkinson and Tardy (2018) and Gevers (2018) posit that there should be a heightened focus on the language development of EAL writers within translingual writing studies, which is currently lacking. This deficit, for example, can manifest in the "linguistic tourism" phenomenon (Matsuda 2014) resulting from an overemphasis on resisting dominant language norms, wherein teachers prioritize intriguing linguistic features over essential language skills. In essence, the spotlight on resistance to dominant language norms might require recalibration to allow students to develop a comprehensive range of language skills, encompassing grammar, syntax, and vocabulary — vital elements for academic success. However, a strong focus on conforming to dominant language norms may overlook the unique linguistic resources of multilingual students, potentially leading to a diminishing of linguistic diversity in the classroom. Therefore, striking a balance between resisting and accommodating language norms through translingual practice is vital in EAL writing education. It enables the fostering of positive, multilingual identities while simultaneously preparing students for academic success.

The concept of translingual practice, which advocates dismantling traditional linguistic, social, and cultural divisions among languages by treating them as collective resources within an integrated repertoire, proposes a unique challenge to the notion of separate languages. This perspective underscores the individuality of each language act in its unique temporal and spatial context. Despite attempts to distinguish translingual practice from other models, as discussed earlier, this approach questions the standard definitions of multilingual writing and writers, thereby inciting a wave of critiques. Some scholars have voiced concerns about the implementation of translingual practice in writing education, highlighting issues such as the paradox of appreciating yet failing to legitimize marginalized languages (Milson-Whyte 2013), complications surrounding codemeshing (Guerra 2016), and the potential to oversimplify language differences in attempts to address them (Gilyard 2016). Such oversimplification or "flattening" of language differences hinders critical discourse on language similarities and disparities. Moreover, critics argue that translingual practice falls short of acknowledging power dynamics and societal inequalities. They claim that the hybrid turn in TESOL and applied linguistics disregards the linguistic history of nation-states and oppressed societies (Flores 2013), applauds individualism and indifference toward differences, and overlooks marginality, inequality, and language imperialism (Kubota 2016). Hence, for the prosperous development of EAL writing education, translingual practice should strive to develop a nuanced understanding of language differences by accounting for linguistic, social, and cultural variations among languages while avoiding over-generalizations.

6. Conclusion

Over recent years, there has been a notable surge in interest in integrating translingual practice into EAL writing education, with numerous scholars endorsing its prospective advantages. One such benefit is that translingual practice champions greater linguistic and cultural diversity in the educational environment, posing a challenge to traditional monolingual norms prevalent in EAL writing instruction. This approach could equip students with vital skills necessary to effectively communicate with a variety of audiences both within and beyond the classroom and foster an understanding of how language use is influenced by social and cultural settings. Moreover, another potential advantage of translingual practice is its emphasis on writer agency and the utilization of multiple linguistic resources. This approach fosters a sophisticated understanding of language use, enabling students to be more critical readers and adept creators of written material. Acknowledging language as a fluid and emerging phenomenon influenced by numerous factors — from the writer's personal experiences and viewpoints to the specific social and cultural contexts of communication — the translingual approach embraces diversity. Furthermore, by advocating for student experimentation with varied linguistic and rhetorical strategies, translingual practice promotes the development of adaptable and flexible writers. Such writers can deftly navigate the complexities of different writing scenarios, thereby potentially enhancing their overall effectiveness and versatility.

Translingual practice, despite its potential benefits, encounters several challenges in the context of EAL writing education. One of the main challenges is the need to distinguish between translingual writing and L2 writing. Both approaches share certain commonalities, such as an emphasis on multilingualism and heterogeneity, yet they differ in significant aspects. Specifically, translingual practice underscores the inventive and context-specific utilization of a multitude of language resources, while L2 writing, in addition to valuing linguistic diversity, underscores the mastery of linguistic forms and writing conventions. The process of distinguishing these methodologies and understanding their implications for EAL writing instruction is pivotal in fostering a more profound comprehension of translingual practice, which could facilitate its wider implementation in classrooms. Another challenge that translingual practice faces is the resistance to language norms, making its integration into EAL writing instruction potentially problematic. Certain students might find the prospect of straying from established norms and conventions daunting, while others may feel that their linguistic and cultural backgrounds are overlooked or undervalued within the educational setting. Addressing these concerns will require a shift in the way that writing is taught and evaluated, placing greater emphasis on the creative and context-sensitive use of language rather than strict adherence to established norms and conventions.

The array of benefits and challenges presented by translingual practice underlines the necessity for educators to refine and adapt translingual pedagogies, responding to relevant conversations based on their specific educational contexts. Although some concerns exist, existing studies suggest that the application of translingual pedagogies can enrich EAL writing education. Educators can address these challenges by tailoring translingual pedagogies to meet the unique needs and circumstances of their students, considering factors such as linguistic backgrounds, cultural identities, and prior writing experiences. In addition to this, the review highlights the potential for a more holistic approach to writing education, achieved by blending translingual pedagogies with other instructional approaches such as genre-based, sociocultural, and cognitive pedagogies. Such a balanced approach can help students cultivate their writing skills across various contexts and genres while capitalizing on the unique benefits that translingual pedagogies offer. This synthesis of approaches ensures a well-rounded and comprehensive writing education, catering to the diverse needs and abilities of students.

In conclusion, translingual practice holds the potential for enriching EAL writing education by fostering linguistic and cultural diversity, enhancing writer agency, harnessing multiple language resources, and equipping students with the skills necessary for a globalized world. Yet, the realization of these benefits necessitates continued refinement and further empirical research on the effectiveness of translingual practices within EAL writing education. By addressing these concerns, EAL writing educators can contribute to a more inclusive and equitable approach to writing instruction that values and recognizes the linguistic and cultural diversity of all students. This study is not without its limitations. Despite efforts to reduce bias, the selection and data extraction processes might have been influenced by our personal opinions. The interpretation of the findings might also be subject to our subjectivity, which could influence the data extraction process. Lastly, the scope of this systematic review is limited to conversations surrounding translingual practice in EAL writing education, which may inadvertently overlook some relevant studies. Thus, while we have endeavored to offer a comprehensive analysis, some aspects may require further exploration.

References

Arnold, L. R. 2016. "This is a field that's open, not closed": Multilingual and international writing faculty respond to composition theory [J]. *Composition Studies* 44(1): 72-88.

Atkinson, D. & C. M. Tardy. 2018. SLW at the crossroads: Finding a way in the field [J]. *Journal of Second Language Writing* 42: 86-93.

Atkinson, D., D. Crusan, P. K. Matsuda, C. Ortmeier-Hooper, T. Ruecker, S. Simpson & C. Tardy. 2015. Clarifying the relationship between L2 writing and translingual writing: An open letter to writing studies editors and organization leaders [J]. *College English* 77(4): 383-386.

Beiler, I. R. & J. Dewilde. 2020. Translation as translingual writing practice in English as an additional language [J]. *The Modern Language Journal* 104(3): 533-549.

Bou Ayash, N. 2016. Conditions of (im)possibility: Postmonolingual language representations in academic literacies [J]. *College English* 78: 555-577.

Brubacher, K. 2022. Print literacy humiliation: Translanguaging and emotions with newcomer children [J]. *Language & Literacy* 24(2): 133-152.

Canagarajah, A. S. 2013a. *Translingual Practice: Global Englishes and Cosmopolitan Relations* [M]. London: Routledge.

Canagarajah, A. S. 2013b. The end of second language writing? [J]. *Journal of Second Language Writing* 22(4): 440-441.

Canagarajah, A. S. 2015. Clarifying the relationship between translingual practice and L2 writing: Addressing learner identities [J]. *Applied Linguistics Review* 6(4): 415-440.

Canagarajah, A. S. 2016. Translingual writing and teacher development in composition [J]. *College English* 78(3): 265-273.

Canagarajah, A. S. 2018. Translingual practice as spatial repertoires: Expanding the paradigm beyond structuralist orientations [J]. *Applied Linguistics* 39(1): 31-54.

Canagarajah, A. S. 2022. Challenges in decolonizing linguistics: The politics of enregisterment and the divergent uptakes of translingualism [J]. *Educational Linguistics* 1(1): 25-55.

Cavazos, A. G. 2017. Translingual oral and written practices: Rhetorical resources in multilingual writers' discourses [J]. *International Journal of Bilingualism* 21(4): 385-401.

Conference on College Composition and Communication. 1974. "Students' right to their own language." Special issue, *College Composition and Communication* 25. http:// www.ncte.org/ library/ NCTEFiles/ Groups/ CCCC/ NewSRTOL.pdf (accessed 26/04/2024).

Cooper, H., L. Hedge & J. Valentine (eds.). 2009. *The Handbook of Research Synthesis and Meta-analysis* (2nd Ed.) [C]. New York: SAGE.

Donahue, C. 2016. The "trans" in transnational-translingual: Rhetorical and linguistic flexibility as new norms [J]. *Composition Studies* 44(1): 147-150.

Ferris, D. 2014. "English only" and multilingualism in composition studies: Policy, philosophy, and practice (book review) [J]. *College English* 77(1): 73-83.

Flores, N. 2013. The unexamined relationship between neoliberalism and plurilingualism: A cautionary tale [J]. *TESOL Quarterly* 47(3): 500-520.

Flores, N. & G. Aneja. 2017. "Why needs hiding?": Translingual (re)orientations in TESOL teacher education [J]. *Research in the Teaching of English* 51(4): 441-463.

Gevers, J. 2018. Translingualism revisited: Language difference and hybridity in L2 writing [J]. *Journal of Second Language Writing* 40: 73-83.

Gilyard, K. 2016. The rhetoric of translingualism [J]. *College English* 78(3): 284-289.

Gómez, M. & M. A. Lewis. 2022. Identifying the assets of emergent bilingual middle school students' writing: Opportunities to validate students' linguistic repertoires and identities [J]. *International Journal of Bilingual Education and Bilingualism* 25(10): 3791-3803.

Gonzales, L. 2015. Multimodality, translingualism, and rhetorical genre studies [J]. *Composition Forum* 31: 1.

Guerra, J. C. 2016. Cultivating a rhetorical sensibility in the translingual writing classroom [J]. *College English* 78(3): 228-233.

Hall, J. & B. Horner (eds.). 2023. *Toward a Transnational University WAC/WID Across Borders of Language, Nation, and Discipline* [C]. Denver, Colorado: University Press of Colorado.

Hartse, J. H., M. Lockett & M. Ortabasi. 2018. Languaging about language in an interdisciplinary writing intensive course [J]. *Across the Disciplines* 15(3): 89-102.

Horner, B. 2001. "Students' Right," English only, and re-imagining the politics of language [J]. *College English* 63(6): 741-758.

Horner, B. 2018. Translinguality and disciplinary reinvention [J]. *Across the Disciplines* 15(3):76-88.

Horner, B. & J. Trimbur. 2002. English only and U.S. college composition [J]. *College Composition and Communication* 53(4): 594-630.

Horner, B. & L. Tetreault. 2016. Translation as (global) writing [J]. *Composition Studies* 44(1): 13-30.

Horner, B. & L. Tetreault (eds.). 2017. *Crossing Divides: Exploring Translingual Writing Pedagogies and Programs* [C]. Boulder, Colorado: Utah State University Press.

Horner, B., M-Z. Lu & P. K. Matsuda (eds.). 2010. *Cross-Language Relations in Composition* [C]. Carbondale, IL: Southern Illinois UP.

Horner, B., S. NeCamp & C. Donahue. 2011. Toward a multilingual composition scholarship: From English only to a translingual norm [J]. *College Composition and Communication* 63(2): 269-300.

Horner, B., M-Z. Lu, J. Jones Royster & J. Trimbur. 2011. Language difference in writing: Toward a translingual approach [J]. *College English* 73(3): 303-321.

Jain, R. 2014. Global Englishes, translingual identities, and translingual practices in a community college ESL classroom: A practitioner researcher reports [J]. *TESOL Journal* 5(3): 490-522.

Kiernan, J., J. Meier & X. Wang. 2017. Translingual approaches to reading and writing: Centering students' languages and cultures within reflective practices of translation [J]. *L1-Educational Studies in Language and Literature* 17: 1-18.

Kubota, R. 2016. The multi/plural turn, postcolonial theory, and neoliberal multiculturalism: Complicities and implications for applied linguistics [J]. *Applied Linguistics* 37(4): 474-494.

Kulavuz-Onal, D. & C. Vásquez. 2018. "Thanks, shokran, gracias": Translingual practices in a Facebook group [J]. *Language Learning & Technology* 22(1): 240-255.

Lee, J. & C. Jenks. 2016. Doing translingual dispositions [J]. *College Composition and Communication* 68(2): 317-344.

Lu, M-Z. 1994. Professing multiculturalism: The politics of style in the contact zone [J]. *College Composition and Communication* 45(4): 442-458.

Lu, M-Z. & B. Horner. 2013. Translingual literacy, language difference, and matters of agency [J]. *College English* 75(6): 582-607.

Lu, M-Z. & B. Horner. 2016. Introduction: Translingual work [J]. *College English* 78(3): 207-218.

Malcolm, K. 2017. Disrupting monolingual ideologies in a community college: A translingual studio approach [A]. In B. Horner & L. Tetreault (eds.). *Crossing Divides: Exploring Translingual Writing Pedagogies and Programs* [C]. Boulder, Colorado: University Press of Colorado. 101-118.

Matsuda, P. K. 1999. Composition studies and ESL writing: A disciplinary division of labor [J]. *College Composition and Communication* 50(4): 699-721.

Matsuda, P. K. 2006. The myth of linguistic homogeneity in U.S. college composition [J]. *College English* 68(6): 637-651.

Matsuda, P. K. 2013a. It's the wild west out there: A new linguistic frontier in U.S. composition [A]. In A. S. Canagarajah (ed.). *Literacy as Translingual Practice: Between Communities and Classrooms* [C]. New York: Routledge. 128-138.

Matsuda, P. K. 2013b. Response: What is second language writing — And why does it matter? [J]. *Journal of Second Language Writing* 22(4): 448-450.

Matsuda, P. K. 2014. The lure of translingual writing [J]. *PMLA* 129(3): 478-483.

Matsuda, P. K. 2021. On the disciplinary identity of second language writing [J]. *Journal of Second Language Writing* 52: 100796.

Milson-Whyte, V. 2013. Pedagogical and sociopolitical implications of code-meshing in classrooms: Some considerations for a translingual orientation to writing [A]. In A. S. Canagarajah (ed.). *Literacy as Translingual Practice: Between Communities and Classrooms* [C]. New York: Routledge. 115-127.

Norris, J. M. & L. Ortega (eds.) 2006. *Synthesizing Research on Language Learning and Teaching* [C]. Philadelphia: John Benjamins.

Pacheco, M. B., S. M. Daniel, L. C. Pray & R. T. Jiménez. 2019. Translingual practice, strategic participation, and meaning-making [J]. *Journal of Literacy Research* 51(1): 75-99.

Pacheco, M. B. & B. E. Smith. 2015. Across languages, modes, and identities: Bilingual adolescents' multimodal codemeshing in the literacy classroom [J]. *Bilingual Research Journal* 38(3): 292-312.

Pratt, M. L. 1991. Arts of the contact zone [J]. *Profession* 91: 33-40.

Ruecker, T. 2014. Here they do this, there they do that: Latinas/Latinos writing across institutions [J]. *College Composition and Communication* 66(1): 91-119.

Sánchez-Martín, C. 2022. Teachers' transnational identities as activity: Constructing mobility systems at the intersections of gender and language difference [J]. *TESOL Quarterly* 56(2): 552-581.

Severino, C. 2017. "Multilingualizing" composition: A diary self-study of learning Spanish and Chinese [J]. *Composition Studies* 45(2): 12-31.

Silva, T. 1997. On the ethical treatment of ESL writers [J]. *TESOL Quarterly* 31(2): 359-363.

Silva, T. & Z. Wang (eds.). 2020. *Reconciling Translingualism and Second Language Writing* [C]. New York: Routledge.

Silva, T., I. Leki & J. Carson. 1997. Broadening the perspective of mainstream composition studies: Some thoughts from the disciplinary margins [J]. *Written Communication* 14(3): 398-428.

Smith, B. E., M. B. Pacheco & C. R. De Almeida. 2017. Multimodal codemeshing: Bilingual adolescents' processes composing across modes and languages [J]. *Journal of Second Language Writing* 36: 6-22.

Sun, Y. 2022. Implementation of translingual pedagogies in EAL writing: A systematic review [J]. *Language Teaching Research* 13621688221090б.

Sun, Y. 2023. Increasing critical language awareness through translingual practices in academic writing [J].

Journal of English for Academic Purposes 62: 101229.

Sun, Y. & G. Lan. 2021a. Enactment of a translingual approach to writing [J]. *TESOL Quarterly* 55(2): 398-426.

Sun, Y. & G. Lan. 2021b. Research trends in 'trans-' studies on writing: A bibliometric analysis [J]. *System* 103: 102640.

Sun, Y. & G. Lan. 2023. A bibliometric analysis on L2 writing in the first 20 years of the 21st century: Research impacts and research trends [J]. *Journal of Second Language Writing* 59: 100963.

Sun, Y., G. Lan. & L. Zhang. 2023. Pedagogical values of translingual practices in improving student feedback literacy in academic writing [J]. *Assessing Writing* 56: 100715.

Sun Y., K. Yang. & T. Silva. 2021 Multimodality in L2 writing: Intellectual roots and contemporary developments [A]. In D. Shin, T. Cimasko, & Y. Yi (eds.). *Multimodal Composing in K-16 ESL and EFL Education* [C]. Singapore: Springer. 3-16.

Tannenbaum, M. 2014. 'With a tongue forked in two': Translingual Arab writers in Israel [J]. *International Journal of Bilingualism* 18(2): 99-117.

Tardy, C. M. 2017. Crossing, or creating, divides? A plea for transdisciplinary scholarship [A]. In B. Horner & L. Tetreault (eds.). *Crossing Divides: Exploring Translingual Writing Pedagogies and Programs* [C]. Boulder, Colorado: Utah State University Press. 181-189.

Tardy, C. M. & E. Whittig. 2017. On the ethical treatment of EAL writers: An update [J]. *TESOL Quarterly* 51(4): 920-931.

Wang, X. 2017. Developing translingual disposition through a writing theory cartoon assignment [J]. *Journal of Basic Writing* 36(1): 56-86.

Williams, J. & F. Condon. 2016. Translingualism in composition studies and second language writing: An uneasy alliance [J]. *TESL Canada Journal* 33: 1-18.

Xie, D. & Y. Sun. 2023. Pedagogical implications of translingual practices for content and language integrated learning [J]. *Applied Linguistics Review*. https://doi.org/10.1515/applirev-2023-0057 (accessed 16/04/2024).

Young, V. A. 2004. Your average nigga [J]. *College Composition and Communication* 55(4): 693-715.

Zhang-Wu, Q. 2023. Rethinking translingualism in college composition classrooms: A digital ethnographic study of multilingual students' written communication across contexts [J]. *Written Communication* 40(1): 145-174.

Zheng, X. 2017. Translingual identity as pedagogy: International teaching assistants of English in college composition classrooms [J]. *Modern Language Journal* 101(S1): 29-44.

About the Authors

Li ZHANG is a first-level English teacher (secondary school) at Yushan Middle School. She received her M.A. from Shanghai International Studies University. Her research interests include English education, translingual studies, and practice-based language teaching.

Yachao SUN (corresponding author) is an assistant professor in the Language and Culture Center at Duke Kunshan University. His research interests include multilingual writing, translingual studies, multimodal composition, and corpus linguistics. Email: ys302@duke.edu

Ruiyun SUN is an associate professor in the College of Foreign Languages at Northeast Forestry University. Her research interests include second language writing and English education.

现状与趋势：国内二语写作焦虑研究现状与趋势可视化分析

胡萍萍[1] 王雨钦[2]

浙江师范大学

摘要：文章以国内2013—2022年间中国知网（CNKI）数据库中有关二语写作焦虑研究的中文期刊文献为数据来源，利用文献计量分析法梳理国内二语写作焦虑研究的基本情况，并运用CiteSpace信息可视化技术绘制二语写作焦虑研究的相关科学知识图谱。研究结果表明，近十年国内二语写作焦虑研究发文量呈现“M”形状的波动态势，仍有较大发展空间；核心文献的研究机构集中在师范类本科院校；研究的核心领域主要包括写作教学、写作能力、写作成绩、教师反馈及焦虑表现等；未来研究需进一步改进核心研究主体未成形、研究对象分布欠均衡和研究内容多元性不足的问题。

关键词：二语写作焦虑；反馈方式；写作教学；可视化分析；文献计量分析

DOI: 10.20081/j.cnki.cjslw.2023.07.003

1. 引言

写作焦虑指学习者在写作过程中所表现出来的焦虑行为，如逃避写作任务，担心自己的作文被他人阅读和评议等（Daly & Miller 1975）。外语写作焦虑是一种产生于特定外语写作学习情境的焦虑（Matsuda & Gobel 2004; Woodrow 2011）。随着人本主义心理学的兴起和发展，外语教学逐渐由“以教师为中心”向“以学生为中心”转变，情感因素对语言教学的影响越来越受到重视，作为情感因素重要组成部分的焦虑情绪也逐渐成为国内外二语习得和外语学习研究的重要内容。

目前，国内专门针对二语写作焦虑的综述性文章主要是基于文献分析法对二语写作焦虑的相关研究进行梳理和分类，目的是厘清二语写作焦虑的发展方向。如王松和曾祥发（2021）在对国内外二语写作焦虑的相关研究进行回顾性分析后发现，该领域的研究内容主要涉及写作焦虑测试量表的编制、写作焦虑与写作能力的相关关系以及写作焦虑的缓解策略等。马洁和董攀（2018）对大数据背景下国内外外语写作焦虑的研究方向进行了梳理，认为二语写作焦虑研究的未来发展总体趋势为深度与广度的拓展。然而，国内基于文献计量法的二语写作焦虑综述研究较少，存在较大发展空间。文献计量法作为一种被广泛认可的研究方法，可以对一个学科的总体发展状况进行梳理（李昶颖、徐锦芬 2018）。鉴于此，本研究运用CiteSpace信息可视化技术对国内2013—2022年间发表的有关二语写作焦虑研究的期刊文献进行分析，绘制相关科学知识图谱，探究国内二语写作焦虑研究的核心领域、新兴研究热点及趋势。具体而言，本文尝试回答以下问题：

1）近十年我国二语写作焦虑研究的总体状况如何？

2）二语写作焦虑研究聚焦的热点有哪些？

3）二语写作焦虑研究的未来趋势如何？

2. 研究设计

2.1 研究方法

本研究采用文献计量法中的词频分析、共词分析等，以中国知网（CNKI）学术资源总库为文献来源，利用知识图谱分析软件CiteSpace进行关键词提取、聚类图生成、突现词提取等语料处理，将文献的结构、规律和分布情况以可视化方式进行呈现（杨艳霞、任静生 2016），解读2013—2022年间中国二语写作焦虑研究的演进历程与特点。

2.2 数据收集与分析

本文数据来源于中国知网学术期刊数据库（CNKI）。在高级检索项中以“写作焦虑”进行主题检索，在主题检索的同时，在全文检索中分别输入“英语”“外语”和“二语”，结果显示数据库的最后更新时间为2022年12月1日。此外，参考徐锦芬和聂睿（2015）和黄慧等（2021）的研究方法，本研究将时间跨度选取为10年，最终确定时间范围为2013—2022年。期刊来源类别为“全部期刊”，文献语种限定为中文，剔除通知、目录、征稿、访谈等文献以及其他不符合条件的文献，最后确定135篇文献作为本研究的研究数据，其中，北大核心/CSSCI核心期刊论文23篇。将135篇文献导入知识图谱分析软件CiteSpace进行关键词提取、聚类图生成、突现词提取等语料处理，并绘制近十年国内二语写作焦虑研究发文量折线图、关键词聚类图、关键词共线图、关键词突现图等图谱，以可视化方式呈现近十年国内二语写作焦虑研究的结构、规律和分布情况，解读国内二语写作焦虑研究现状与趋势。

3. 结果与讨论

3.1 国内二语写作焦虑研究发文情况

3.1.1 发文数量及其年度分布

某一学科领域科研成果的数量在一定程度上体现了该领域的发展情况和研究水平，因此有必要对发文数量及其年度分布进行统计分析。将CiteSpace时间切片设置为一年，并对数据进行逐年统计（见图1）。由图1可以看出，近十年间国内二语写作焦虑研究的发文量呈现“M”形状的波动。具体而言，2013年发文量共13篇，随后呈现增长趋势，并在2015年达到峰值（20篇）。2016年发文量有所下降，但在2017年又迎来另一个高峰（16篇）。白丽茹（2017）在《写作焦虑测验》（Daly & Miller 1975）和《二语写作焦虑量表》（Cheng 2004）的基础上，以240名英语专业二年级学生为调查对象，尝试编制了《英语写作焦虑诱发因素量表》，为我国大学英语学习者课堂英语写作焦虑相关研究提供了科学规范且简便易行的本土化工具，这大大激发了国内学者对于二语写作焦虑的研究热情。2018年后虽然每年的发文量都不及两个峰值，但总体呈现波动上升趋势，这从侧面说明国内二语写作焦虑研究仍有较大发展空间。

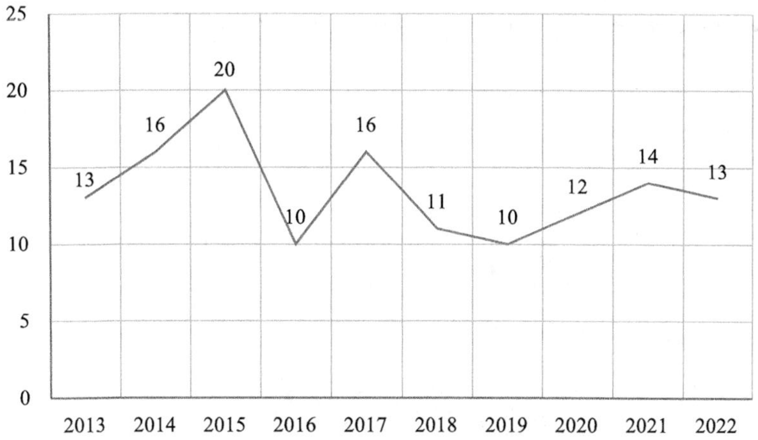

图1　2013—2022年国内二语写作焦虑研究发文量

3.1.2 研究机构及作者分布

从研究机构来看，2013—2022年国内二语写作焦虑研究全部期刊论文的发文机构集中在师范类本科院校和其他本科院校的外国语学院，如北京师范大学（6篇）、东北师范大学（2篇）、延安大学外国语学院（2篇）、安徽工程大学外国语学院（2篇）、南京大学外国语学院（2篇）等。核心期刊论文发文机构以师范类本科院校为主，如北京师范大学、东北师范大学等。发文作者中，影响力最大的是李航与刘儒德（316次被引），发文量最多的是李航（4篇）；合作作者占比约为30%，其中同机构合作作者占比约75%，跨机构合作作者占比约25%。

由此可见，二语写作焦虑的研究主体为师范类本科院校和其他本科院校的外国语学院，核心文献的发文机构主要集中在师范类本科院校。研究者之间的跨机构合作较少，深耕该领域的量产作者较少。因此，二语写作焦虑研究者应加强跨机构合作，从初期零散、低层次的研究向系统化、深层次、聚合性的研究发展（傅恒2022）。

3.2 国内二语写作焦虑研究的核心领域

运用CiteSpace绘制国内二语写作焦虑研究的关键词聚类知识图谱，具体操作如下：时间跨度选择为2013年1月—2022年12月，时间切片设置为1，词汇来源同时选择主题、摘要、关键词和附加关键词，节点类型选择关键词，其他设置均按照软件默认设置。得到的结果显示2013—2022年间国内二语写作焦虑研究共有21个聚类。使用CiteSpace过滤功能筛选出具有分析意义的聚类（见图2），得到的社团结构显著，聚类非常理想（图谱模块值Q=0.6099，平均轮廓值S=0.9052），聚类节点从大到小依次为：写作教学、英语写作、外语焦虑、写作能力、写作成绩、互动关系、焦虑值、教师反馈、焦虑表现、外语学习焦虑。由于部分概念过于宽泛，且受篇幅限制，下文将重点讨论写作教学、写作能力、写作成绩、教师反馈以及焦虑表现五个核心研究领域。因为写作能力无法量化，所以现有研究通常将写作成绩作为写作能力的衡量方式，因此下文将写作能力与写作成绩合并讨论。

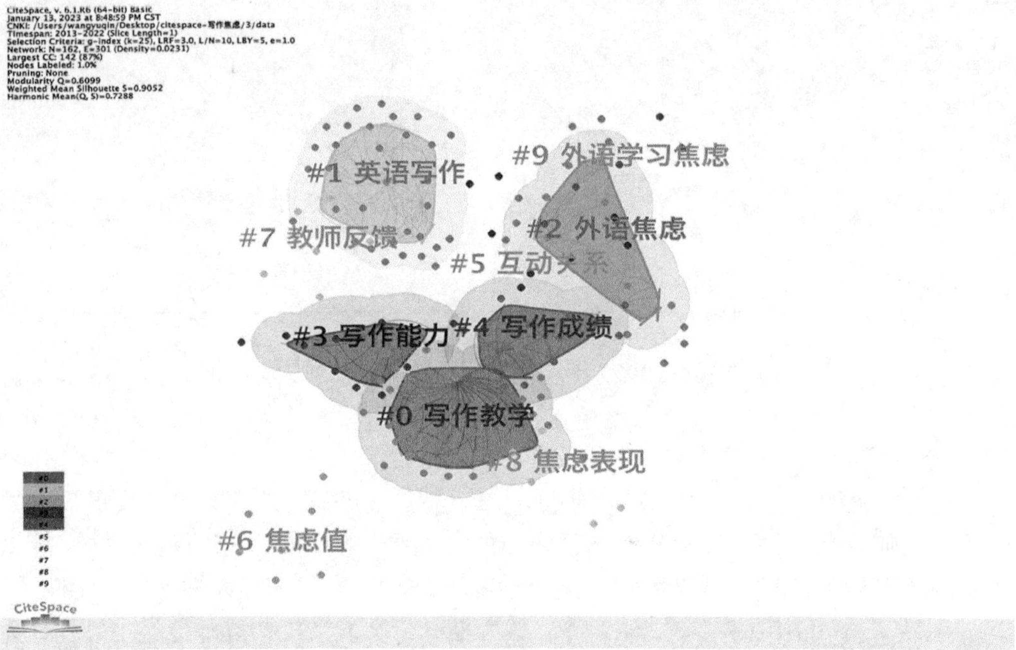

图2 2013—2022年国内二语写作焦虑研究关键词聚类知识图谱

3.2.1 写作教学对二语写作焦虑的影响

此研究主题的研究方法主要有实验研究、问卷调查、反思性日志以及访谈，研究内容主要为不同写作教学模式与英语写作焦虑的相关性研究，如郭士香（2016）在进行教学实验后发现实施AAWP（Authentic writing task-motivated，Application-oriented，Writing skill-targeted，Project-checked）英语写作教学模式的实验班在英语写作总焦虑、躯体焦虑、自信焦虑和评价焦虑等方面有显著降低；甄荣（2013）基于混合式教学构建了一种将多媒体网络教学与传统课堂教学相结合、将任务型教学模式和自主型学习模式相融合的新型英语写作教学模式，这一模式能够有效缓解学生的英语写作焦虑，并为推动传统写作教学改革提供了一个新的方向；张琳和秦婷（2020）通过对相关的测试、问卷和反思性日志实验数据进行定量研究发现读后续写有助于降低学习者的写作焦虑，尤其是在减少回避行为和缓解构思焦虑方面有显著作用；钟含春和范武邱（2018）通过为期一年的定量追踪研究发现CLIL（Content and Language Integrated Learning）教学模式能有效降低学生的外语写作总体焦虑，其中课堂教学焦虑和构思焦虑受到的影响最为显著，回避行为次之，自信焦虑受到的影响较为不明显，且该教学模式对不同水平学生的影响程度也不尽相同，对缓解中、低水平学生的写作焦虑效果尤为显著。

3.2.2 二语写作焦虑对写作能力与写作成绩的影响

此研究主题的研究方法主要有实验研究、问卷调查以及质性访谈，研究内容主要为二语写作焦虑与写作能力和写作成绩的相关性研究。国外学者研究发现二语写作焦虑与写作成绩和写作能力之间存在显著负相关关系，高焦虑水平学生的写作成绩往往比低焦虑水平学生差（Tahmouresi & Papi 2021；Zabihi 2018）。国内学者也对英语写作教学中的焦虑情绪进行了诸多研究，发现二语写作焦虑情绪在我国英语学习者中也普遍存在，且与写作能力呈负相关关系，严重阻碍了英语学习者写作能力与成绩的提升，印证了国外学者的研究结果。郭燕和徐锦芬（2014）开展的英语学习焦虑多维度研究显示，在写作焦虑维度上，学生写作主动性因子的焦虑值达到高频范围，表明其写作练习主动性非常差；自信及评价忧虑因子的焦虑值也接近高频范围，表明英语学习者写作信心不足，对教师评价产生抵触和焦虑情绪。詹剑灵等（2022）对比研究了续写与命题写作中的二语写作焦虑后，发现二语写作焦虑与写作成绩呈显著负相关关系，且在不同写作任务中，对写作成绩产生负面影响的焦虑因子有所不同，对比续写中的写作成绩仅与构思焦虑呈显著负相关关系，而命题写作中的写作成绩与所有焦虑因子均呈显著负相关关系。张家强和郭丽（2021）探讨了外语写作焦虑与写作质量的关系，发现外语写作焦虑程度与体现写作质量的三个词汇丰富性指标（词汇变化度、词汇复杂度和词汇密度）之间存在显著关系，焦虑程度越高，词汇变化度和词汇复杂度越低，写作篇章越短、句子结构越简单且词组使用越少，进而导致词汇密度越高，表明焦虑情绪对写作能力的发挥及写作质量产生明显的负面影响。

3.2.3 教师反馈对二语写作焦虑的影响

此研究主题的研究方法主要有实验研究、文本分析、访谈（包括半结构化访谈和刺激回忆访谈）、个案研究以及问卷调查。研究内容集中于：1）教师反馈与其他反馈模式的对比研究。如周一书（2013）通过问卷和访谈调查了大学生对三种写作反馈方式（教师反馈、同伴反馈和网络反馈）在缓解写作焦虑程度、增强写作兴趣等方面的满意度。结果表明，教师反馈在缓解写作焦虑程度和增强写作兴趣这两方面的得分要低于另外两种反馈方式，原因在于学生对教师评阅存在敬畏心理，感到紧张不安。吴育红（2013）考察了同伴互评对大学生英语写作自我效能感的影响。研究发现，与接受传统教师反馈的学生比较，参与同伴互评的学生获得了更多积极的情感体验，其写作自我效能感得到显著提升。2）不同类型的教师反馈（如口头反馈、书面反馈、即时反馈、延时反馈等）对学生写作的影响，尤其是书面反馈的研究，集中探讨教师书面纠错的有效性和教师反馈对学生写作焦虑水平的影响。牛瑞英和张蕊（2018）采用个案研究法跟踪了一位经验型专业英语写作教师书面反馈的焦点、策略及其成效，并通过访谈法调查了学生对教师反馈的态度，研究发现该教师对学生作文中语言问题的反馈显著多于对内容和结构的反馈，所用策略主要为间接反馈，且负面反馈占主导地位；虽然学生能够对大部分教师反馈点进行成功修改，但访谈结果表明教师的负面反馈会让学生感到焦虑，适当的正面反馈更能激发其写作信心与投入。3）多元反馈模式的构建与研究。在多元互动环境中，学习者的反馈投入呈现三种类型，即同伴—教师并重型、批改网—教师并重型和批改网—同伴—教师并重型（徐锦芬、龙在波 2022）。相较于教师反馈，人机混合反馈能够显著提高学习者的学习投入，激发学习者的积极情感（张亚、姜占好 2022）。陈功和宫明玉（2022）通过对教学的深度观察以及相关数据的细致分析发现，融合了机器反馈、同伴反馈和教师反馈的"N+2+1"多元反馈模式可以促成深度学习的发生，减少学生焦虑，促进全体学生共同进步。佘雨新（2021）探索了"师生合作评价"（TSCA）模式对不同水平非英语专业学生英语写作焦虑的影响，研究结果表明，TSCA模式对于降低英语写作焦虑起到积极作用，且对低水平学生整体写作焦虑的缓解程度要优于高水平学生。

3.2.4 二语写作焦虑的表现

此研究主题的研究方法主要有问卷调查和访谈，研究内容主要为二语写作焦虑的来源和诱因。白丽茹（2017）认为《写作焦虑测验》（Daly & Miller 1975）的研究对象为母语学习者，调查内容涉及焦虑因素的题项相对较少，故而不能有效测量外语学习者在特定写作语境下产生的焦虑情绪，而《二语写作焦虑量表》（Cheng 2004）中的量表题项和构成成分不能涵盖第二语言写作焦虑特质及诱发因素，且由于语言环境、教育背景以及学习者英语水平不尽相同，该量表也不完全适用于中国大陆地区英语教学语境。鉴于此，白丽茹（2017）以240名英语专业二年级学生为调查对象，尝试编制了《英语写作焦虑诱发因素量表》，研究表明英语写作焦虑诱发因素主要包括写作者个体诱发因素和写作过程诱发因素，前者涉及表达能力、语言能力和篇章能力，后者涉及评语反馈、任务特征和输出方式。秦晓晴等（2015）通过对受试进行问卷调查和访谈，发现英语写作障碍由写作任务复杂性、语言系统障碍、内容障碍、写作态度障碍、写作信心障碍和结构障碍等因素构成；英语写作焦虑由构思焦虑、课堂焦虑、回避行为和自信焦虑等因素构成；引起写作障碍和写作焦虑的原因主要是自身原因、英语语言能力，以及教师原因、汉语写作能力和英语写作目的等因素。

3.3 研究热点与趋势

3.3.1 高频关键词

关键词作为文章的核心与精髓，是文章主题的高度概括和凝练，高频出现的关键词通常被认为是该领域的研究热点（徐锦芬、聂睿 2015）。运用CiteSpace绘制国内二语写作焦虑研究的关键词共现知识图谱（见图3），图中节点代表关键词，其大小与关键词的出现频次成正比。如图3所示，出现频次超过5次（包括5次）的关键词依次是写作焦虑、英语写作、写作能力、写作成绩、焦虑、同伴互评、写长法、写作、写作教学。各关键词频次、中心性以及初始发表年份见表1。

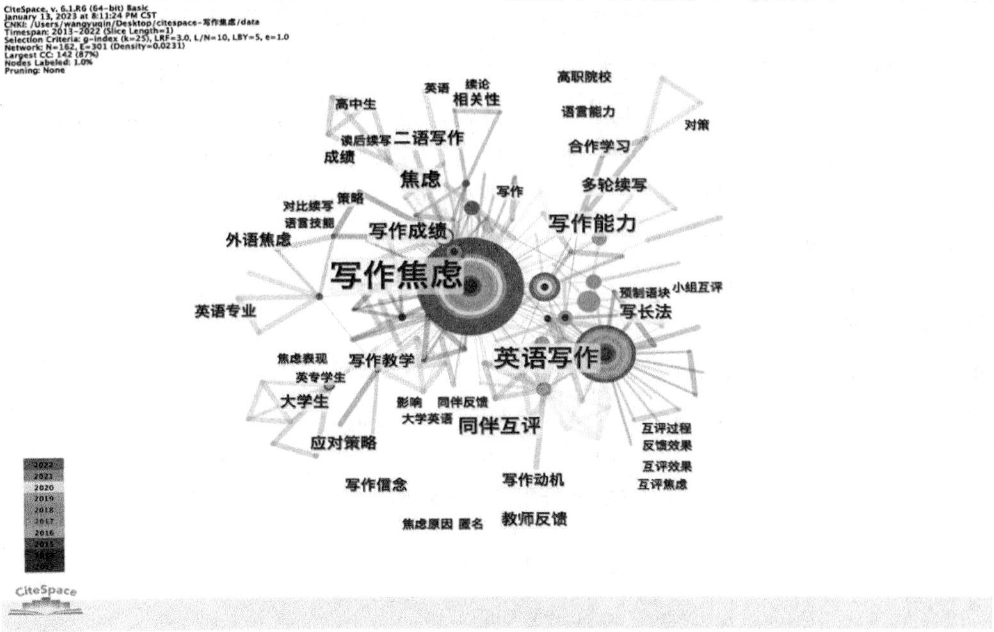

图3 2013—2022年国内二语写作焦虑研究的关键词共现图谱

表1 2013—2022年国内二语写作焦虑研究高频词列表

序号	关键词	中心性	频次	年份
1	写作焦虑	1.24	57	2013
2	英语写作	0.37	22	2013
3	写作能力	0.08	13	2014
4	写作成绩	0.01	13	2013
5	焦虑	0.14	10	2014
6	同伴互评	0.05	8	2016
7	写长法	0.03	5	2014
8	写作	0.01	5	2013
9	写作教学	0.01	5	2013

从表1可以看出，近十年国内二语写作焦虑研究主要聚焦英语课堂写作教学，英语写作、写作能力、同伴互评等关键词中心性数值较大，表明其核心地位突出，是国内二语写作焦虑研究领域的研究热点。写作教学与二语写作焦虑的相关性研究

也获得了较高的关注，其中外语写长法的中心性和关键词出现频次相较于其他写作教学法略高，是目前比较流行的缓解二语写作焦虑的教学方法。此外，写作能力和写作成绩出现的频次较高，推测其原因可能是研究二语写作焦虑的最终目的是帮助学生提高写作能力与写作成绩。国内学者研究发现写作焦虑能够显著负向预测写作成绩。大学生写作焦虑与写作自我效能感呈负相关，写作焦虑水平越高的大学生其写作自我效能感越低，面对写作任务时的动机水平越低，并产生强烈的回避行为，这会对其的写作认知过程产生妨碍性干扰，影响其写作质量，最终降低其写作成绩（李航 2017；李航、刘儒德 2013；李航等 2013）。尽管写作自我概念和写作自我效能对学生的写作成绩没有直接的显著影响，但仍可通过写作焦虑的中介作用间接地促进学生的写作学习，进而提高其写作成绩（郭继东 2018）。

3.3.2 新兴研究热点与趋势

突现词指短时间内使用频率较高的词，体现了阶段时间里研究热点的活跃程度，同时还能反映该领域研究热点的演变和发展趋势（屈琼等 2021）。本文运用CiteSpace绘制了国内二语写作焦虑研究的关键词突现图（见图4）。由图4可见，2013到2014年间国内学者尝试从二语习得理论的视角研究二语写作焦虑。2014到2017年间的突现词与写作教学和缓解写作焦虑的应对策略相关，合作学习（2014—2015年）和写长法（2014—2017年）均被国内学者证实能有效缓解二语写作焦虑情绪。

图4　2013—2022年国内二语写作焦虑研究关键词突现图

随着国内二语写作焦虑研究的不断深入，2014到2015年间涌现了大量与缓解二语写作焦虑的应对策略相关的研究。吴荣辉和何高大（2014）调查了合作学习在大学英语写作教学中的应用效果，研究发现师生平等的面对面交流有助于减少因不能顺畅表达意图而引发的交际焦虑，避免教师对学生交际错误、写作错误的纠错而造成的消极评价焦虑，合作学习使学生有机会接触到同伴解决问题的方法和思维过程，学会解决写作问题和克服写作困难，有助于消除写作认知焦虑。马洁和董攀（2017）通过问卷调查发现大学生英语写作焦虑自我调节策略包括行动策略、构思策略、回避策略和情感策略四种类型，且使用频率总体上随焦虑程度的加深而降低，进而提出通过针对性写作任务、写前构思训练和个性化鼓励引导大学生使用积极的自我调节策略从而减缓写作焦虑情绪。

2016年前国内二语写作焦虑研究的重点研究对象是大学生，包括英语专业学生和非英语专业学生。例如，周俊良（2014）采用混合研究法探究了写作焦虑对英语专业学生写作策略使用的影响，研究发现各年级英语专业学生均存在英语写作焦虑情绪，而焦虑值会显著负向影响学生三大类写作策略（准备阶段策略、过程策略和修改策略）的使用，焦虑程度越低的学生对这三大类写作策略的使用频率和实践程度越高，反之则反。李航（2015）以330名非英语专业大学生为受试探究英语写作焦虑和写作成绩之间的关系，研究结果显示，就学生整体而言，学期初的焦虑程度能够负向预测学期末的写作成绩，但学期初的写作成绩无法预测学期末的焦虑程度，说明写作焦虑是写作成绩的影响因素；就学生个体而言，经过一学期的写作训练，学生的写作成绩较学期初有所提升，同时焦虑值也有所上升，但始终保持在中等水平，表明适度焦虑不会阻碍学生写作成绩的进步。2015到2016年间以大学生为研究对象的二语写作焦虑研究大量突现，推动了国内二语写作焦虑研究对象的扩展。随着英语教育的普及和英语教育低龄化趋势的发展，未来研究还可将研究对象进一步延伸至普通高中学生、初中学生、小学生乃至学前儿童。

2017到2018年间“写作信念”的突现表明国内学者开始关注写作信念、写作焦虑等个人因素之间的相互关系。写作信念不仅能够促使学习者在写作过程中兼顾内容与形式，努力提高写作效率，影响学习者的写作自信和写作动机，还能够引导学习者对写作焦虑情绪形成正确的认知，从而缓解其写作焦虑（任风雷 2018）。

2018到2022年间“同伴互评”的突现表明同伴互评因其自身具备的调节性和社会交互性，逐渐引起了学者的广泛关注（屈琼等 2021）。现有研究表明，学生完全可以信任同伴的语言能力和互评能力。通过同伴互评，学生不仅是在互相帮助，而且在掌控自己的学习，发展自主学习和自我规约的能力（高瑛等 2018）。同伴互评的效果受到多种因素影响，其中起到决定性作用的是评语采纳环节（高瑛等 2019）。还有研究关注写作焦虑对同伴互评时学生提供评语数量、质量和形式的影响，结果分析显示虽然写作焦虑与评语总量和质量不具有显著相关性，但对给出修改建议/办法形式的评语具有较强负向预测力（高瑛、刘杭松 2021；梁忠庶等 2020）。此外，解冰等（2020）在现有研究基础上编制了同伴互评感知量表，不仅是本土化研究工具开发的有益尝试，还对调查和分析中国外语学习者英语写作同伴互评感知具有借鉴意义。

写作能力作为国内二语写作焦虑研究的核心领域，其在2020到2022年间的再次突现预示着未来写作能力仍将是国内二语写作焦虑研究的核心领域和热点话题。现有研究通常将写作成绩作为写作能力的衡量方式，因此二者间的关系往往被直接画上等号。但成绩的高低有时并不能代表能力的强弱，未来研究应进一步明确写作能力和写作成绩之间的联系与区别。

4. 研究总结与展望

国内二语写作焦虑的文献计量分析表明，过往十年我国二语写作焦虑研究成果数量呈现波动上升态势，研究领域不断拓展，研究视角日益多元，但仍存在有待改进之处。

首先，核心研究主体未形成。研究机构及作者分布的现状表明，深耕该领域的量产作者较少，稳定的、高质量的核心研究者队伍尚未形成；研究者之间缺乏跨机构合作，各研究机构之间暂未建立联系密切的学术共同体。核心作者群体和研究机构在二语写作焦虑研究中起着重要的奠基和引领作用，因此亟须通过专项资助、专题探讨等途径，加强研究者、研究机构之间的交流与合作，构建核心学术共同体，并赋予其一定的学术职责和历史使命，鼓励其持续深入地进行研究，为二语写作焦虑研究开辟全新的发展道路。

其次，研究对象分布欠均衡。国内二语写作焦虑研究已有成果研究对象多为大学生和高职高专生，以中小学生为研究对象的研究开展较少。教育部颁布的《普通高中英语课程标准（2017 年版）》和《义务教育英语课程标准（2022年版）》均对学生的书面表达能力提出了较高水平的学业质量要求。然而，学生英语写作的实际水平与理想要求之间存在一定差距，经常出现英语知识储备不足、使用中式英语、不善于用英语思考等现象，导致一些学生对英语写作产生厌恶、排斥、焦虑等负面情绪。因此，未来仍然需要不断扩充样本群体，进一步完善各个教育阶段中二语写作教学的衔接。

最后，研究内容多元性不足。国内二语写作焦虑研究在研究内容方面存在较大程度的重复。首先，在写作焦虑与写作能力相关性方面，虽然研究成果丰富，但系统性的多维度研究较少，各中介变量仍然较为零散。今后研究应围绕研究目的完善研究设计，将焦虑这一情感因素与成就动机、态度等变量相结合，运用结构方程模型等更先进的统计方法，全面深入探索焦虑情感因素对写作水平的影响。其次，在二语写作焦虑的缓解策略方面，已有研究大多倾向于从外部因素出发，主要围绕教学方法、教学组织形式和反馈方式三个维度展开，而从学习者内部因素出发的自我调节策略研究较少。未来研究可以进一步拓宽对写作焦虑自我调节策略和写作自我效能感的研究。

5. 结语

本文以国内2013—2022年间中国知网上有关二语写作焦虑研究的中文期刊文献为数据来源，对国内二语写作焦虑研究现状进行了文献计量分析，并通过CiteSpace软件绘制了相关知识图谱。研究发现，近十年来，国内二语写作焦虑研究呈现“M”形状的发展态势，从2013年起，发文量显著增加，并分别于2015年和2017年出现了两次发文高峰，其后发文量有所下降但整体仍呈现波动上升趋势；研究主体为师范类本科院校和其他本科院校的外国语学院，而核心文献的研究机构集中在师范类本科院校；国内二语写作焦虑研究的核心领域包括反馈方式、写作教学、对策及焦虑表现等；未来二语写作焦虑研究可着力于打造核心学术共同体，进一步扩展研究对象的范围，拓展研究内容的广度和深度。

本文只分析了国内二语写作焦虑研究的情况，且时间跨度较短。未来可进一步分析国外相关研究与文献，并延长时间跨度，更深层次地挖掘国内外二语写作焦虑研究的核心领域和变化趋势，从而为国内相关研究提供启示。

参考文献

Cheng, Y. S. 2004. A measure of second language writing anxiety: Scale development and preliminary validation [J]. *Journal of Second Language Writing* 13(4): 313-335.

Daly, J. & M. Miller. 1975. The empirical development of an instrument of writing apprehension [J]. *Research in the Teaching of English* 9(3): 242-249.

Matsuda, S. & P. Gobel. 2004. Anxiety and predictors of performance in the foreign language classroom [J]. *System* 32(1): 21-36.

Tahmouresi, S. & M. Papi. 2021. Future selves, enjoyment and anxiety as predictors of L2 writing achievement [J]. *Journal of Second Language Writing* 53. doi: 10.1016/j.jslw.2021.100837.

Woodrow, L. 2011. College English writing affect: Self-efficacy and anxiety [J]. *System* 39(4): 510-522.

Zabihi, R. 2018. The role of cognitive and affective factors in measures of L2 writing [J]. *Written Communication* 35(1): 32-57.

白丽茹，2017，英语写作焦虑诱发因素量表编制 [J]，《外语界》(5)：74-82。

陈功、宫明玉，2022，多元反馈模式促进深度学习的行动研究 [J]，《外语教学》(3)：60-66。

傅恒，2022，中国金融英语研究二十年回溯与展望——基于知识图谱的文献可视化分析 [J]，《外语界》(4)：64-71。

高瑛、刘杭松，2021，英语写作同伴互评中提供反馈的作用与影响因素研究 [J]，《外语电化教学》(6)：87-93+14。

高瑛、汪溢、Christian D. Schunn，2019，英语写作同伴反馈评语采纳及其影响因素研究 [J]，《外语电化教学》(2)：17-24。

高瑛、张福慧、张绍杰、Christian D. Schunn，2018，基于Peerceptiv互评系统的英语写作同伴反馈效果研究 [J]，《外语电化教学》(2)：3-9+67。

郭继东，2018，写作自我概念和自我效能对大学生英语写作成绩的影响：写作焦虑的中介作用 [J]，《外语学刊》(2)：69-74。

郭士香，2016，AAWP英语写作教学模式对英语专业学生写作焦虑影响的实证研究 [J]，《解放军外国语学院学报》(4)：111-118+160。

郭燕、徐锦芬，2014，非英语专业大学生英语学习焦虑多维度研究 [J]，《外语界》(4)：2-11。

黄慧、陈翠翠、丁松，2021，国内近十年外语教育研究中的技术工具使用情况分析 [J]，《外语电化教学》(4)：73-79+11。

李昶颖、徐锦芬，2018，我国语言学研究国际发表状况及未来趋势——基于2000—2017年SSCI论文的分析 [J]，《外语电化教学》(4)：30-37。

李航，2015，大学生英语写作焦虑和写作成绩的准因果关系：来自追踪研究的证据 [J]，《外语界》(3)：68-75。

李航，2017，英语写作自我效能感对非英语专业大学生写作成绩的影响研究 [J],《外语教学理论与实践》(3)：57-63+79。

李航、刘儒德，2013，大学生外语写作焦虑与写作自我效能感的关系及其对写作成绩的预测 [J],《外语研究》(2)：48-54+112。

李航、刘儒德、刘源，2013，大学生外语写作自我效能感在写作焦虑对写作成绩影响中的中介效应 [J],《心理发展与教育》(4)：385-390。

梁忠庶、高瑛、解冰、贺文婧，2020，英语写作同伴互评焦虑及其对互评的影响研究 [J],《外语电化教学》(3)：41-46+67+7。

马洁、董攀，2017，大学生英语写作焦虑自我调节策略研究 [J],《外语界》(5)：83-89。

马洁、董攀，2018，大数据背景下国内外语写作焦虑研究 [J],《外语电化教学》(2)：32-37。

牛瑞英、张蕊，2018，二语写作教师书面反馈焦点、策略及成效个案研究 [J],《解放军外国语学院学报》(3)：91-99+160。

秦晓晴、杨京京、毕劲，2015，英语写作障碍和写作焦虑的构成及影响因素研究 [J],《外国语文研究》(1)：97-106。

屈琼、刘媛媛、兰宁艺，2021，国内二语写作反馈研究现状与趋势的可视化分析 [J],《外语电化教学》(3)：37-43+6。

任风雷，2018，动机、信念和焦虑对大学生英语写作的影响 [J],《广西民族师范学院学报》(3)：113-116。

佘雨新，2021，“师生合作评价”模式对不同水平英语学习者写作焦虑的影响研究 [J],《二语写作》(1)：47-57+131-132。

王松、曾祥发，2021，大学英语写作焦虑相关研究综述及其对策分析 [J],《高教学刊》(2)：55-57+62。

吴荣辉、何高大，2014，合作学习在大学英语写作教学中的应用效应研究 [J],《外语教学》(3)：44-47。

吴育红，2013，同伴互评对自我效能感的影响——一项基于大学英语写作的实证研究 [J],《山东外语教学》(6)：68-72。

解冰、高瑛、贺文婧、梁忠庶，2020，英语写作同伴互评感知量表的编制与探索性应用 [J],《外语教学》(3)：67-72。

徐锦芬、龙在波，2022，多元互动环境下学习者写作反馈投入研究 [J],《外语与外语教学》(5)：21-31+144-145。

徐锦芬、聂睿，2015，基于 CiteSpace 的国际二语写作研究动态可视化分析（2004-2014）[J],《外语电化教学》(4)：3-9。

杨艳霞、任静生，2016，我国外语批判性思维研究可视化分析与反思 [J],《外语界》(3)：50-56+80。

詹剑灵、姜琳、黄灵灵，2022，对比续写中的二语写作焦虑研究 [J],《解放军外国语学院学报》(2)：61-69+160。

张家强、郭丽，2021，外语写作焦虑与写作质量：词汇丰富性差异研究 [J],《二语写作》(1)：26-36+131。

张琳、秦婷，2020，读后续写对英语专业学生写作焦虑和写作能力的影响研究 [J],《外语教学》(6)：72-76。

张亚、姜占好，2022，人机混合反馈环境对学习投入和二语写作水平的影响研究[J],《外语界》（4）：40-48。

甄荣，2013，基于混合式教学的英语写作教学[J],《外国语文》（4）：142-144。

钟含春、范武邱，2018，CLIL模式对英语专业学生写作焦虑影响的定量追踪研究[J],《解放军外国语学院学报》（4）：111-119。

中华人民共和国教育部，2017,《普通高中英语课程标准（2017年版）》[M]。北京：人民教育出版社。

中华人民共和国教育部，2022,《义务教育英语课程标准（2022年版）》[M]。北京：北京师范大学出版社。

周俊良，2014，英语专业学生写作焦虑对写作策略使用影响的实证研究[J],《广西师范学院学报（哲学社会科学版）》（4）：117-121。

周一书，2013，大学英语写作反馈方式的对比研究[J],《外语界》（3）：87-96。

作者简介：

胡萍萍，浙江师范大学外国语学院副教授，博士。主要研究领域：外语教学理论与实践、外语课程与教学论、教师专业发展、以及研究方法论。电子邮箱：beth@zjnu.cn

王雨钦，浙江师范大学外国语学院硕士研究生。主要研究兴趣：外语教学理论与实践。

混合式教学背景下大学英语专业写作教学策略的行动研究

杨 熙

长治学院

摘要：近年来，写作教学研究从原本相对离散的状态逐步形成了完善的专业网络，其中写作教学策略研究是最重要的研究方向之一。结合疫情时代“双线”教学的应用，以及大数据和人工智能助推下大量英语写作助学软件的涌现，研究混合式教学背景下教师教学策略选择及效用对写作教学发展具有重要意义。本研究是在太原某独立院校英语专业大二年级写作课堂开展了为期一学期的行动研究，以“后方法”教学理论为框架，探索混合式教学背景下教师教学策略的发展与变化。研究发现，利用“后方法”理论框架的宏观策略赋能教师进行写作教学策略的融合与改编，对学生写作水平有明显提升作用；其中，高分组学生写作水平发展平稳，中等分数组学生进步最为显著。通过主题分析发现，学生个体差异、环境因素和任务特点对写作水平发展影响较大，教师应在进行教学设计时重点关注。

关键词：英语写作；教学策略；行动研究；“后方法”理论

DOI: 10.20081/j.cnki.cjslw.2023.07.004

1. 引言

“后方法时代”（Post-method Era）语言教学观是对传统教学方法的反思，旨在创建一种“由下至上”的教学理论体系，适用于具体的教学情境和教学实践者自身，并倡导教师自主性的回归（杨熙 2015）。经过20年的发展和演变，“后方法”在外语教学领域逐渐形成了一定的研究基础，一些理论研究探讨了“后方法”理论对外语教师和外语教学课堂的重塑作用，发现“后方法”理论在一定程度上在教学目标、教学内容、教学过程、教学评价、教师发展等方面对夯实教学理论、创新教师发展路径、优化“情景化”教学模式具有积极影响（Kamali 2021；齐放、张军 2017；万垚 2020）。由于混合式教学模式结合了传统教学方法和数字化、网络化的在线学习手段，强调教师教学的多样性和自主性，“后方法”理论对于推动混合式教学模式的发展从理论上看具有相辅相成的作用。“后方法”理论能帮助教师找到适合具体课堂、有时效性的教学方案，在英语写作课堂中可以基于教学实际实现多重教学方法和教学策略的有机结合，但将两者相结合的实证研究尚不多见，因此“后方法”理论渗透下的混合式教学模式对教师英语写作教学策略的影响及其效果是本研究的焦点。

1.1 英语写作教学策略

英语写作教学模式在近十年中经历了较大变革。我国大学英语写作教学一直以来以成果教学法为主导，这种教学法以行为主义理论为基础，认为写作是一个“刺激—反应—强化”的过程，教学围绕范文和语法知识讲解展开，重点关注写作的结果。成果教学法忽视写作过程，不能及时发现和解决写作中出现的问题，学生的写作状态十分被动，教学效果不显著（姚香泓 2010）。21世纪初，许多专家致力于探索更有效的写作教学法，如“过程教学法”“体裁教学法”等，其中过程教学法的基础是交际理论，强调写作的认知过程。但也有学者指出该教学法不利于学生英语基础知识的学习（张效国 2007）。为了能够在语言知识、写作过程、写作体裁之间找到一个平衡点，近年来“任务教学法”在英语写作教学中得到广泛应用（Ahmad 2020）。该教学法是交际教学法的发展，其核心是让学生在完成有现实意义的任务的过程中习得语言。它把学习者的外语交际能力放在首位，强调“做中学”。写作教学模式的转变不但表明我国对英语写作教学的重视，也给教学一线的英语写作教师以启示，写作教学应避免形式单一，做到策略化教学，进一步丰富课堂教学形式。

1.2 混合式教学与“后方法”

混合式教学是将传统课堂面对面教学与线上教学相结合的一种“双线教学”模式，自2020年起在世界各地得到了广泛应用，通过教学设计和技术支持有效开展教学活动，具有学习时间地点更灵活、资源更易分享、交互性更强等优势（李宝敏等 2022）。混合式教学的挑战性在于这一模式需要教育者重新审视并重构教学实践，将课堂上所教授的知识和技能通过不同形式组织在一起，并共同参与学习过程。关于混合式教学对学生学习的影响的研究结果并不一致，有研究发现混合式教学比传统教学更能促进学生课程成绩提高，并能提升学习动机，而一些研究发现混合式教学相较于传统面授教学对学生成绩产生负面效应（李宝敏等 2022）。例如，相关研究显示，混合式教学对学生课程成绩具有显著的促进作用，同时能提升学生的学习动机（Lin et al. 2016）。另一方面，Wong et al.（2020）发现混合式教学与传统教学在学生学习成绩方面的影响并无显著差别，二者效果相当。还有一些研究发现混合式教学的效果并不一定优于传统教学，混合式教学相较于传统面授教学对学生成绩甚至存在负面效应（Demaidi et al. 2019）。因此，有学者提出线上线下融合教学实践目前仍处于探索初期，还未实现线上线下模式的有效结合（祝智庭、胡姣 2021）。

外语教学中的“后方法”理论是近四十年来在西方外语教学界兴起的一种教学思想，其内核强调从意识到行为超越传统“教学法”范畴，其代表人物和理论开拓者是Kumaravadivelu教授，其理论主张和实证理据发表于Kumaravadivelu（1992，1994，2001，2003a，2003b，2006）论著中，这标志着“后方法时代”的开启（齐放、张军 2017）。“后方法”理论的提出源于对传统教学方式的不满，在大多数情况下传统教学方式未能使学习者运用他们的外语知识进行有效交流（Hazratzad &

Gheitanchian 2009）。“后方法”理论具有三条基本属性：首先，它本身不是另一种方法而是一种方法转化的探索过程，采取不同的教学方法是一种“自上而下”的选择产物，相反寻求方法转化却是“自下而上”的形成性过程（Kumaravadivelu 2006）。这就要求我们首先能够重新考虑语言教学理论研究者和实践者之间的关系，如果传统的方法观认为理论研究者是建构教学法理论的专家，那么“后方法”理论则赋予教学实践者形成个人实践理论的能力。如果传统方法观认为理论家掌握教学法的决定权，那么“后方法”理论则认为每一个教学实践者具有产出其基于教学具体场景、基于课堂的创新型教学策略的权力（Kumaravadivelu 2003a）。

其次，教师自主性是“后方法”理论的必要条件。对于教学方法的传统解读“忽视了教师在其学生时期获得的教学经验和相关知识”（Freeman 2016：35），但是“后方法”理论则重视教师在课程、教材、学校等学术或管理约束内可以自主发挥的创造力，并且注重激发和提升教师进行批判性教学的能力。因此，不仅是教学专家，普通教师亦可通过自己的教学经历、课堂观察、分析和反思去构建全新的教学方法。

最后，“后方法”理论强调原则性实用主义，这要求我们先厘清两个概念：“折中主义”和“宏观策略”。前者是一种基于将现有理论合并的应用，后者是基于“理论与实践关系、观点和现实关系”而形成的教学法实用主义（Widdowson 1990：30），从而达成对课堂教学过程的重构。目前我国基于“后方法”的实证研究较少见，本文的课堂设计和教学策略构建试图从“最大化学习机会”“促进协商式互动”“提高学习自主性”“激活直观启发”“综合语言技能”五条宏观策略出发，进行混合式教学背景下微观教学策略设计和探索。

1.3 研究问题

随着教育、文化、科技的进步和教育理念的发展，混合式教学和“后方法”逐步结合，利用“后方法”对教学方法灵活性和实用性的强调，并注重根据实际情况进行线上和线下的教学资源的整合，着力培养学生的英语学习能力和综合素质，是一项符合当代重视个性化学习、教育教学创新的有效尝试，然而此类实证研究在我国外语教学界较少涉及。

本文采用行动研究方法，在中国一所地方二本高校的英语专业学生中，探索混合式教学背景下融合性教学策略是否有助于提高英语写作课堂教学质量和教学效果。研究意义首先在于利用“后方法”教学法及行动研究的组合形成适用于特定教学场景的教学方法，从而形成混合式教学背景下的有效教学策略，具有一定的教学参考价值；其次对于处于后疫情时代的中国外语教育，研究结果和形成的结论对于外语写作教学策略的理论发展亦有价值，是一次对“后方法”理论“自下而上”的课堂教学理论构建的实践。研究问题如下：

1）“后方法”理论对教师英语写作教学策略的应用有何影响？

2）“后方法”理论下的英语写作课堂教学效果如何？

2. 研究方法

本研究采用了行动研究方法，通过“问题分析—行动干预—教学反思”循环进行的三个步骤形成基于具体课堂的“后方法”英语写作教学设计，此过程通过搜集分析定量与定性数据回答研究问题。因篇幅有限，定性数据中关于学生英语写作水平只截取写作的衔接连贯性为例进行分析论证。

2.1 研究对象

本次行动研究以太原某高校英语专业二年级四个平行班共96名学生为研究对象，采取方便抽样方法确定80名同学为被试，将其分成两个大班上课，80名学生均已进行了一个学期的相同教材、同一教师指导的写作训练，并全部参加了写作期末考试，统计结果显示（表1），两班学生的英语写作水平相当，无显著差异（p=0.475>0.05）。在第二学期的行动研究中，两班上课统一使用同一教材，由同一教师授课，对照组教师采用传统教学法进行教学，实验组教师采取了“后方法”理论指导的教学设计。

表1 两个参与实验的班级第一学期期末写作成绩对照

班级		n	均值	标准差	p 值（双侧）
第一学期成绩	对照组	40	75.8000	5.60311	0.475
	实验组	40	74.9250	5.29822	

注：*p<0.05

2.2 研究工具

研究工具包括一次访谈、四次写作测试和一次学生活动报告。首先，在行动研究最初对学生进行随机访谈，主要围绕以下三个问题：1）你知道什么是衔接连贯吗？2）你知道的衔接连贯方式有哪些？3）你认为写作中的衔接连贯重要吗？其次，在为期十周的行动研究过程中，对被试进行了四次英语专业四级写作模拟测试。每次测试均按照英语专四考试要求，在规定时间、规定地点进行集中测试，测试内容为三段式议论文写作。将学生写作中的衔接连贯手段使用情况进行统计，然后进行错误分析，并针对具体问题进行面对面访谈以了解其产生的深层原因。最后，合作写作活动结束后，要求每小组提交一份合作写作活动报告，内容包括本次活动后的感受、本学期写作课的收获，以及对自己写作水平发展情况的反思和评价。

2.3 研究设计

2.3.1 第一阶段（第1周）

问题分析

通过收集学生第一学期期末考试成绩，针对学生写作的主要问题，对学生进行了第一次结构式访谈（详见研究工具），访谈主要内容是了解学生对写作的衔接和连贯性的理解。主要表现出的问题为：1）概念不清，即学生无法很好地理解和区分衔接和连贯的概念；2）学生意识不到衔接连贯的重要性；3）学生对写作策略学习并不感兴趣。

行动干预

课堂教学策略：通过交互式课堂教学提高学生对英语写作课的热情。采用基于任务的交互式教学方法，在课堂上让学生通过小组讨论、合作学习等方式完成学习任务。具体实施的做法是，成对地在课堂上展示语篇，并使学生通过小组讨论发现两个语篇的区别，然后选出感觉流畅的语篇。在学生们经过充分讨论得出自己的见解后，引导学生发现和总结通顺的语篇中分别使用了哪些不同的衔接手段，本阶段结束后进行了第一次英语专业四级写作模拟测试。

线上教学策略：引入线上批改软件，让学生在批改软件上提交作业，提交前需自己根据软件批改意见修改两次作文。

教学反思

交互式课堂对改善写作课堂沉闷的气氛较为有效，调动了学生的积极性。第一次模拟作文的衔接连贯统计发现，学生普遍存在的问题为生硬地照搬模板，衔接连贯词汇使用单调。学生对线上批改软件的使用还不熟悉，没有习惯多次修改的过程写作，大部分学生对文章两次修改的内容只是根据机器批改出的明显错误进行了修改。

融合型策略打破了学生对于写作课的预期，学生们积极和老师同学沟通线上交作业的问题，课堂氛围、课堂秩序、师生关系均有所改善。

2.3.2 第二阶段（第2—6周）

问题分析

解决词汇使用单调最重要的方法之一是加强语言输入。课本是主要教学资源和依据，但绝不是唯一来源。在教学过程中，结合大纲要求和学生的实际情况，充分开发课本以外的教学资源，将文本素材和影音素材相结合，这样不仅能扩大学生的知识面，更可以激发学生的学习兴趣和课堂参与热情。

行动干预

1）课堂教学策略：翻转课堂，要求学生积累在阅读材料中读到的好词好句，在每节课前留出15到20分钟请五位学生为全班讲解自己收集到的词句，在自己积累和学习其他同学的基础上要求每位学生建立自己的词汇库。

2）线上策略：为提高学生写作兴趣，在布置记叙文写作任务时，不是传统命题写作，而是要求学生课下观看指定的视频片段并改写成一篇记叙文。所用视频软件是一个英语口语跟读软件，学生跟读电影片段并录制视频作为作业的一部分，跟读软件会对学生口语进行智能评分，这种手段不仅有助于促进写作作业多元化、提高趣味性，也可以帮助学生加强英语听说练习。同时，依然采用线上批改软件提交作业的方式，要求学生进行两次修改后再提交。此阶段结束后，进行第二次英语专业四级写作模拟测试。

教学反思

学生课堂参与度有很大改善，学生愿意分享自己的词汇库，也乐于展示自己的作品让教师发现自己的不足。根据作业批改和学生反馈的情况，学生的衔接连贯意识有很大提高，但是依然存在衔接连贯手段错用或非恰当使用的情况。

2.3.3 第三阶段（第7—8周）

问题分析

随着学生整体衔接连贯意识的提高，词汇输入量的增多，学生作业中的问题趋于多样化。有同学词组搭配不当，有同学复杂句语法错误，还有同学有冠词使用错误等情况。为解决学生在衔接连贯中表现出的不同问题，第三步行动干预是建立"循环型"反馈手段，教会学生作文修改策略，帮助其形成良好写作习惯。

行动干预

"循环型"反馈手段是指批判融合地使用写作批改手段。有效的作文批改是写作教学中非常重要的环节，纠错的明晰程度、纠错时机以及学习者对反馈的理解都会影响到纠错效果。本次研究中纠错方案包含以下三点设计。1）批改软件辅助修改：收集学生电子版作文，利用作文批改软件统计出文章当中的语法和拼写等错误，将软件评分数据和人工批改结合，来发现学生常犯错误；2）同伴互评：每两周安排一次批改自习时间，利用一个小时让同学们与同桌进行同伴互评，当场纠错并讨论后改正；3）面批：同伴互改后，老师与学生进行面对面批改，了解学生写作过程中真实的心理过程和出错原因，并对上两次批改中学生存在的疑惑进行解答，最终给出得分和评语。此阶段结束进行第三次英语专业四级写作模拟测试。

教学反思

软件批改方式虽高效但难免存在批改错误，因此无法完全替代人工批改；学生对面批手段表现出很大热情，在有限时间里学生都积极争取更多面批机会。但面批确实很费时，作者对面批方式进行了一定的改良，在进行同伴互评和面批前老师先进行一次批改示范，即选取一篇包含典型错误的学生作文以PPT演示形式在全班进行批改，访谈数据显示80%的学生认为此做法很有用；同伴互评的效果并不明显，有的学生不能认真对待同伴的作文，还有一部分学生不能正确识别错误，其原因可能与学生自身水平和环境因素等有关。

2.3.4 第四阶段（第9—10周）

问题分析

同学们在经历前三轮教学行动干预后，对衔接连贯手段的重要性、主要手段、写作方式等有了较好的理解和提高，但在形成文章段落内部和段落间逻辑连贯方面仍存在概念不清的问题，不能统一上下文间的逻辑顺序和视角。经访谈了解到，学生没有对文章整体结构的提前构思，没有过程写作意识。

行动干预

最后阶段的主要任务是巩固本学期所学知识点和学习策略，研究者设计了一次真实的体验式教学，即将合作学习和过程写作相结合。具体做法是把学生分成小组，布置了一次合作写作活动。该写作活动持续两周，要求每个小组自行分工完成一次记叙文写作任务。参照过程写作的写前准备、写初稿、修改、反馈修改、重写五个阶段（邓鹂鸣等 2003）的流程来合作完成，并要求每小组以PPT的形式将他们合作写作的成果进行汇报展示，其中要明确每个步骤的负责人和阶段性成果。任务完成后要求每个小组呈交一份活动报告，并进行了第四次英语专业四级写作模拟测试。

教学反思

通过合作写作完成的文章较之前几周的文章在衔接连贯的使用上有明显的提高，学生能够清晰地介绍自己文章中哪些部分使用了衔接连贯和使用该衔接连贯手段的目的和必要性。通过小组分工，同学们明确了过程写作的各个步骤和每个阶段应形成的作品。借助批改软件和小组间批改，对形成的初稿进行多次完善，形成的作文内容充实、衔接连贯手段使用恰当，每位同学都对过程写作有了深刻的认识。

十周行动研究结束后，学生的写作中仍然存在一些未解决的问题。首先，对于某些衔接词汇使用僵化，如and、but、firstly、secondly，以及对on one hand、on the other hand等词的错用；其次，在记叙文写作中，学生能使用时间顺序排列事件，但时间标记词汇的使用仍然较为贫乏，个别同学全文只能用and、then等低级词汇进行连接；最后，议论文写作缺乏逻辑连贯性，对于隐性的衔接连贯手段重视不够，如论据的排列顺序混乱，不能做到逻辑连贯和条理清晰。

3. 研究结果与讨论

3.1 “后方法”理论促进多元化英语写作教学策略应用

首先，教师在灵活应用各种写作教学策略，进行“因地制宜”的教学设计方面有了显著提升。一是教师能通过“后方法”教学理论框架中的宏观策略对教学策略进行合理选择与优化。二是教师能通过再造自身教学身份，从单纯的“知识传授者”向“学习推动者”“知识建构者”身份转化，更新教学模式、提升教学效果。所以相关研究提出，“后方法”的关键贡献在于对教师身份定义的变革和持续推向深入，教师在塑造自我教学身份、师生关系，并被授权创造特定教学方法的过程激发了其教学的自主性，直接受益者是学生（Golzar 2020；Kamali 2021）。

其次，通过数据分析可见，学生写作表现也有良好发展。通过对比学生第一次访谈与最终形成的学习报告可以看出，学生在衔接连贯手段运用、过程写作法、词汇多样化使用等方面有了明显提高。 仍然明显存在的问题包括词汇量不足、写作修辞法掌握不够灵活、写作焦虑等。

最后，将对学生在本次行动研究中对模因写作、合作学习、纠错反馈三种写作教学策略的效果评价进行总结。

模因写作教学策略可以排除母语的干扰，减少错误，补充外语学习脱离目的语环境之不足（郭亚玲、蒋宝成 2009）。在写作课堂设计建立词汇库任务是应用模因论的一个体现，学生在之后的作业中试着使用多种表达来丰富自己的用词，措辞更为地道。在活动报告中，大部分学生表示大量有效输入对写作很有帮助，丰富了她们的措辞和句式。不过作者也发现，不少同学对这种方法能否真正提高写作提出了质疑。例如，有的学生写道："有帮助，但是写的时候想不到，想到觉得语篇风格不合适。"也有学生提到："背东西还是有用的，可以用得到的地方很多，但写完又忘了。"因此对于输入方式，包括介绍单词句式的深度和广度，强化输入的方式手段等都需进一步研究。如何把这些知识点从短期记忆变成长期记忆，也是一个重要的课题。

合作学习方法强调以学习者为中心，从教学过程的集体性出发，着眼于学生之间的互动性，认为学习者是知识意义的主动构建者，教师对学生的意义建构起帮助和促进作用。实证研究证明，合作学习法运用于写作教学有助于学习者发展其元认知能力，即学习者控制、掌握学习过程，适时调整学习策略的能力并在互教互学的过程中掌握所学内容，学会自主学习（Alexandra 2005；孙丽明等 2009）。本次研究发现，合作学习过程极大地激发了学生的课堂参与热情，使每个学生都对过程写作和作文修改的重要性和优越性有了新的认识。以下为部分学生在合作写作结束后在活动报告中记录的体会。

> 在完成各自的片段之后，我们三人互相修改交流，将一些最基本的时态语态问题及时进行了修正，理顺了各自片段的逻辑关系，使文章得以连贯通顺。两个片段之间的衔接问题也是我们重点讨论的范畴，目的就是做到片段不会遗漏情节，保持故事的完整性。我们也体味到了合作的快乐，大家都竭尽全力去把这个故事写好、写完整，合作的学习方式我们也会继续运用到以后的学习中。(B 组：2021-06-16)
>
> 在帮助别人改的时候，也同时发现了自己的错误，对自己的写作有一定提升。大家一起完成一件事情并将它完美是很开心的，并能从中学习到很多。（E 组：2021-06-18）
>
> 写作要抓住文章的主旨大意，时间顺序，事情的先后发展都要清楚。语言要组织恰当、语法正确、用词恰当，前后两部分文章要浑然一体，段落层次分明。(H 组：2021-06-12)
>
> 现在写文章会先打草稿，然后再修改。背的句子、单词都挺有用，但是有时会懒得背，除了老师要求背。现在也开始注意文章是否达到衔接连贯了，中文写作对我的英文写作影响还是挺大的，中式思维还是难以克服。制定了好多学习计划，想提高自己的水平，但是往往懒得练习。（K 组：2021-06-20）

纠错反馈的重要性不言而喻，而保证作文修改效果有两个必要条件：一是保证学生对评改后的作文作出反应；二是注意评改方法，努力提高评改质量。建立学生和教师之间的循环机制是纠错反馈的关键：正向反馈是指教师对学生的作文作出评价，而教学实践中教师较少关注负向反馈，即从实际评改过程中接收信息，了解学生的学习情况并进一步完善课堂教学（杨敬清 1996）。同伴互评和教师一对一批改方式都对学生写作质量总体上有提升效果（孔文等 2013），因此本次行动研究中的同伴互改和面批两种修改方式正是实现教师与学生之间循环机制的实践，不仅建立了学生和老师之间的循环，也建立起学生与学生之间的循环。几乎所有学生在活动报告中都表示非常愿意进行同伴互改，80%的学生表示希望老师能尽可能多地进行面批，主要原因可总结为以下几点：1）同伴互改和面批可以适度增加学生的焦虑感，提高注意力，从而在写作过程中投入更多的努力；2）同伴互改的过程可以进一步促进学生对相关知识的巩固，并在写作中对类似问题提高注意；3）面批过程能够做到因材施教，解决每个个体不同的问题，并搭建起教师与学生更好沟通的情感纽带。

3.2 “后方法”理论下英语写作教学课堂教学效果的提升

3.2.1 写作成绩显著提高

表2为第二学期实验结束后两个班级期末写作成绩对照表，作文由两位非任课老师在卷子密封状态下进行流水线评分。由于第二学期与第一学期的考试内容和评分标准存在较大差异，因此不进行两学期之间的纵向比较。利用SPSS软件对两班测试结果进行了独立样本检验，统计结果显示（见表2）对照班成绩均值为70.825，实验班成绩为77.125，实验班平均成绩高于对照班，$p<0.05$，证明两者之间成绩相等的假设不成立，两组间平均值存在显著差异。

表2　实验组与对照组下半学期期末写作成绩对照

班级		n	均值	标准差	*p* 值（双侧）
第二学期成绩	对照	40	70.825	7.538	*0.001
	实验	40	77.125	8.013	

注：*$p<0.05$

由表2可见，两个班的均值相差较大（6.300），说明实验班和对照班的写作成绩经过一学期的教学实验后发生了较大的变化，实验班的成绩要明显优于对照班。统计结果表明该差异达到了统计学上的显著性水平。实验证明“后方法”教学理念指导下的混合式教学模式有利于提高英语专业学生的英语写作水平。究其原因，“后方法”理论所主张的“教师不拘泥于某种教学法”，而是考虑具体的语言环境、课程目标、学生的水平与需求、教学设施等因素，选择适当的原则指导自己的教学过程，并创造出各种不同的微观策略去完成写作教学，使得写作教学变得富有特定性、实用性、可能性（肖丽艳 2010）。

3.2.2 写作衔接连贯度提升

研究者从实验班中良好（>80）、中等（70—80）、及格（60—70）三个成绩段随机挑选了三名同学作为重点个案分析，观察不同成绩段学生的写作水平进步情况。表3为这三位学生的个案分析，其中A代表高分段学生个案，B为中等分段学生个案，C为低分段学生个案。表3记录了三名学生在此次教学实验中的四次模拟测试中衔接连贯手段的使用情况。

表3 不同水平组的三名学生在四次测试中衔接词汇使用次数统计

连词类型		增补连词			转折连词			因果连词			列举连词			总计		
学生		A	B	C	A	B	C	A	B	C	A	B	C	A	B	C
测试	测试1	3	3	3	1	1	2	3	4	2	5	2	2	12	10	9
	测试2	5	4	3	3	2	2	3	1	2	5	7	3	16	14	10
	测试3	6	8	5	3	1	3	2	1	2	7	2	3	18	12	13
	测试4	7	8	4	2	2	2	5	3	4	5	6	4	19	19	14

图1为三名学生在四次测试连词使用总数趋势图，A、B和C三名学生在四次测试中，各类连词使用情况总体上均呈上升趋势。第一次测试到第四次测试的连词使用总数上，A生提高58%，B生提高90%，C生提高55%。从发展趋势看，A生发展趋势平缓稳定；B生虽总体进步最大，但发展过程最不稳定；C生在第一、二次测试中进步较不明显，而在第三、四次测试中取得较为快速的进步，从第二次到第四次测试阶段中最大进步40%（A生18.7%，B生35.7%）。笔者结合写作文本，对三名学生在面批时进行了回顾性访谈。A生认为自己的进步和课堂上老师的指导是分不开的，在多种教学方法中，该生认为词汇库建立最有用，很好地扩大了连词选择的范围；B生在第三次测试中连词总数明显下滑，原因是该生对第三次测试写作主题较为陌生，因此写作字数和衔接词汇使用都明显少于另外几次测试，B生表示过程型写作这种方式有助于理清写作思路，对提高写作衔接连贯帮助很大。

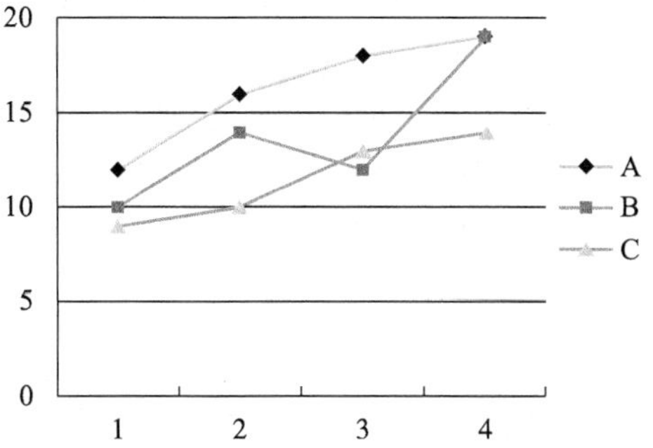

图1 不同水平组的三名学生在四次测试中衔接词汇使用总量变化趋势

图2以低分组C生在四次测试中衔接词汇使用情况为例，深入探索该生衔接连贯使用情况的变化趋势和发生变化的原因。

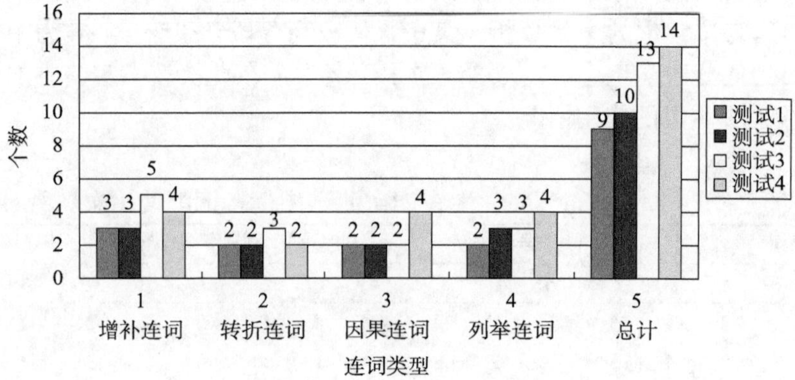

图2　C生四次测试衔接词汇使用情况

从C生四次测试衔接连词使用发展的柱状图可以看出，C生在四次测试中正确使用衔接手段的数量有一定提升，连词使用总数明显增多。其中并列连词在数量上变化不大，但通过阅读其文本发现，在第一、二次模拟中，该生使用的并列连词只有and，而从第三次测试开始，可以使用furthermore、that is to say这些高级的并列连词；第二类是转折连词的使用，四次测试中该生分别在第一、二、四次测试中使用了三次on the other hand，但是前两次均为错用。通过两次面批后，该生在第三次测试回避使用该转折连词，而在第四次测试中重新使用并运用正确，这说明对于相对来说较为顽固或已经石化的错误，采用面批对其进行纠正效果较为明显；最后可以明显看到该生在后两类连词的使用上进步显著，前两次测试中，该生列举论据时不使用举例类连词，而在后两次测试中均正确恰当地使用了举例连词。特别是时间连词的使用，从一开始只使用了nowadays，到第四次测试中使用时间短语in the meanwhile，该生在衔接连词多样性上取得较大进步。C生认为面批这种批改策略对其写作水平提升有明显帮助，这与一些研究提出的纠错反馈中直接反馈比间接反馈更具优势的结论相一致（Karim & Nassaji 2020；Leow 2015），因为直接反馈可以帮助学习者短期内更高效地避免语法混淆、词义混淆，从而短期内提高语法及用词准确性等。从以上分析可知，多样化的写作教学策略对学生写作水平发展有明显正向影响，但由于个体差异、环境因素和任务本身的区别，每种策略对于不同学生的影响不同。

4. 结语

本研究回答了两个研究问题：第一，在“后方法”教学理论指导下教师利用多样化的写作教学策略形成符合课堂实际的混合式教学方法，通过主题分析对模因写作、合作写作、纠错反馈等写作教学策略高频词的作用进行了分析和论证；第二，

“后方法”教学理论影响下的写作教学较之传统写作教学法对于提高英语专业学生写作成绩有更好表现。通过个案分析发现，学生个体差异（如学习动机、多元智能等）、环境因素（如学习环境、语言环境等）和任务特点（如任务复杂度、任务内容熟悉程度等）都对混合式教学对学生的英语写作成绩有着不同程度的影响。

通过实践“后方法”的五项宏观策略，本研究构建了如下混合式教学的设计逻辑。1）“学习机会最大化”：“双线”融合教学，对于学生形成课后自学自评的学习习惯有积极作用；翻转课堂，提高学生课堂参与和完成作业的积极性。2）“促进协商式互动”：同伴互评和教师面批结合，通过师生间、学生间的交流互动建立良好的教学生态环境、提高作业完成度。3）“提高学习自主性”：合作学习，以分组任务式教学激发学生的学习动机和热情。4）“激活直观启发”：丰富教学资料，线上直播课、电影跟读、小说仿写等教学活动都有助于激发学生的语言系统，达成综合性语言教学目的；用图示法讲解过程写作的基本流程，用思维导图带学生进行“头脑风暴”练习，用生动形象的图形概念强化学习结果。5）“综合语言技能”：模因论指导下开展“读—记—写”综合写作教学模式，超越写作课程本身对学生进行多方面语言训练。

本研究对英语专业写作教学主要有以下启示。一是写作教学应采用过程型写作而非结果型写作，可以培养学生强烈的写作程序意识和语篇意识；二是写作课堂任务和教学手段应多样化，但需保证任务的针对性和完成过程的可监控性；三是“双线”教学趋势下融合性教学的发展之道应更强调教师通过双线渠道实现与学生的交际沟通，最大化学习机会并激发学生的直观启发；四是有效利用融合型手段建立“可循环型”作文批改策略，充分调动学生在学习上的互助性和学习主动性。

参考文献

Ahmad, Z. 2020. Action research in EFL: Exploring writing pedagogy through a task-based lesson delivery [J]. *Journal of Language Teaching and Research* 11(3): 379-388.

Alexandra, A. 2005. The process of writing a text by using cooperative learning [J]. *Profile* 6: 47-57.

Demaidi, M. N., M. Qamhieh & A. Afeefi. 2019. Applying blended learning in programming courses [J]. *IEEE Access* 7: 156824-156833.

Freeman, D. 2016. *Educating Second Language Teachers* [M]. Oxford: Oxford University Press.

Golzar, J. 2020. Teacher identity formation through classroom practices in the postmethod era: A systematic review [J]. *Cogent Education* 7(1): 1-19.

Hazratzad, A. & M. Gheitanchian. 2009. EFL teachers' attitudes towards postmethod pedagogy and their students' achievement [R]. *Proceedings of the 10th METU ELT Convention* 1989. https://dbe.metu.edu.tr/convention/proceedingsweb/Attitudes.pdf (accessed 16/04/2024).

Kamali, H. C. 2021. "Deconstructionist" as the role of a teacher in postmethod pedagogy [J]. *Technium Social Sciences Journal* 19: 67-75.

Karim, K. & H. Nassaji. 2020. The revision and transfer effects of direct and indirect comprehensive corrective feedback on ESL students' writing [J]. *Language Teaching Research* 24(4): 519-539.

Kumaravadivelu, B. 1992. Macrostrategies for the second foreign language teacher [J]. *Modern Language Journal* 76(1): 41-49.

Kumaravadivelu, B. 1994. The postmethod condition: Emerging strategies for second/foreign language teaching [J]. *TESOL Quarterly* 28(1): 27-48.

Kumaravadivelu, B. 2001. Toward a postmethod pedagogy [J]. *TESOL Quarterly* 35(4) : 537-560.

Kumaravadivelu, B. 2003a. A postmethod perspective on English language teaching [J]. *World Englishes* 22(4): 539-550.

Kumaravadivelu, B. 2003b. Beyond methods: Macrostrategies for language teaching [M]. New Haven: Yale University Press.

Kumaravadivelu, B. 2006. TESOL methods: Changing tracks, challenging trends [J]. *TESOL Quarterly* 40(1): 59-81.

Leow, R. 2015. *Explicit Learning in the Classroom: A Student-Centered Perspective* [M]. New York: Routledge.

Lin, Y. W., C. L. Tseng & P. J. Chiang. 2016. The effect of blended learning in mathematics course [J]. *EURASIA Journal of Mathematics, Science and Technology Education* 13(3): 741 -770.

Widdowson, H. G. 1990. *Aspects of Language Teaching* [M]. Oxford: Oxford University Press.

Wong, K. T., G. J. Hwang, P. S. ChooGoh & S. K. Mohd Arrif. 2020. Effects of blended learning pedagogical practices on students motivation and autonomy for the teaching of short stories in upper secondary English [J]. *Interactive Learning Environments* 28(4): 512-525.

邓鹂鸣、刘红、陈芃、陈艳、章毓文，2003，过程写作法的系统研究及其对大学英语写作教学改革的启示 [J],《外语教学》(6)：58-62。

郭亚玲、蒋宝成，2009，从语言模因论看ESL写作教学的历史性回归——基于调查数据的实证分析 [J],《河北师范大学学报（教育科学版）》(8)：42-46。

孔文、李敦东、余国兴，2013，L2写作动态评估中同伴中介干预和教师中介干预比较研究 [J],《外语界》(3)：77-86。

李宝敏、余青、杨风雷，2022，混合式教学对学生学习成效的影响——基于国内外106篇实证研究的元分析 [J],《开放教育研究》(1)：75-84。

齐放、张军，2017，"后教学法"时代视阈下对我国外语教学策略与技巧的再思考 [J],《外语教学》(5)：54-59。

孙丽明、高帆、戴峥峥，2009，合作型过程写作在英语写作教学中的实践与启示 [J],《教法研究》(27)：133-134。

万垚，2020，后方法时代英语教学理论的范式重构 [J],《教学与管理》(18)：110-112.

肖丽艳，2010，试论后方法时代的写作教学 [J],《教育与职业》(15)：152-153。

杨敬清，1996，提高英语写作评改有效性的反馈机制——实验与分析 [J],《外语界》(3)：41-45。

杨熙，2015，"后方法"教学视角下的大学英语写作教学行动研究 [D]，太原理工大学。

姚香泓，2010，过程体裁法和成果法教学对学生写作应用策略及写作能力的影响 [J],《外语与外语教学》(3)：30-34。

张效国，2007，认知语言学在多媒体辅助"过程写作教学"中的应用 [J],《江南大学学报（教育科学版）》(2)：69-72。

祝智庭、胡姣，2021，技术赋能后疫情教育创变：线上线下融合教学新样态 [J],《开放教育研究》(1)：13-23。

作者简介：

杨熙，长治学院，二级翻译，博士生。主要研究领域为外语教学、二语习得、跨文化交际。

电子邮箱：yangxi1990@czc.edu.cn

双语体裁视角下汉英学术写作实践研究*

陈宁阳

苏州大学

摘要：在新时代国际化人才竞争背景下，需要思考如何培养兼具母语和外语表达能力，熟谙本土与国际规则，积极参与本土与全球知识构建的高水平人才。在帮助学生掌握英语作为国际学术通用语的同时，也应重视汉语作为母语的学术能力的发展研究和教学。本文从双语体裁视角出发，考察了新手作者汉英学术写作的实践场景、体裁知识储备及其双语写作实践中体裁知识的应用情况。研究发现新手作者实践场景和涉及体裁较为丰富，汉语在学术写作实践中占有重要地位；体裁知识储备缺乏全面性、系统性；汉英学术写作实践呈现仿拟与杂糅、对比与借鉴的知识应用特点。基于实践反思，本文还从体裁入手探讨立足本土实际的学术写作教学实践，助力学生汉英双语学术读写能力的提升，从而能够更为自信地参与本土和世界范围的知识构建。

关键词：双语体裁视角；体裁知识；学术写作；汉语；英语

DOI: 10.20081/j.cnki.cjslw.2023.07.005

1. 引言

日益深化的高等教育国际化进程中，人才培养面临新机遇的同时也面临新挑战。就语言教育而言，为适应面向全球化趋势下丰富多变的语言景观，语言教学的重点逐渐由单一模式下的外语人才培养向外语专业复合型人才和外语赋能的专业型人才方向转变。在各种教学改革尝试中，需要关注国家人才需求和社会宏观发展趋势。一方面，新时期国家发展大背景下的外语人才需要兼具国家意识和全球视野（文旭等 2020），在培养外语能力基础上要加强本土语言文化的学习掌握。另一方面，全球流动性带来个体跨国学习经历（cross-national learning experience）普及化（Jiang 2021）和出国低龄化（晋浩天 2015）等新趋势，海外教育对本土学生语言文化认知和语言能力发展产生一定影响（Fang et al. 2017）。从个案经验看，英语为主导的学术培养环境可能导致个体学术语言能力发展失衡，导致用母语进行学习研究的能力欠缺甚至缺失。近年来，国内不少高校在学术用途英语（English for Academic Purposes）和英语作为教学语言（English as Medium of Instruction）方面做了不少努力，这些尝试尽管加速了国际接轨的进程，但对本土人才的母语学术读

* 本文系教育部人文社会科学研究青年基金项目“中国人文社科学者汉英双语学术写作实践研究”（项目编号：21YJC740005）的阶段性研究成果。本文的撰写得到苏州大学人文社科交叉研究团队“汉外语言文化对比研究”（项目编号：5033720623）团队的支持，谨致谢忱。

写能力的发展存在潜在影响（Galloway et al. 2020）。从语言系统本身看，英语主导的国际学术交流和科研发表对本土学术语言的发展有制约作用（Flowerdew 2015）。一味趋从英语学术话语而忽视本土学术话语的写作实践可能造成认识论层面的潜在蚀失（陈宁阳 2021），带来学术领域广泛关注的“认识论危机”（epistemicide）（Bennett 2007；Zhao 2019）。如何在英语强势地位仍旧显著、汉语学术话语蓬勃发展的当下，在本土高校教学中提升学生的学术语言综合运用能力，使其未来能够自信地参与本土和全球范围的学术交流与知识建构，需要新时代语言教育决策者和工作者认真思考、积极回应。在该现实背景下，本文尝试从双语体裁视角出发，将本土英语专业本科生作为新手作者群体，分析其学术写作实践中的知识储备和应用情况，探讨开展汉语为基、汉英并进的学术写作教学的可能性，助力面向未来的外语人才培养。本研究具体围绕以下三个问题展开：

1）新手作者汉英学术写作的实践场景有哪些？有何特点？

2）新手作者汉英学术写作的体裁知识储备如何？

3）新手作者汉英学术写作实践中体裁知识的应用有哪些特点？

2. 双语体裁视角下的学术写作研究

写作研究中对体裁的关注由来已久。尽管体裁视角下的分析研究层出不穷，但大多着眼于单一语言中的写作实践，即一语或二语学习者如何应对不同体裁的写作任务，对多语作者跨语言写作能力和写作表现的关注相对较少（Gentil 2011；Pérez-Llantada 2021）。针对该研究缺口，Gentil（2011）开拓出双语体裁研究视野，提出需要将双语语言能力和体裁研究结合起来，全面考察双语作者实践中涉及的语言知识和体裁知识的复杂关系。一项个案研究（Canagarajah 2006）比较了一位斯里兰卡学者用一语泰米尔语和二语英语撰写三篇主题大致相同的研究文章的写作经历，作者需要通过把握不同体裁特征，以适应一语本土发表、二语本土发表、二语海外发表三种修辞情境。研究发现，不同修辞情境和话语团体对体裁期待不同，作者需要足够的修辞灵活性和体裁能力，以协调不同语言和话语团体之间的要求。另一项个案研究（Mein 2012），考察了一位美墨边境西语母语研究生的就读经历研究发现双语作者能够通过策略性调用一语体裁知识资源，驾驭跨学科领域的二语学术表达任务。

在针对双语作者语言能力的讨论中，Cummins（2008）指出以日常交际能力作为衡量二语水平的传统做法存在局限性。需要区分个体语言能力中会话流利度、语言技能和学术语言能力三个维度，口语流利度与学术语言能力之间不存在直接的迁移关系（Cummins & Yee-fun 2007）。语言共同基础能力（common underlying proficiency）为学术语言能力的发展创造了条件，作者可以借助已有的一语能力巩固共同基础能力，提升二语学术语言能力。体裁作为典型化的社会惯习具有跨语言的共性，但同时具有语言所在的社会文化背景的个性。个体的双语体裁能力以跨语言的体裁知识和意识为基底，在此基础上为适应不同表达任务需求发展出具有语言特征的体裁知识（language-specific genre knowledge）和体裁意识（awareness of language-specific genres）。高水平的双语作者可以灵活调用不同语言中的体裁知识和修辞策略，驾驭面向不同话语团体和交际需求的写作任务（Gentil 2011）。

与丰富的英语二语写作研究文献（邓鹂鸣、肖亮 2022）相比，仅有少量研究考察了汉语二语写作中的体裁差异（师文、陈静 2019），而针对汉英双语写作中体裁问题的探讨尚未展开。造成该悬殊差异的原因主要有认识和实操两方面。认识方面，在学术"母语优势"观的影响下，类似"外语学术写作能力需要通过系统性学习获得提升，母语学术写作能力可通过多读多写自然掌握"的观念较为普遍，学术汉语的研究和教学存在一定的认识盲区（陈宁阳 2021）。实操方面，由于一语和二语写作研究传统和范式等方面存在明显差异（Matsuda 2010），汉语学界和外语学界在学术写作方面研究的交流互鉴有限，加之研究者对双语语料的掌握情况和分析能力不平衡，在不同程度上限制了双语写作研究的开展。就体裁知识而言，目前研究主要集中研究生阶段的写作实践（如彭玉洁、徐昉 2021），对其他语言发展阶段作者的调查相对较少。该研究现状为本研究的开展提供了实践契机：研究聚焦英语专业本科生，将其作为一个汉英双语学术写作新手作者群体，以体裁知识为切入口，考察该新手作者群体的双语学术写作实践。

3. 研究设计

作为一名英语（大类）专业本科一线教师，笔者在开设"学术英语写作"课程三年（2021学年、2022学年、2023春季学期）过程中，利用授课机会，通过自愿报名参与的方式，在告知研究目的、过程、数据使用等细节后，承诺参与者数据的匿名和保密处理，对征得同意的选课学生在课堂之外进行了调查问卷、结构性访谈、个案跟踪、文本民族志（text ethnography）等形式的数据收集。本文集中汇报的实证研究数据包括课前调查问卷以及接受问卷调查中三名学生的跟踪访谈和历时写作文本。

调查问卷分为学术用途语言使用情况和体裁知识两部分。问卷设计参考前期学术英语调研结果，扩充增加了相应的汉语使用场景部分，题目设置为多选，要求勾选出符合自己真实学习情境的能力需求，主要目的是了解学生在使用汉英两种语言的主要学术实践场景及实践方式。体裁知识部分参考四维度模型（见表1），基于主要写作体裁（课程论文、读书报告等）要求学生自评其体裁知识掌握情况，并辅以体裁比较和开放式反思问题。

表1　体裁知识的四大维度（Tardy 2009）

体裁知识维度	内容
形式知识	体裁特定的词汇语法特征、结构语步以及体裁沟通的模式和媒介
过程知识	体裁的实施过程，包括实施过程中的必要步骤
修辞知识	体裁的预期目的，所处社会修辞语境中的修辞情境、话语团体和作者身份
内容知识	体裁内撰写或讨论特定话题所需要的专业知识

问卷调查涉及英语大类（英语、翻译、师范专业）三年级学生101人，回收有效问卷96份。访谈录音累计时长18.5小时，文本资料逾12.8万字。结果的统计和分析、访谈录音的转写和编码、历时写作文本的整理和标注均遵照相应的操作规范，文中引用文本和访谈语料均得到允许，对作者和受访人做了匿名处理。

4. 研究发现

4.1 汉英学术写作实践场景

从整体反馈情况看（表2），尽管调查对象为英语专业大类学生，专业课学习的工具语言和研习对象为英语，汉语在典型学术实践场景中使用频率仍然很高，包括信息检索、阅读文献、撰写课程论文等。值得注意的是，在听学术报告、撰写项目申报书、参加学术交流三项典型学术实践场景中，汉语使用需求较英语更为普遍。通过访谈交流发现，大部分学生在本科阶段参加的学术报告和论坛交流以汉语为多，仅有少数学生参加过以英语或其他语言为工作语言的国际学术报告和论坛活动。在撰写项目申报书方面，除个别学生有申请参与国际项目的经验外，大部分学生只申请过本科生科研培育项目、大学生创新创业训练计划项目等，而这些项目的申报材料均需要用汉语撰写。

表2　新手作者汉英学术实践场景及实践方式（n=96）

	实践场景（提及比例）	实践方式
汉语	信息检索（100%）	检索网页、数据库、图书馆等资源，收集信息
	阅读文献（100%）	阅读专业学习资料（包括翻译文献）、应试备考及其他材料
	课程学习（100%）	完成通识课、跨专业选修课等课程的课堂任务和课外作业
	课程论文（95.8%）	撰写通识课、跨专业选修课及部分专业课的期中或期末论文
	专业考试（89.6%）	参加考研及其他资格考试（如教师资格证）
	讲座报告（48.3%）	参加专业讲座、听学术报告、记笔记
	项目申报（26.0%）	撰写大学生科研创新项目等的申请材料
	通讯文稿（18.7%）	撰写学术活动通讯稿、宣传新闻等
	学术交流（12.5%）	参加国内学术论坛、学术会议等
英语	信息检索（100%）	检索网页、数据库、图书馆等资源，收集信息
	阅读文献（100%）	阅读专业学习资料（包括英文论文）、应试备考及其他材料
	课程学习（100%）	完成专业课程的课堂任务和课外作业
	课程论文（100%）	撰写专业课的期中或期末论文
	专业考试（100%）	参加专业水平测试（如专四专八）、考研及其他考试（如雅思）
	留学申请（43.2%）	撰写出国留学申请材料等
	讲座报告（23.4%）	参加专业讲座、听学术报告、记笔记
	项目申报（8.7%）	撰写科研实践等项目的申请材料
	学术交流（5.2%）	参加国际学术论坛、学术会议等

结合访谈数据，我们发现新手作者汉英学术写作的实践场景较为丰富，主要包括课程学习相关的写作任务和科研活动相关的写作任务。涉及体裁种类除面向通用学术用途的文本类型（如读书报告、课程反思、课程论文）外，还涉及面向专门学术用途的文本类型（如专业领域内的项目申报和学术交流）。在语言使用方面，尽管专业课学习以英语为主，但汉语在新手作者的学术写作实践中占有重要地位，尤其在专业学术性较强的科研活动相关的写作任务中，汉语使用频率高于英语。此外，大部分新手作者的汉语学术写作实践先于英语（逾八成同学认为“自己的第一篇‘学术’文章是用汉语写的”）。

4.2 汉英学术写作的体裁知识储备

新手作者体裁知识储备的自评结果（图1）显示，过程知识储备最高，学生较为清楚撰写小论文包括查阅文献、收集材料、写作、修改等步骤。形式知识次之，学生对学术体裁文本的词汇语法、结构语步等特征有一定认识。相比之下，修辞知识和内容知识储备较为有限，学生对学术体裁的预期目的和所处修辞语境特点了解不多，撰写或讨论专业话题所需知识也相对欠缺。

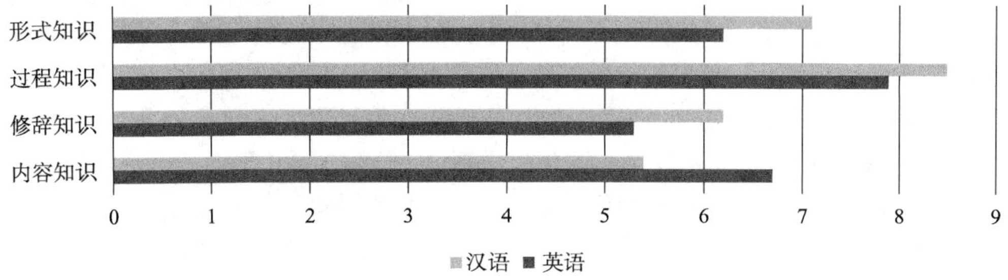

图1　新手作者汉英学术写作的体裁知识自评（0—10分）

比较基于两种语言的体裁知识，汉语写作的体裁知识在形式、过程、修辞维度高于英语，但在内容知识方面低于英语。主要可能原因是新手作者的汉语学术写作实践以跨专业选修课的课程论文为主，在参与非本专业学科讨论时，普遍感觉专业知识不足。

尽管从自评结果看，新手作者掌握了一定的学术体裁知识，但在现实中的体裁辨识和认知方面，存在模糊和分歧。比如，在问卷“你认为以下几种写作任务属于‘学术’写作吗？”一题的李克特五级量表评分中，近半数学生（43.8%）认为高考语文作文等级为“3”，逾半数学生（56.3%）认为高考英语作文等级为“1”。访谈中学生普遍表示，入校前自己接触最多，也最为熟悉的写作体裁是“高考作文”，但却无法说清“高考作文”属于哪个体裁（有些认为是“议论文”，有些认为是“考试文”）。其次，体裁知识的储备的来源以实践经验为主，缺乏系统性。受调查学生在选修“学术英语写作”前普遍没有“学术写作的相关课程或培训经历”，仅在平时写作实践中“观察发现”了汉语和英语学术类文章的一些特点和规律，部分学生提及教师课堂上偶有提及过学术语言的正式性等特点。

4.3 汉英学术写作实践中体裁知识的应用

4.3.1 汉语学术写作中的仿拟与杂糅

受调查的多数新手作者将自己的汉语学术写作实践追溯至大一的课程论文，认为课程论文是自己修读课程前完成过的最“学术”的写作任务（在对各项写作任务的“学术”性判断中，课程论文任务的评分最高，50%学生评价等级为“4”，25%学生评价为“5”）。然而，学生对于学术小论文的定义和特征并不明朗。参考《普通高中语文课程标准（2017年版2020年修订）》中的解释：

> 学术性小论文不同于一般的议论文，其写作的重点在表达研究成果，可参阅学术论著的基本格式和语言表达。理论推导、数据引用等应坚持学术规范，不作假，不抄袭，不强词夺理。尊重他人研究成果，引用资料应注明出处，文末应注明参考书目。（2020:32）

该解释尽管区别了“学术性小论文”与“一般的议论文”，但并未明确给出具体区别和体裁特征；“可参阅学术论著的基本格式和语言表达”提出了作者自行参考仿拟的建议。尽管通过阅读摸索找到了一些学术写作的行文规律，如法炮制出了自己的“第一篇学术论文”，但部分学生提到自己在阅读汉语学术论著时，常常会对不同作者的风格差异（尤其是不同年代学者的论著）感到困惑，不清楚什么应该是汉语学术写作的“基本格式和语言表达”。以下是刘同学大一（上）学期跨专业选修课期末课程论文的摘要部分：

> 内容提要：必修一的第三章的那页上写着，引自翟中和院士等主编的《细胞生物学》，“我确信哪怕一个最简单的细胞，也比迄今为止设计出的任何电脑更精巧！”细胞质遗传就是细胞精妙的一环，而其与细胞核遗传的相互作用，两者在遗传上相互协调和制约，反映了核与质两个遗传体系相互依存和联系的统一关系，与我国传统文化中的“和合”亦有共同之处。借此机会，就让我们来细细探讨一下高中时期学习生物被潦草讲述过的细胞质遗传，本篇文章将从与其有关的历史，应用，疾病等等方面展开。（2022.12.8）

刘同学选修的“DNA：生命的秘密”这门课程要求学生基于课堂所讨论话题中自己感兴趣的某一话题展开论述，写一篇不少于2500字的小论文，并要求引用文献。刘同学提交的课程论文总长3645字，共引用了11条文献（10条汉语文献、1条英语文献），形式上符合课程论文要求。论文题为“细胞质遗传”，摘要部分引用了课程主要参考书上的内容，以突出选题的重要性，随后介绍了本文作者的主要思考和文章的大致内容。刘同学解释这是自己“看过教材和多篇论文之后花尽心思”写成的摘要。仔细分析，不难看出学生通过自主探索注意到论文类体裁学术写作相对明显的形式特征（如文内引用等），但对于较为隐性的修辞特征把握不够到位，误将直接引用放在摘要中。同时，由于缺少修辞知识，对课程论文体裁的认识有限，作者产出的一些文句，如“借此机会，就让我们来细细探讨一下高中时期学习生物被潦草讲述过的细胞质遗传”偏离了体裁预期。

在汉语学术写作实践中，新手作者普遍采用仿拟和杂糅的方式，通过网络信息搜索和文献资料阅读，获得写论文的步骤方法和文本特征的主观感受。较为显见的过程知识和形式知识（如词汇、句法、结构特征）得到了一定程度的应用和转化，但由于自行探索中存在风格差异等困扰因素，对特征把握存在模糊性。较为深层的修辞知识和内容知识的应用和转化则相对困难，由于缺乏经验，新手作者普遍对论文体裁所处社会修辞语境中的修辞情境、话语团体和作者身份修辞情境、话语团体和作者身份认识不足，在实践之初无法准确使用符合预期的规范表达。

4.3.2 英语学术写作中的对比与借鉴

整体而言，尽管没有正式接触学术写作的相关知识，新手作者在观察和实践中形成了一些主观想法，在阅读中有意识地比较汉英学术文本，如张同学解释了她所认识到的汉英学术体裁的异同：

> 我觉得中国人眼中的“学术”指那种系统的、专门的学问，提到学术，我脑海里立马想到的一些关联词是硕士、博士、大家、专家、论文，总感觉这是一种很高大上的很理论性的东西，英语中的academic我觉得倾向于对某一个问题或者某一个领域的钻研。[……]读文章的时候，感觉汉语论文喜欢谈那种宏大的理论，英语论文则谈得很细，比较重逻辑论证。但整体感觉都会用很专业很难的词，结构都比较固定。而且很多汉语论文的结构和英语很像，好像是英语的翻版。(2022.3.1)

新手作者基于对比，往往可以发现汉英学术体裁中较为明显的形式特征，比如结构和词汇语法特征等。值得注意的是，多数学生发现汉语学术论文“和英语很像”，在一定程度上印证了英语学术语篇模式的向心驱动作用（Bennett 2007）。基于该相似性，新手作者尝试进行英语学术写作。

> In China, many translators and researchers have applied performability with speakability to their works or adopted them in their study, including both C-E and E-C translations in literary works (Qi Yan, 2023) and practical texts. But the complexity and profound meaning of SL often make it difficult for translators to put speakability into practice. [···] some scholars are also considering that the

focus of domestic drama translation should be transferred from performance-oriented to reading-oriented. (Zhengjun Zhao, 2022)（2023.4.28）

以上写作文本来自杨同学的过程性产出。作业要求对个人研究选题的文献检索结果用英文进行小结概括。可以发现，作业中作者误将汉语文内引用的格式用在英语学术写作中（如括号内人名写法、句末标点和括号的相对位置），而此类现象在作业中较为普遍。新手作者往往会基于自己的汉语学术写作经验，将某些文本特征直接移植入英语写作。在对英语学术体裁形式和修辞知识了解不全面的情况下，容易出现“失误”的借鉴。

5. 讨论

结合现实，可以从体裁经历和体裁期待方面，反思新手作者汉英学术写作实践的特点。研究发现，新手作者在高等教育之前的体裁经历与高校学习中的体裁期待之间存在一定差距。尽管在入校前，学生普遍有较好的汉语语言基础，具备多体裁文本的阅读能力，但汉语写作的体裁知识并不完善，典型学术体裁的汉语写作任务接触较少。《普通高中语文课程标准（2017年版）》对现代文阅读内容及相关能力层级要求中将“学术论文”归入“论述类文本”，解释为“阅读中外论述类文本。了解政论文、学术论文、时评、书评等论述类文体的基本特征和主要表达方式。阅读论述类文本，应注重文本的说理性和逻辑性，分析文本的论点、论据和论证方法”（中华人民共和国教育部 2017：33）。在2020年修订版中增加了“学术论著专题研讨”任务群，与“汉字汉语专题研讨”“中华传统文化专题研讨”“中国革命传统作品专题研讨”“中国现当代作家作品专题研讨”“跨文化专题研讨”并置，定位为课程的选修内容。在2021年高考语文考试大纲中，写作部分的要求提及论述类、实用类和文学类，并未具体提及论述类文本中的子类。从高考语文历年试卷分析看，论述类文章写作的要求大多是“命题作文”形式，即就某个话题进行主观论述，与高校场景中常见的“学术论文”类写作体裁存在较为明显的区别。

相比之下，学生英语语言基础在知识和能力方面与汉语相比存在明显差距，对学术体裁的认知有限，在入校前很少触及学术体裁写作任务。在《普通高中英语课程标准（2017年版）》中以“学术”为检索词，仅在选修（提高类）中有两次提及，一次将“学术论文摘要”划入议论文范畴，与报刊社论、专栏文章、书评、影评并置；另一次将“科研和学术报告”列入“其他语篇类型”，与专题类文章并置。而在2021年的高考英语考试大纲中，仅笼统描述了写作任务的表达要求和语言知识运用，未对体裁类型给出明确说明。从高考英语历年试题分析看，以应用文写作为主（常见书信或命题作文），2021年高考改革后增加了记叙文体裁的读后续写，对应用文写作任务没有明确的体裁界定。尽管学生在高中学习中积累了丰富的语文知识，但面对高校的学术写作任务仍需要一定的教学支持。在对“学术语言非任何人的母语”这句话的理解反馈中，93.8%的新手作者认同“作为汉语母语者，自己尚需要系统学习，掌握学术汉语”，且认为在高校“有必要开设‘大学语文’和‘汉语学术写作’两门课程”。

在典型双语社会（如加拿大）中两种语言在学术用途使用场景中发挥的功能相当，学习者在两种语言中的体裁经验和预期相近（Gentil 2011）。这与我国高校情况不同。除少数学校（如中外合作办学和国际学校）有英语教学环境外，我国多数高校以汉语为教学语言，学术用途英语的口语与书面语使用场景不平衡，不同学科对接受性技能与产出性技能要求存在差异。近年来，随着我国高等教育国际化不断深入，教学资源和学习机会得到了极大的丰富，学生的学术语言需求呈现多元化发展趋势。而研究发现，学生对学术写作体裁知识的掌握不够完备，认识存在局限，需要借助系统学习弥补体裁知识的缺漏，并通过有针对性的练习操练所学体裁知识，以适应高校环境中的学术写作任务。

为此，需要充分考虑新手作者的特殊性，分析作者所处的体裁场景，包括特定环境中对写作实践的期待、要求、呈现、反馈方式等系列活动及其发生的场域。在本研究涉及的英语专业大类学术写作教学过程中，尽管教材和参考资料以英语材料为主，但学生的学术写作经验以汉语为主。因此，可以在专业学术写作课程中加入跨语言材料和练习，帮助学生提高学术体裁的整体意识。从学生的文本经验出发，结合学生在必修和选修课阅读过的文献和写过的汉语课程论文，引导学生反思学术文本的特点，开展跨体裁、跨语言比较。在比较和探索过程中，教师主要起引导作用，提供学术写作、文体学等相关的文献供学生自行参考，为比较和反思提供一定的理论支持。在课程中加入反思性作业，促使学生关注相近体裁在不同语言中的表现形式，有助于培养宏观体裁意识（genre awareness），为进一步培养基于专业知识构建规律的微观体裁意识（the awareness of genres）打下基础（Cheng 2018）。同时，可以提供具有目标特征的材料（如在“引用规范”教学中选择密集使用典型引用例证的学术语篇作为阅读材料）为输入，以此为基础有针对性地展开讲解和讨论，促成教学（文秋芳 2015）。在体裁教学内容的先后顺序方面，可以先模糊语言分界，突出体裁特征。在学生掌握学术书面语整体特征后，再引入语言维度，引导学生比较汉英学术语篇的异同。这一教学思路符合由笼统到具化的认知规律。此外，可以根据学生自身所需的不同使用场景，通过观察、分析、比较、总结，基于较为熟悉的体裁文本的特征，自主探索陌生体裁文本的特征，形成思考探索的学习习惯。

6. 结语

本文从双语体裁视角出发，以国内某高校英语专业本科生作为新手作者群体，考察了新手学术作者的汉英双语写作实践。通过分析发现：新手作者有丰富的体裁实践场景，但体裁知识储备不够充足，缺乏系统性，体裁知识的应用过程中能够自主探索，但仍需要教学引导实现有效的体裁知识学习和体裁知识转化。基于实证考察，研究者应进一步思考适应本土高校教学环境的以汉语为主导、汉英双语共同发展、加强语言共核能力和跨语言学术素养的必要性和可能路径，从更为广泛的实践场景中获取实证证据，以丰富助益写作教学实践的研究文献（孙厌舒、王俊菊 2015；徐锦芬、聂睿 2015）。在学术写作教学实践中可以尝试通过跨体裁、跨语言比较的教学方法，引导学生掌握体裁特征的分析步骤和策略，将体裁方法应用于自身发展所需的个性化学习场景。该思路下的学术写作教学旨在为新时代人才培养服务，在理论和实践上着眼本土经验、贡献本土智慧。

参考文献

Bennett, K. 2007. Epistemicide! The tale of a predatory discourse [J]. *The Translator* 13(2): 151-169.

Canagarajah, S. 2006. Toward a writing pedagogy of shuttling between languages: Learning from multilingual writers [J]. *College English* 68(6): 589-604.

Cheng, A. 2018. *Genre and Graduate-Level Research Writing* [M]. Ann Arbor: University of Michigan Press.

Cummins, J. 2008. BICS and CALP: Empirical and theoretical status of the distinction [A]. In B. Street & N. H. Hornberger (eds.). *Encyclopedia of Language and Education, 2nd Edition, Volume 2: Literacy* [C]. New York: Springer. 71-83.

Cummins, J. & E. M. Yee-fun. 2007. Academic language: What is it and how do we acquire it? [A]. In J. Cummins & C. Davison (eds.). *International Handbook of English Language Teaching* [C]. Boston, MA: Springer. 797-810.

Fang, F. G., L. Hu & J. Jenkins. 2017. Overseas Chinese students' perceptions of the influence of English on their language and culture [J]. *Journal of Asia TEFL* 14(1): 144-161.

Flowerdew, J. 2015. Some thoughts on English for research publication purposes (ERPP) and related issues [J]. *Language Teaching* 48(2): 250-262.

Galloway, N., T. Numajiri & N. Rees. 2020. The "internationalisation", or "Englishisation", of higher education in East Asia [J]. *Higher Education* 80(3): 395-414.

Gentil, G. 2011. A biliteracy agenda for genre research [J]. *Journal of Second Language Writing* 20(1): 6-23.

Jiang, S. 2021. The call of the homeland: Transnational education and the rising nationalism among Chinese overseas students [J]. *Comparative Education Review* 65(1): 34-55.

Matsuda, P. K. 2010. The disciplinary division of labor: A decade later [Z]. Plenary address given at the 2010 Symposium on Second Language Writing. Spain: University of Murcia.

Mein, E. 2012. Biliteracy in context: The use of L1/L2 genre knowledge in graduate studies [J]. *International Journal of Bilingual Education and Bilingualism* 15(6): 653-667.

Pérez-Llantada, C. 2021. Genres and multiliteracies [A]. In C. Pérez-Llantada (ed.). *Research Genres Across Languages: Multilingual Communication Online* [C]. Cambridge: Cambridge University Press. 129-160.

Tardy, C. M. 2009. *Building Genre Knowledge* [M]. West Lafayette, IN: Parlor Press.

Zhao, W. 2019. *China's Education, Curriculum, Knowledge, and Cultural Inscriptions: Dancing with the*

Wind [M]. London: Taylor & Francis.
陈宁阳，2021，关注学术用途汉语的研究与教学 [N]，《社会科学报》，09-09（005）。
邓鹂鸣、肖亮，2022，体裁与二语写作研究：焦点、方法及发展趋势 [J]，《二语写作》（2）：81-95。
晋浩天，2015，基础教育应培养孩子世界眼光 [N]，《光明日报》，01-30（006）。
彭玉洁、徐昉，2021，体裁知识视角下研究生对国际期刊审稿反馈的认知投入特征 [J]，《中国外语》（6）：74-81。
师文、陈静，2019，汉语二语写作语言特征的体裁差异研究 [J]，《汉语学习》（6）：76-85。
孙厌舒、王俊菊，2015，二语写作体裁教学研究的回顾与反思 [J]，《解放军外国语学院学报》（1）：44-50。
文秋芳，2015，构建"产出导向法"理论体系 [J]，《外语教学与研究》（4）：547-558。
文旭、文卫平、胡强、陈新仁，2020，外语教育的新理念与新路径 [J]，《外语教学与研究》（1）：17-24。
徐锦芬、聂睿，2015，基于CiteSpace的国际二语写作研究动态可视化分析（2004-2014）[J]，《外语电化教学》（4）：3-9。
中华人民共和国教育部，2017，《普通高中英语课程标准（2017年版）》[M]。北京：人民教育出版社。
中华人民共和国教育部，2020，《普通高中语文课程标准（2017年版2020年修订）》[M]。北京：人民教育出版社。

作者简介：

陈宁阳，苏州大学外国语学院英文系讲师。主要研究领域：汉英比较、汉英学术写作、双语学术素养发展。电子邮箱：rosaliechen@126.com

思辨性学术英语写作教学模式建构及效果验证*

吴 琼

福建师范大学

摘要：《大学英语教学指南（2020 版）》将学术英语教学放于重要的地位。目前，国内许多高校都在进行大学英语教学改革，将学术英语教学纳入大学英语教学体系。本项目基于学术英语的规约性、社会性、情境性、动态性和开放性的认知，从思辨能力培养的视角开展思辨性博士生学术英语写作教学，并进行三轮实证研究，以验证此教学模式对博士生学术英语写作是否具有促进作用。研究发现，使用思辨技能对学术英语规约性特征进行思考、探究、评价和质疑，使用思辨标准来衡量学术语篇文本，进行具有思辨情感的学术英语社会实践写作，将社会实践意义建构、写作者学术身份建构以及学习者批判性思维能力的发展作为博士生公共英语教学的主要目标，能有效改变学生对英语学习的传统认知，增强学生的思维能力和学术英语表达能力，培养学生的学术英语素养，构建其学术身份。

关键词：学术英语；思辨能力；思辨性学术英语写作教学

DOI: 10.20081/j.cnki.cjslw.2023.07.006

1. 引言

学术英语写作是中国学者在国际间进行沟通和交流的手段，是中国学者的声音能够被听见和被理解的重要方式（Lyda & Warchal 2014）。博士生是中国学者团体的重要组成部分和中国学术领域的主力军，但在各种国际研究索引和数据库中，其研究实力未能得以充分体现。其中部分原因在于受其学术英语写作能力的限制，他们的研究成果无法在国际学术领域传播。

学术英语写作是学术英语素养培养的有效途径，其意义不仅在于写作技能的提高，更在于意义的建构、思维的发展、以及批判性意识的养成。国内博士生学术英语写作教学多从局部视角出发，聚焦体裁视角下的语步分析和学术语言特征应用（孙瑜 2021；郑飞 2021；朱效惠 2021），强调对学术英语静态语言特征的掌握和应用，忽略了学术英语语篇形成的系统性知识，未能利用思维的发展来探索学术英语写作的社会性、情境性、动态性和开放性特征（Duff 2007）。鉴于此，本研究将从思辨角度探讨学术英语写作教学，通过实证研究构建思辨性的学术英语写作教学框架。

* 本研究系2022年第十一批“中国外语教育基金”项目“博士生公共英语教学过程中学术英语素养的培养研究”（项目编号：ZGWYJYJJ11A106）的阶段性研究成果。

2. 国内外相关研究

学术英语（English for Academic Purposes，简称EAP）是指在学术语境下进行交流的英语。学术英语写作教学从早期对学术语篇中的词汇、短语以及句子结构的关注逐渐转向学术英语写作教学过程中的学术英语素养培养。越来越多的学者认为学术英语素养的培养包含思辨能力的发展，并且致力于探讨思辨能力与学术英语写作之间的关系。熊淑慧和邹为诚（2012）认为在学术语篇构建过程中，需要利用思辨技能对观点进行整合、分析和反应，才能产生和创造新知识。Evans et al.（2014）指出学术写作中的讨论部分是作者展示思辨技能的最重要的部分。濮实（2018）认为文献综述部分更能体现学术写作对思辨的要求，并通过对思辨能力维度进行探究，澄清了论述能力和评价能力的内涵和外延。陈则航等（2022）对学术语篇讨论部分的思辨表征进行研究，促进了学生思辨水平和写作质量的提高。马利红（2021）基于论证效度对写作中思辨能力的评价进行验证，提供了评分推论和外推推论环节的效度证据，对思辨能力的培养具有启发意义。以上研究表明了思辨对于学术英语写作的不可或缺性。

目前，有关思辨能力和学术英语写作的研究大体可分为三类：一是认为思辨论证是学术语篇的基本表达方式（Kuhn & Moore 2015；Suppe 1998）；二是认为对学术英语语言特征的认知与应用需要思辨能力的参与（Biber et al. 2011；Hyland 2017；Schleppegrell 2004；Uccelli et al. 2020；吴琼 2022）；三是认为学术语篇的构建是思辨技能显性和隐性作用的结果（Burgess & Ivanič 2010；Matsuda 2015；陈则航等 2022；濮实 2018；熊淑慧、邹为诚 2012）。

随着社会文化视角的介入，学术英语写作能力被视为个体发展的要素（Lei & Hu 2015；Woodward-Kron 2004）。在语言和文化的多样性以及全球化进程中，意识形态模式下的学术语言除了具有原有的规约性，还呈现出社会性、情境性、动态性和开放性的特征（Duff 2007），学术英语写作的维度也得以延伸和扩展，强调学术英语写作的社会文化属性，包含意义建构、身份建构、反思精神和独立批判性能力的培养（Benesch 2001；Morgan 2004；Spack 1997）。

因此，本研究以语篇论证、学术英语语言特征和学术语篇构建为基础，从学术英语的规约性、社会性、情境性、动态性、开放性的特征出发，认为学术英语写作教学不仅应传授学术英语语言知识，还需通过体裁知识的传授，帮助学生构建学术身份，融入话语社区；通过对学术语篇的分析和批判，培养学生的思辨意识和反思精神。本研究旨在回答以下两个问题：1）思辨性学术英语写作教学模式是否有效？ 2）思辨性学术英语写作教学模式对学生的学术英语写作具体有何影响？

3. 理论基础

3.1 学术英语写作理论

早期学术英语写作的相关理论经历了从结构范式到社会文化理论范式的发展

过程。结构范式下的学术英语写作是在英语语言中融入学术化的内容（Snow & Uccelli 2009），有相对特定的语言使用形式和话语表达模式。在这一范式下，学术语篇的写作核心在于遣词造句、语篇衔接和典型学术语言特征的应用。随着社会文化理论的发展，Swales（1990）将语篇的社会功能（function）与语言表达形式（form）相结合，借助结构语步分析方法（Sheldon 2011），在学术语篇的规约性基础上，强调语篇的社会性和情境性，通过体裁概念实现语篇社会实践意义的建构。

在后结构主义影响下，学术英语写作受到批判主义范式的影响。Bhatia（2004，2015）提出话语的多视角模式（见图1），以及批评体裁分析（Critical Genre Analysis，简称CGA），从三大空间（语篇空间、社会认知空间和社会空间）来审视学术语篇，从宏观层面探究不同语篇体裁特征的共时差异和历时变化。批判主义范式让人们意识到学术语篇不单具有规约性，其体裁更具有复杂性、动态性、社会性等特点。

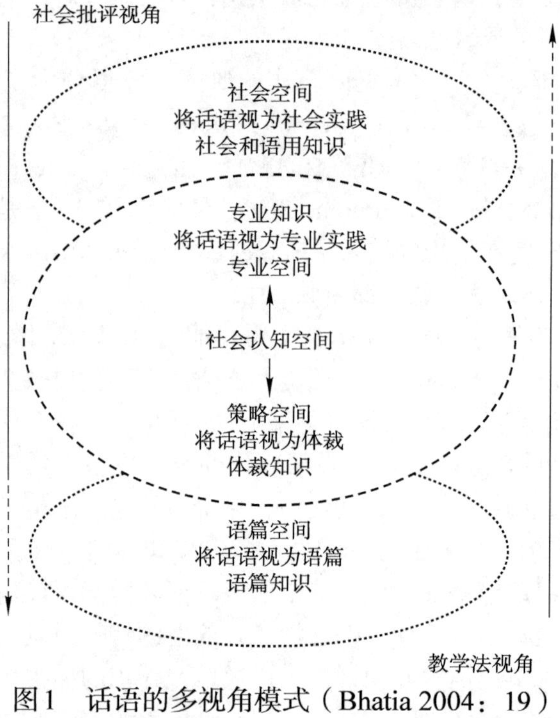

图1　话语的多视角模式（Bhatia 2004：19）

同时，此时期的大量学术英语写作研究还表明论证是学术语篇中批判主义的主流形式（马利红 2021；濮实 2018）。学术语篇的生成涉及概念表达、人际交流、语篇结构和观点评述等，具有开放性的特点。从系统功能语言学的角度出发，学术英语写作中的论证能力包含逻辑推理能力、文献引用能力、对论据的理性评估能力以及清晰的论证步骤等（鞠玉梅 2004）。因此，在学术英语写作过程中，作者需要将批判性思维能力融入学术英语语篇的论证过程中（Street 2008）。

学术语篇还强调语篇社团的规范性和语域层面的得体性（余莉、梁永刚 2006），即不同学科的学术文本都在各自知识建构基础上实现本专业学术语篇的话语功能；学术语篇的写作与社会文化大语境和个人心理认知之间具有密切关系。学术英语写作的过程是个体通过不断参与，逐渐进入学术实践共同体的过程，是个体通过具体的社会实践创造意义、建构自己学术身份的过程。Snow和Uccelli（2009）在话语的多视角模式下，从人际立场、信息承载量、语篇组织、词汇选择、信息呈现、体裁差异、推理策略以及专业知识八个方面（见表1）帮助和引导学习者在自己的研究领域构建自己的学术身份。

表1 学术英语语言特征（Snow & Uccelli 2009：119）

1. 人际立场（Interpersonal stance）	无偏见、客观、权威的学术立场
2. 信息承载量（Information load）	内容简洁、信息量大
3. 语篇组织（Organization of information）	注重衔接与连贯、话语标志词显著、言据性话语、论证严密
4. 词汇选择（Lexical choices）	词汇多样、表达书面化、用词精确、术语广泛使用
5. 信息呈现（Representational congruence）	紧凑、非一致性语法（名词化表达、嵌入结构）
6. 体裁差异（Genre mastery）	学科学术体裁
7. 推理策略（Reasoning strategies）	学术性论证
8. 专业知识（Disciplinary knowledge）	具有学科特征

在对学术英语写作的研究中，研究者们从原先关注文本语言表层的静态分析到探索文本外的各个元素，关注现实学术语篇的复杂性、动态性和社会性，着重社会实践价值、着重学术语篇体裁的形成机制。这意味着学术英语写作不是简单的短期“技能培训”，而是与思维能力相互促进的长期发展过程，是融合社会视角和批判视角的动态性和情境性的写作过程。

3.2 思辨能力

批判性思维能力（critical thinking ability）也被称为思辨能力，被认为是21世纪高等教育人才所需培养的核心能力。早在20世纪90年代，德尔菲项目组将思辨定义为理解、分析、推理、评价、解释和自我修正等认知能力（critical thinking skill）和追求真理、公正、思想开放、自信等情感特质（critical thinking disposition）。文秋芳等（2009）融合了Facione（1990）的双维结构模型、林崇德（2006）的三棱结构模型以及Paul和Elder（2006）的三元结构模型的主要特征，构建了思辨能力层级模型（见表2）。该模型将思辨能力分为两个层级，并将第二层级的思辨能力分为思辨认知和思辨情感。其中思辨认知包含三种主要技能（分析、推理和评价），这三种主要技能里又包含更小的子技能。对于技能达成的标准则包含清晰性、相关性、逻辑性、深刻性和灵活性五个方面，同时发展好奇、开放、自信、正直、坚毅的思辨情感。思辨能力层级模型的提出清晰阐释了思辨的内涵并指出了思辨培养的方向和目标。

表2 思辨能力层级理论模型（文秋芳等 2009）

元思辨能力（自我调控能力）——第一层次		
思辨能力——第二层次		
认知		情感
技能	标准	好奇（好疑、好问、好学） 开放（容忍、尊重不同意见，乐于修正自己的不当观点） 自信（相信自己的判断能力、敢于挑战权威） 正直（追求真理、主张正义） 坚毅（有决心、毅力、不轻易放弃）
分析（归类、识别、比较、澄清、区别、阐释） 推理（质疑、假设、阐述、论证等） 评价（评判预设、假定、论点、论据、结论等）	清晰性（清晰、精确） 相关性（切题、详略得当、主次分明） 逻辑性（条例清晰、说理有理有据） 深刻性（有广度与深度） 灵活性（快速变化角度、娴熟自如地交替使用不同的思辨技能）	

文秋芳和孙旻（2015）指出需将思辨活动有效融入各项具体课程，尤其是技能课程。思辨技能的应用和思辨情感的培养有利于学习者思辨特质的发展（Facione 2011）；思辨的标准能较好地评价和衡量写作能力目标的达成。学者们从各维度论述了思辨在写作中的重要性，包含从论证的逻辑性、有效性等视角对写作进行评价（Osana & Seymour 2004；Qin & Karabacak 2010；Stapleton 2001）；从清晰性、准确性、精确性、相关性、逻辑性、公正性等方面对写作文本进行衡量（Benesch 2001；董焱宁 2017；穆从军 2016）；建立语篇的思辨能力评估指标（陈则航等 2016；马利红 2021；濮实 2018），等等。虽然目前的相关研究具有一定的深度和广度，但如何将思辨活动融入学术英语写作教学的相关研究并不多见。

4. 思辨性学术英语写作教学模式的构建

文秋芳等（2009）实证研究表明，任何一项思维活动都涉及不同的思辨维度，单一的思辨维度很难完成复杂的思维任务。因此，只有在活动中将写作任务分解，设置不同的写作教学内容，安排具体的写作教学活动，才能将思辨能力培养与学术英语写作教学有机融为一体。本研究利用思辨的相关技能来输入学术英语写作的相关知识，用思辨的标准来评估思维和写作的质量，并在教学过程中隐性发展学生的思辨情感来培养学生的写作态度。

本研究以Bhatia（2004，2015）的三大空间理论和Snow和Uccelli（2009）所阐述的学术英语特征为基础，综合考虑学术英语的规约性、社会性、情境性、动态性和开放性特征，将学术英语教学内容分为语言形式知识、语篇论证知识、人际互动知识、社会实践知识（见表3）。语言形式知识帮助学生掌握一定的学术语篇语言特征，如主题句特征、名词化特征等；语篇论证知识包含篇章结构教学，如衔接手段以及论证能力的培养；人际互动知识在于帮助学生进行身份构建，向学生介绍多种话语资源，对话语资源所实现的社会交际功能进行分析和思考，以及利用话语资源来建构自己的学术身份，如评价话语、模糊语和加强词、情态词汇、言据性话语的使用等，在具体的语境中实现话语权力；社会实践知识将语篇的写作和社会实践结合，围绕各种社会问题进行开放式学术写作，注重社会问题的复杂性，分析社会实践中不同学术文本体裁的差异性以及影响因素，以及如何利用语步完成学术研究的交际功能，加强语篇论证结构的社会合理性和基础论证的逻辑性，强调论据的恰当使用以及对反方观点进行反驳等。这四个知识板块相互交融。在思辨性学术英语教学中，任何部分知识的习得都与其他知识的学习息息相关。写作者在写作过程中对这四个知识板块进行思辨性学习，有利于知识的内化，对学习者写作文本的社会实践意义建构、学术身份建构以及批判性思维能力的发展具有积极的影响。

表3 思辨式学术英语写作教学内容

语言形式知识	语篇论证知识	人际互动知识	社会实践知识
学术表达词汇特征 学术句法结构特征 隐喻性语言	语篇结构 图尔敏论证结构 衔接和连贯	元话语资源 （引导式话语资源、 互动式话语资源）	结合学科内容的论证 实现社会实践意义的语步结 构学科间体裁差异

思辨性的学习，指的是在教学过程中，将思辨意识通过思辨技能的各项活动贯穿每个教学内容。博士生学术英语思辨教学在博士生第一学期开展授课，总教学时数为64学时，每周4学时连续课时，以教师讲授、师生互动、生生讨论合作为主要课堂教学模式。思辨性学术英语教学模式基于思辨式学术英语写作教学内容，设置了五个课堂教学基本步骤（见图2），分别为文本导入环节、概念引入环节、文本分析环节、文本创作环节和评价反思环节。首先教师导入典型性文本，引导学生使用思辨技能对文本进行充分性阅读和自主分析与评价；接着教师引入相关学术英语写作概念，使学生对概念的特征、使用方法、意义以及功能进行归纳和掌握；在此基础上，学生再次对导入的文本进行分析、推理、评价和质疑，加深对学术英语写作概念的理解；在文本创作环节，学生采取小组讨论、合作的方式将所学的学术英语写作概念应用于实践写作。评价反思环节，每组将所创作的文本在小组间分享、对比、讨论、批评、修改和自我反思，形成反思性报告。

在整个教学流程中，教师引导学生利用思辨标准（清晰性、相关性、逻辑性、深刻性和灵活性）审视自己和同伴的思维以及产出的文本；学生对语篇文本和思维过程进行自我提问和相互批评，发展和改进自己的思想。比如在论证过程，学生审视自己所提供的论据是否和论点相关联；自己的主题思想是否表达清晰；哪些词汇表达能更好地实现自己的话语权力；是否了解问题的复杂性；是否从不同的角度来看待问题等。正如Paul和Elder（2006）所指出的，批判性思维需要掌握基本的智力标准，这些标准指的就是清晰、准确、精确、相关、深度、广度、逻辑，意义和公平。

思辨性学术英语写作教学在教学各步骤中融合思辨技能和思辨标准，这在一定程度上可促进学生思辨情感（好奇、开放、自信、正直、坚毅）的发展。思辨情感是思辨的基础，是人们对思辨活动的信念、态度和意愿，是人心理潜在的动机和进行思维活动的心理驱动力；同时，学术思辨情感推动学生理性思维的生产，提高学生学术写作能力，从而形成了良性循环的发展路径。

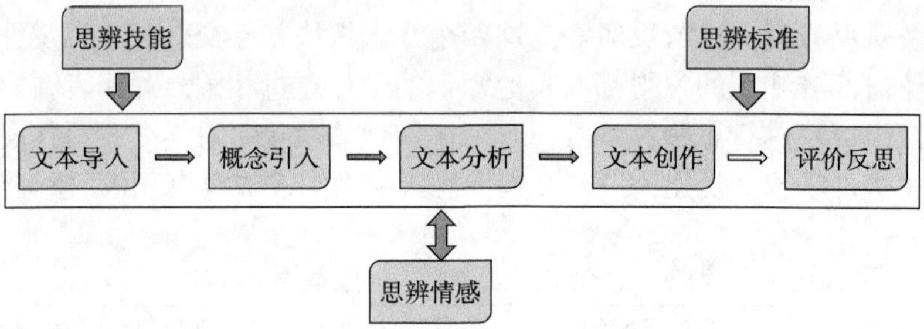

图2 思辨式学术英语写作课堂教学模式

5. 思辨性的学术英语写作教学实践效果验证

为观察思辨性的学术英语写作教学模式对学生的学术英语写作能否带来积极影响，本研究采用行动研究方法，基于思辨性学术英语写作教学模式，开展三轮教学实验来验证教学有效性并使用课程满意度问卷调查来论证这一教学模式的可行性。同时，本研究对学生的论说文和科研小论文进行分析，以了解学生在这一教学模式下是否提升了批判性思维能力和学术写作能力。本研究在实验前后收集学生的写作文本并进行多维度的对比分析。实验前收集学生论说文语篇36份，共12971字；科研小论文引言部分语篇36份，共10774字。实验后收集学生论说文语篇41份，共36907字；引言部分语篇41份，共23042字。语料被分成两个语料包，分别为论说文语料包和引语语料包。

语料处理包括两个阶段。第一阶段，为了保证标注的准确性，两个语料包各选取2篇学生习作，四位从事学术英语教学的老师根据学术英语具体教学内容的评价维度一同进行标注，并将各自标注结果进行对比。四位教师就分歧处进行探讨分析，直到意见达成一致。第二阶段，将剩下的78份学生习作分成两组（每组39份），每组由两位老师使用电脑进行独立手动标注，并进行组内标注结果对照，两组信度分别达到0.96和0.94，之后老师们对分歧处再进行讨论，最终达成一致。最后使用AntConc 3.5.8软件分别提取不同类型写作特征，统计其频率。

首先考察学生批判性思维能力是否得到提升。批判性思维发展的指标主要体现在论说文写作是否清晰有条理。Langan（2014）认为，论说文需具有清晰明确的论点、合理的论证、详细的论据。在论证过程中，作者需要时时质疑自己论据是否充分、是否将问题分析透彻、对于反方观点能否予以反驳等等。因此，本研究采用思辨能力的标准（清晰性、相关性、逻辑性、深刻性和灵活性）对论说文进行衡量。实验选取六个维度分别进行标注和统计："论点明确（CC）"来反映思辨标准中的清晰性，"有分论点（ST）"体现逻辑性，"论述有一定的理据（BW）"反映相关性，"多角度分析（MA）"和"见解有一定的深度（OD）"体现深刻性，"进行反驳（OR）"体现灵活性。具体统计结果如下（见表4）：

表4　学生论说文写作样本部分维度实验前后对比

评价标准部分子维度	前测文本 （平均文本字数360）	后测文本 （平均文本字数513）
论点明确	26.2%	72.6%
有分论点	23.1%	87.3%
论述有一定的理据	12.6%	76.9%
多角度分析	35.7%	52.2%
见解有一定的深度	23.5%	26.1%
进行反驳	2%	68.7%

从表4可以看出，学生后测论说写作文本篇幅明显增长，在六个维度上都有一定变化，尤其是论点更加明确，采用分论点，形成金字塔形的论证模式，写作文本的逻辑性明显增强；另外在论证过程中更注意理据的应用以及对反方观点进行反驳，思维更加缜密，以及能用积极开放的心态进行质疑和挑战。

以实验后学生习作为例，从例1学生的写作文本可以看出，学生在语篇写作的开头明确地提出论点，即新媒体对传统媒体提出挑战，接着从新媒体的速度和便利性两个方面展开论述，分论点清晰。例2中的学生文本开始有意识使用一定的理据，包括事实和数据，并且对造成现象产生的原因作出进一步分析。

例（1）：Given new media offers the unsurpassed benefits of speed and convenience, in contrast to other traditional media, more people are choosing to utilize new media as their information conduits, which challenges traditional media's leading position. Similar to the views of Matthew Maron, many traditional paper media, like Newsweek, have started to change into new media as people's habits of reading news information gradually change from the paper end to the screen end.（学生习作）

例（2）：In general, a number of people consider that traditional media will soon lose its appeal to the public and that the future of print is in a precarious position. The statistics of a survey of teenagers between the ages of 18 and 24 show that, as of 2010, 28% of them were more likely to rely on online media to read the news or receive information, a proportion that is significantly greater than the percentage of people who use newspapers to do so. Additionally, the circulation of the *British Daily Mirror*, *Daily Express*, and *Daily Telegraph* has decreased over the past 30 years, going from 3.819 million copies to 1.565 million, 2.312 million copies to 777,000, and 1.3 million copies to 892,000 copies, respectively. This issue also affects the *People's Daily* in our country. The main reasons for this are as follows. Firstly ...（学生习作）

同时，学生实验后的论说性文本在很大程度上体现了学生能自主对社会实践进行观察和思考，能较明确地提出自己的见解和观点、确立自己的立场、进行数据收集，并对理据进行评估，审视论证逻辑，具有一定深度和广度的思考，从而在学术英语思辨写作过程中提高了写作的自信心。

其次，学术论文是学术共同体高度规约的语篇类型，它具有独特的语步结构。本研究对学生的科研小论文的语步进行分析，目的在于了解学生是否掌握一定的学术英语写作能力，实现学术语篇的社会意义建构。本研究以学生科研小论文中的引言部分为统计分析对象。引言部分是学术论文的重要组成部分，具有总览全文的功能，具有很强的步骤性和规约性。引言的写作目的主要是介绍写作背景以及确立研究范围，引发读者对研究的兴趣，使之意识到研究的重要性并了解研究的意义。因此引言部分需要通过一定的语步来吸引读者、说服读者，同时帮助读者更好地理解整篇学术论文。引言部分通常包含以下六个语步：介绍主题（M1）、宣称研究主题重要性（M2）、引用前期研究（M3）、作出评价（M4）、进行总结（M5）、指出研究空白（M6）。实验对学生科研小论文中引言的六个语步分别进行标注和统计，结果如表5所示。

表5　学生引言部分写作样本语步维度实验前后对比

百分比	总字数 / 平均字数	M1 频次	M2 频次	M3 频次	M4 频次	M5 频次	M6 频次
前测文本	（10774/388）	66.64%	21.22%	100%	0	12.3%	0
后测文本	（10982/562）	100%	98.31%	100%	82.16%	61.54%	25.6%

注：介绍主题（M1）、宣称研究主题重要性（M2）、引用前期研究（M3）、作出评价（M4）、进行总结（M5）、指出研究空白（M6）

通过实验可发现（见表5），实验前学生引言部分的语步大多只包含1—2个语步，局限于介绍前人研究，并未对前人的研究成果进行评价、对比、概括和分析，语步策略较少，无法达到有效的学术交际目的，无法凸显自己的学术观点和立场。思辨性的学术英语教学在教学过程中，引导学生分析语篇语步，推断各个语步的功能，鼓励学生对相关性文献进行评价等。教学实验结束后，学生文本语步种类和频次都明显增加，学生通过对文献进行筛选、归纳、比较、分析、评价、归类和总结，来展示对该领域研究的熟悉程度，为自己的研究范围确定空间并通过语步论证的方式来说服读者认可本研究的必要性和合理性，从而达到交际目的。

思辨性学术英语教学关注元话语教学，学生通过对语篇文本的分析、比较和推理，意识到元话语在学术英语写作中对语篇信息传递、文本交际以及学术身份自我构建等方面具有重要的作用。其中评价话语是语言表达态度的资源，评价话语的应用在一定程度上可以反映写作者在充分利用自己的思辨能力，对交流命题和内容进行的有态度、有立场以及有价值的判断。本文以引言语料中的评价话语为例，以态度标记词（attitude markers）的统计进行说明。实验参照Coffin（2009）的评价立场分类，将学生引言部分的态度标记词分为中性、疏离、反驳和赞同四种：中性立场的词汇如reflect、anticipate、conceive；疏离立场词汇如believe、doubt、suppose、suspect；反驳立场的词汇如disagree、dispute、hold the view against；赞同立场词汇如agree、understand、conform、establish。实验对文本中态度标记词进行标记、编码、统计，结果如表6所示。

表6 学生文献综述部分写作样本作者立场实验前后对比

		中性	疏离	反驳	赞同
前测文本	原始频次	100	2	1	68
	百分比	58.47%	1.12%	0.06%	39.77%
后测文本	原始频次	102	10	23	81
	百分比	47.22%	4.63%	10.65%	37.5%

注：因四舍五入，表格中的百分比相加结果可能不足100%

实验前后学生文本中的中性和赞同的立场表达占态度标记词总数的主要地位，但很明显，实验后学生写作文本中的疏离和反驳相关的词汇明显增加，实验前，show、say、point out、believe出现的次数频繁，实验后表达立场的词汇更加丰富，出现了suggest、argue、claim、doubt、dispute、satisfied、novel、clear等。这表明学生在做文献综述的过程中，不再仅仅只是展示自己的阅读内容，开始有意识地对文献作出一定的批判性分析，并选用适当的词汇表达自己的声音和立场（如例3、例4）：

例（3）：Although, Ariffin（2013）pointed out that there is a close relationship between airport image and passengers delight, little is known about consumer preferences regarding the design of airport.

例（4）：The theory proposed by Clayton Christensen dissatisfied with all walks. Some experts argued that the reason is that there is no technology core in many industries ...

评价话语在学生学术英语写作中的应用，反映了学生在经过思辨性的学术英语教学后，意识到学术写作并非是完全客观和中立的，学术英语写作是作者运用批判性思维来构建具有社会性、互动性的学术语篇，也是体现写作者学术身份的窗口。

在每一轮实验教学结束后研究者都会对学生进行问卷调查，对部分学生进行访谈，了解学生对课程的满意度，结合学生的反思日记和自我评价表，对本课程的教学进行分析和思考，不断调整思辨性学术英语写作教学各环节，以完善博士生的学术英语写作教学框架。

思辨性学术英语写作教学模式经过三年实践，取得良好效果，课程结束后学生的满意度分别达到74.06%、86.23%、92.18%。学生在课堂调查问卷中有如下的反馈："老师的课程设计非常适合我们现阶段的研究需要，也对我们未来的写作以及学术报告打下一个坚实的基础"；"该课程对于科研论文写作、演讲汇报、阅读均有很大的帮助，而且最重要的很培养学生的思维，非常nice的一门课程"；"该课程对于学术英语写作有较大的帮助，指出了许多写作过程中常见的错误，同时从思辨性、逻辑性上加以训练，不管是图尔敏的论证理论、名物化还是元语言等，都对学术英语的写作有所裨益"；该课程使"思考变得更有条理性"，"让我的学术思维更加敏捷，思维框架更加清晰"。

6. 结语

本文介绍了思辨能力概念以及学术英语的相关概念，探讨思辨能力的发展与学术英语写作能力培养之间的关系，进一步探索如何将思辨能力的培养与学术英语写作教学融为一体。本研究的重点落在两个方面，一是探讨思辨框架下的学术英语写作教学内容和教学模式，二是用实验数据来验证思辨性的学术英语写作教学对学生的学术英语写作能力有明显的促进作用。本研究在经过三轮的实践教学与反思后，给出了实际的解决方案，为学术英语写作教学与研究提供了参考方向。本文的局限性在于未能构建完整的评价体系，因此在接下来的研究中可细化思辨能力与学术英语写作能力的相关维度，设计出较全面的显性的测量方法来反映思辨能力发展框架下的学术英语写作水平；同时，结合博士生的专业知识，基于各学科写作的共性和差异，开展具有真正融合意义的思辨性跨学科学术英语写作教学，以帮助博士生更为有效地驾驭其领域的学术英语写作。

参考文献

Benesch, S. 2001. *Critical English for Academic Purposes: Theory, Politics and Practice* [M]. New Jersey: Lawrence Erlbaum Associates Inc.

Bhatia, V. K. 2004. *Worlds of Written Discourse* [M]. London: Continuum.

Bhatia, V. K. 2015. Critical genre analysis: Theoretical preliminaries [J]. *Hermes-Journal of Language and Communication in Business* 54: 9-20

Biber, D., B. Gray & K. Poonpon. 2011. Should we use characteristics of conversation to measure grammatical complexity in L2 writing development? [J]. *TESOL Quarterly* 45(1): 5-35.

Burgess, A. & R. Ivanič. 2010. Writing and being written: Issues of identity across timescales [J]. *Written Communication* 27(2): 228-255.

Coffin, C. 2009. Incorporating and evaluating voices in a film studies thesis [J]. *Writing & Pedagogy* 1(2): 163-193.

Duff, P. 2007. Problematizing academic discourse socialization [A]. In H. Marriott, T. Moore & R. Spence-Brown. (eds.). *Learning Discourse and the Discourse of Learning* [C]. Melbourne: Monash University Press. 117-121.

Evans, D., P. Gruba & J. Zobel. 2014. *How to Write a Better Thesis* [M]. Switzerland: Springer.

Facione, P. 1990. Critical thinking: A statement of expert consensus for purposes of educational assessment and instruction: The Delphi Report [R]. Millbrae, CA: The California Academic Press.

Hyland, K. 2017. Learning how to write for academic purposes: Specificity and second language writing [A]. In J. Bitchener, N. Storch & R. Wette (eds.). *Teaching Writing for Academic Purposes to Multilingual Students: Instructional Approaches* [C]. London: Routledge. 24-41.

Kuhn, D. & W. Moore. 2015. Argumentation as core curriculum [J]. *Learning: Research and Practice* 1: 66-78.

Lei, J. & G. Hu. 2015. Chinese university EFL teachers' perceptions of plagiarism [J]. *High Education* 70: 551-565.

Lyda, A. & K. Warchal. 2014. *Occupying Niches: Interculturality, Cross-culturality and Aculturality in Academic Research* [M]. London: Springer.

Matsuda, P. K. 2015. Identity in written discourse [J]. *Annual Review of Applied Linguistics* 35: 140-159.

Morgan, B. 2004. Teacher identity as pedagogy: Towards a field-internal conceptualisation in bilingual and second language education [J]. *International Journal of Bilingual Education and Bilingualism* 7(2): 172-199.

Osana, H. P. & J. R. Seymour. 2004. Critical thinking in preservice teachers: A rubric for evaluating argumentation and statistical reasoning [J]. *Educational Research and Evaluation* 10(46): 473- 498.

Paul, R. & L. Elder. 2006. *Critical Thinking: Learn the Tools the Best Thinkers Use* [M]. Columbus, OH: Pearson Prentice Hall.

Qin, J. & E. Karabacak. 2010. The analysis of Toulmin elements in Chinese EFL university argumentative writing [J]. *System* 38(3): 444-456.

Schleppegrell, M. J. 2004. *The Language of Schooling: A Functional Linguistics Perspective* [M]. New York: Routledge.

Sheldon, E. 2011. Rhetorical differences in RA introductions written by English L1 and L2 and Castilian Spanish L1 writers [J]. *Journal of English for Academic Purposes* 10: 238-251.

Snow, C. & P. Uccelli. 2009. The challenge of academic language [A]. In D. R. Olson & N. Torrance (eds.). *The Cambridge Handbook of Literacy* [C]. New York: Cambridge University Press. 112-133.

Spack, R. 1997. The acquisition of academic literacy in a second language: A longitudinal case study [J]. *Written Communication* 14: 3-62.

Stapleton, P. 2001. Assessing critical thinking in the writing of Japanese university students [J]. *Written Communication* 8(4): 506 -548.

Street, B. V. 2008. New literacies, new times: Developments in literacy studies [A]. In B. V. Street & N. H. Hornberger (eds.). *Encyclopedia of Language and Education, Volume 2: Literacy* (2nd Ed.) [C]. New York: Springer. 3-14.

Suppe, F. 1998. The structure of a scientific paper [J]. *Philosophy of Science* 65(3): 381-405.

Swales, J. M. 1990. *Genre Analysis: English in Academic and Research Settings* [M]. Cambridge: Cambridge University Press.

Uccelli, P. E., P. Galloway & W. Qin. 2020. The language for school litcracy: Widening the lens on language and reading relations [A]. In E. Moje, P. Afflerbach, P. Enciso, N. Lesaux (eds). *Handbook of Reading Research, Volume V.* [C]. New York: Routledge. 155-179.

Woodward-Kron, R. 2004. "Discourse communities" and "writing apprenticeship": An investigation of these concepts in undergraduate education students' writing [J]. *Journal of English for Academic Purposes* 3(2): 139-161.

Langan, J. 2014，《美国大学英语写作（第九版）》[M]。北京：外语教学与研究出版社。

陈则航、庞培、岳昕珂，2022，中国学者学术语篇讨论部分思辨表征研究 [J]，《中国外语》(5)：51-61。

陈则航、邹敏、李晓芳、陈思雨，2016，构建英语写作中思辨能力表征框架 [J]，《中国外语教育》(3)：11-19。

董焱宁，2017，二语写作中的思辨能力评分量表：探索与实践 [J]，《中国外语教育》(1)：23-30+100-101。

教育部高等学校大学外语教学指导委员会，2020，《大学英语教学指南（2020 版）》[M]。北京：高等教育出版社。

鞠玉梅，2004，体裁分析与英汉学术论文摘要语篇 [J]，《外语教学》(2)：32-36。

林崇德，2006，思维心理学研究的几点回顾 [J]，《北京师范大学学报（社会科学版）》(5)：35-42。

马利红，2021，基于论证的英语写作思辨能力评价效度研究 [J]，《现代外语》(9)：694-703。

穆从军，2016，英语专业学生的写作思辨能力调查 [J]，《现代外语》(5)：693-703。

濮实，2018，学术写作中元思辨能力的构成要素研究 [J]，《外语界》(6)：28-35。

孙瑜，2021，中国博士生学术英语写作问题分析 [J]，《扬州大学学报（高教研究版）》(3)：76-82。

文秋芳、孙旻，2015，评述高校外语教学中思辨力培养存在的问题 [J]，《外语教学理论与实践》(3)：6-12+94。

文秋芳、王建卿、赵彩然，2009，构建我国外语类大学生思辨能力量具的理论框架 [J]，《外语界》(1)：37-43。

吴琼，2022，博士生公共英语课程教学路径——学术思辨英语语言能力的培养 [J]，《中国 ESP 研究》(2)：97-106+117。

熊淑慧、邹为诚，2012，什么是学术英语？如何教？——一项英语专业本科生"学术英语"的课堂试验研究 [J]，《中国外语》(2)：54-64。

余莉、梁永刚，2006，英语科技论文摘要的写作范式研究 [J]，《外语教学》(1)：34-37。

郑飞，2021，基于项目的博士研究生学术英语写作阶段教学法 [J]，《北京航空航天大学学报（社会科学版）》(6)：133-139。

朱效惠，2021，学术英语写作课程建设的探索与实践 [J]，《语言教育》(4)：17-21。

作者简介：

吴琼，福建师范大学外国语学院副教授，硕士生导师。研究方向为语篇分析、学术用途英语写作。电子邮箱：335655184@qq.com

From Needing Help to Seeking Help: Examining Chinese College Students' Needs for English Writing Support and Writing Center Usage and Perceptions*

Jing ZHANG Fan FANG

Shantou University

Abstract: English writing centers have gained scholarly attention in China in recent years as a promising means to supplement traditional English writing instruction. To address the lack of empirical research on Chinese writing center praxis, this study collected 388 sets of survey responses, four writing center tutorial recordings, and four post-tutorial retrospective student interviews at a Chinese normal university with the aim of examining Chinese college students' writing center usage and perceptions in light of their self-perceived needs for English writing support and writing-related help-seeking behaviors. Our study revealed the following: (1) The surveyed Chinese students perceived strong needs for English writing support for various types of writing, yet their writing-related help-seeking did not match their expressed needs; (2) Only a small portion of students reported having heard about or used the writing center, and tutorials tended to focus more on global issues than local issues; (3) Students perceived their writing center experiences as being positive, highlighting individualized tutorials as a dialogic space that helped them acquire transferable writing knowledge. Pedagogical and research implications are offered for those who hope to provide students with individualized writing support in Chinese higher education and to contribute the Chinese voice to the international writing center community.

Keywords: writing centers; student needs on writing; writing support; writing tutorial
DOI: 10.20081/j.cnki.cjslw.2023.07.007

1. Introduction

As a U.S.-rooted writing pedagogy with global influence (Okuda 2017), writing centers entered China at the end of the twentieth century (Hayward 1994) and have gained increasing interest among Chinese scholars and educators (e.g., Chen & Wang 2023; Gao & Du 2022; He 2018, 2019, 2021; Zhang 2019). Priding itself on its focus on customized feedback, a process approach to writing, and long-term writerly growth (Lerner 2014; North 1984), writing centers offer a writer-focused orientation that is rarely available in traditional large-size English writing classrooms where students often fail to receive individualized attention and timely feedback. Thus, with the current English writing education yet to meet Chinese college students' demand for second language (L2) writing

* 本研究系汕头大学科研启动经费项目"中国大学生'写好中国故事'二语写作文化生态重构和创新"（项目编号：STF22013）的阶段性研究成果。

development (Jiang et al. 2023), writing centers have been considered a promising site of innovation to supplement traditional English writing instruction in Chinese higher education (Zhang & Liu 2023).

However, despite the momentum of establishing English writing centers to support Chinese college students (Song 2018), research on Chinese writing center praxis is scant and unsystematic, lacking an empirical basis (Zhang 2021). There also exists a particular dearth of inquiry into Chinese college students' utilization of writing centers in light of their needs for writing support and help-seeking behaviors. To address this gap, the present study draws on survey responses, writing center tutorial recordings, and post-tutorial retrospective interviews to examine Chinese college students' writing center usage and experiences in light of their self-perceived needs for English writing support and writing-related help-seeking behaviors. Implications are offered to develop writing centers as effective supplementary support for English writing education in China and to contribute the Chinese voice to the international writing center community.

2. Literature Review

2.1 Writing center research in China

Writing centers, with signature features such as individualized writing tutorials, a collaboration-based conferencing method, and a student-centered orientation (North 1984), have expanded from North America to EFL (English as a Foreign Language) contexts, resulting in various indigenous practices with local features (Barnawi 2018; Lee 2014; Tan et al. 2017; Zhang & Liu 2023). To ensure the effective localization of writing centers — a Western approach imported and adapted in EFL contexts — an important question needs to be answered regarding whether and how writing centers serve local students' needs for English writing support (McKinley 2010). It thus requires scholarly efforts to investigate writing center usage and experiences in light of student needs, expectations, and perceptions.

Because of the general lack of research on writing center praxis in China (Zhang & Liu 2023), it remains largely unclear whether and how English writing centers in China are meeting their goals of serving Chinese students' needs for English writing support. So far, only a few empirical studies have offered a scattering of knowledge regarding the impact of writing centers on Chinese students. One line of inquiry highlighted the positive impact of the writing center approach on Chinese college students, such as He's (2018; 2019) two empirical studies, both of which emphasized the effectiveness of writing centers in supplementing classroom teaching and facilitating Chinese students' autonomous learning of English writing. Despite the empirically attested benefits arising from individualized writing support at writing centers, the only study that directly examined Chinese students' needs in the writing center context was Kwan's (2022) case study, which showed a Chinese student's expectation for writing center tutorials, including formative feedback, directive guidance, and tutor-tutee-negotiated agenda. However, Kwan's (2022) study focused on a single student's interview data and can only offer limited knowledge. Thus, based on the paucity of Chinese writing center research that takes students' writing-related needs into consideration — which stands in stark contrast to the writing center's traditional commitment to providing students with individualized writing support — studies of larger scales are needed to further probe into how English writing centers serve Chinese local students, especially with an eye toward the specific needs and expectations of Chinese student writers.

2.2 Need-based writing center research in North American and EFL contexts

Looking at the thriving scholarship on North American writing centers and growing research on EFL writing centers, one can clearly see the value and benefits of investigating writing center praxis by considering students' voices and expectations (e.g., Bond 2019; Denny et al. 2018; McKinley 2010; Moussu 2013; Raymond & Quinn 2012; Thompson et al. 2009; Winder et al. 2016). To begin with, based on their study on working-class students' perceptions of the writing center, Denny et al. (2018: 69) cautioned that research on writing centers "do not function the way we imagine they do". It has emphasized the need to understand students' real needs in the writing process. Likewise, Severino et al.'s (2020) study revealed that a generalization among writing center practitioners — which associates multilingual writers with the demands for sentence-level assistance by default — turns out to be false; instead, their study suggested that native English-speaking (NES) and non-native English-speaking (NNES) students' requests for writing feedback both ranged across all feedback types without significant differences, thus stressing the importance of investigating student needs empirically rather than impressionistically. Similarly, in the EFL context, Winder et al.'s (2016) study on students' and tutors' perceptions of tutorial experiences at the writing center revealed discrepancies between students' and tutors' perceptions and preferences. This finding echoes Raymond and Quinn's (2012) study, which discovered mismatches between students' concerns/goals and the actual issues addressed by writing center tutors. Therefore, this again cautions that it is crucial to ground writing center support in student needs and perceptions that are empirically examined rather than basing decisions on mere impressions or generalizations.

Furthermore, Williams and Takaku (2011: 6) argued that "what affects students' writing performance is not the writing center tutoring per se but rather the students' help-seeking behavior — whether it is frequent and based on perceived need". The study highlighted student writers' self-perceived needs and help-seeking behaviors, showing how these are vital elements in the equation of writing improvement. Hence, the present study aims to examine Chinese college students' self-perceived needs for English writing support and their help-seeking behaviors, along with their writing center usage and experiences. Specifically, the following research questions guided the present study:

(1) How do Chinese college students perceive themselves as English writers — in terms of their English writing proficiency, needs for English writing support, and writing-related help-seeking behaviors?

(2) How do Chinese college students utilize the writing center?

(3) How do Chinese college students perceive their writing center experiences?

3. Methodology

3.1 Research context and participants

The present study took place at a normal university in Northern China, as well as its English writing center. Founded in the spring of 2019, this writing center is housed in a joint-venture, English-medium program that provides students with opportunities to gain dual degrees from the Chinese host university and an American university. Students in this program take compulsory, credit-bearing English composition courses that are delivered through a writing program. Because of this, the joint-venture program has a strong foundation and expertise in English academic writing, and the English writing center represents an effort to expand the English writing support to reach other programs and departments within the university. The director of this writing center described their mission statement as follows:

> The Writing Center exists to provide an accessible space designed to equip students with the cultural capital and academic fluency to navigate their own way through a project, be it an essay or paper, a personal statement, a resume, or an application letter. The Writing Center operates in a way that is sympathetic to the specific needs of Chinese L2 students and will seek to incorporate the best of international composition pedagogy while tailoring practice to reflect the Center's professional understanding of the particular requirements of students. (Email exchange with Writing Center Director, Sep 10, 2020)

The mission statement above demonstrates the writing center's readiness and flexibility to cater its services to meet the specific needs of Chinese EFL students. This writing center is open to the entire student body, as well as faculty, and offers both asynchronous email tutorials and synchronous in-person tutorials. Although the writing center caps their in-person sessions at 25 minutes, in practice, tutors work with students for as long as necessary.

Our research participants consisted of 388 student survey respondents, 2 tutors, and 4 student writers/tutees. As Table 1 shows, the respondents included 122 freshmen, 26 sophomores, 53 juniors, 37 seniors, 128 master's students, and 22 doctoral students from a myriad of majors such as Finance, Chinese Literature, Communication, Physical Education, Fine Arts, Geography, Chemistry, Japanese, Psychology, Educational Technology, Math Education, Environmental Studies, Biology, Economy, Accounting, Marketing, Marxism Studies, and Music. Most survey respondents self-identified as female (n=307), with others self-identifying as male (n=65) and a few who preferred not to disclose their gender identity (n=16); such an imbalanced gender ratio is typical at normal universities in China. In terms of English learning background, half of the respondents (n=194) reported having studied English for more than 10 years, followed by those with 7 to 10 years of experience studying English (n=154) and those with 3 to 6 years (n=37) of experience.

Table 1. Description of survey respondents

Year of Study	Freshman	Sophomore	Junior	Senior	Master's student	Doctoral student
No. Percentage	122 (31%)	26 (7%)	53 (14%)	37 (9%)	128 (33%)	22 (6%)
Self-reported Gender	Female		Male		Not to disclose gender identity	
No. Percentage	307 (79%)		65 (17%)		16 (4%)	
English Learning Background	More than ten years		Seven to ten years		Three to six years	
No. Percentage	194 (50%)		154 (40%)		40 (10%)	

In addition, six focal participants — two tutors and four student writers — participated in recorded tutorials and follow-up interviews, including a British faculty tutor (who was also the director of the writing center), a Chinese peer tutor, two undergraduate students, and two doctoral students; their demographic information is offered in Table 2.

Table 2. Description of focal tutor/tutee participants

Tutor (T)/ Student Writer (S)	Gender	Ethnicity	Education Level
T1 (Director, instructor, tutor)	Female	British	M.A. in Social and Cultural Theory
T2 (Peer tutor)	Male	Chinese	Senior in Supply-chain Management
S1	Male	Chinese	Junior in Finance
S2	Female	Chinese	Ph.D. candidate in Educational Technology
S3	Female	Chinese	Ph.D. candidate in Educational Technology
S4	Female	Chinese	Senior in Finance

3.2 Data collection

With institutional approval from the investigated university, we distributed an online survey, obtained audio recordings of four tutorials, and conducted post-tutorial interviews with four Chinese student writers. First, an original anonymous online survey (Appendix A) was distributed via Qualtrics to Chinese students with the help of their writing center director and via a snowball method through the researchers' personal network. Apart from demographic information, the survey consisted of Likert scale items, multiple-choice questions, and open-ended questions regarding students' self-perceived English writing proficiency, needs for English writing support, writing-related help-seeking behaviors, and their writing center usage and experiences. In total, 388 valid survey responses were collected.

Then, with the help of the writing center director, four writing center tutorials were recorded with a digital recording device. The four students in these tutorials consented to participate in the present study by signing an informed consent form that listed the procedures, benefits, and potential risks involved. Supplementary materials, such as assignment sheets and notes taken during the tutorials, were also collected. The duration of the recorded tutorials ranged from 19 to 29 minutes, resulting in 87 minutes of tutorial data. Tutorial recordings were first transcribed verbatim and then reformatted into close vertical transcripts to capture the details and complexity of tutorial conversations based on Gilewicz and Thonus's (2003) close vertical transcription convention (Appendix B).

Within a week or so, after obtaining the tutorial recordings, individual, semistructured, retrospective interviews were conducted with the four student writers via Tencent Meeting, a video conferencing application. A few days prior to the interviews, an edited transcript of the recorded tutorials was shared with the student writers, along with the tutorial recording, to help them reflect on their tutorial experiences. During the interviews (Appendix C), the student writers were prompted to identify and discuss what they considered effective moments of discussion during the tutorials, that is, utterances or exchanges that they perceived as conducive for improving the student's text and/or for contributing to the student's learning and writerly development. Students were also asked to discuss their overall experience of utilizing the writing center and their perceptions of the conferencing method of writing center tutorials. The interviews lasted between 41 and 63 minutes, which resulted in 188 minutes of interview data.

3.3 Data analysis

Statistical and qualitative analyses were conducted based on the nature of the data. In response to the first research question regarding students' self-perceptions as English writers, descriptive statistical analyses were performed in SPSS 28 (Statistical Package for the Social Sciences) on the numerical survey data. Then, based on descriptive statistical results, inferential statistical analyses were conducted to further examine potential correlations (e.g., correlations between students' self-perceived English writing proficiency and their reported help-seeking). In response to the second research question regarding students' writing center usage, descriptive statistical analyses were performed on the numerical survey data to examine the students' utilization of the writing center. In response to the third research question regarding students' perceptions of their writing center experiences, descriptive statistical analyses were first performed on the numerical survey data; then, open, thematic analyses were performed on three sources of data, including responses to the open-ended questions in the survey, tutorial recordings, and post-tutorial interviews. Drawing on Saldana (2009), exploratory thematic coding and pattern coding were conducted in NVivo 12 to generate themes that could best capture the students' perceptions of their recorded tutorial experience at the writing center.

4. Findings

4.1 Students' self-perceptions as English writers

In response to the first research question, this section offers a macro understanding of Chinese students' self-perceptions of English writers in terms of their self-perceived English writing proficiency, needs for English writing support, and writing-related help-seeking behaviors by drawing on 388 sets of survey responses.

4.1.1 Self-perceptions: Proficiency, needs, and help-seeking

As Table 3 shows, the responses to the seven 7-point Likert scale statements in our survey indicated that, in terms of English writing proficiency, Chinese college students (n=388) somewhat disagreed that they were good English writers (M=3.35) and were ambivalent regarding having a concept about what good writing is (M=4.44); they agreed or somewhat agreed that English was challenging for them (M=5.49). In terms of English writing support, they needed help with English writing (M=5.79) and held a positive attitude toward the helpfulness of one-on-one tutorials (M=5.48) and discussing their writing with a writing tutor (M=5.91). Despite their perceived needs for English writing support, they remained neutral or somewhat agreed that they often sought help with English writing (M=4.87).

Table 3. Self-perceived English writing proficiency, needs, and help-seeking

Area	Mean	Std. Dev.
Good at English writing	3.35	1.436
Have a clear concept of good English writing	4.44	1.455
English writing is challenging	5.49	1.233
Need help with English writing	5.79	1.193
One-on-one tutorial helps	5.48	1.334
Discussing with tutors helps	5.91	1.106
Seeking help often	4.87	1.524

To further examine the relationships among students' self-perceived English writing proficiency, needs for English writing support, and writing-related help-seeking, a series of Spearman's rho correlation tests[1] were performed on the data in SPSS. Four statistically significant correlations emerged, including a statistically significant, strong, positive correlation between students' self-perceived English writing proficiency and their self-perceived knowledge of what good writing is (rs=0.500, n=388, p=0.000), between students' perceptions regarding how challenging English writing was and that regarding how much help they needed with English writing (rs=0.650, n=388, p=0.000), and between students' perceived helpfulness of one-on-one tutorials and that of discussing writing with a writing tutor (rs=0.639, n=388, p=0.000); in addition, a statistically

1 Spearman's rho correlation test was selected because we consider Likert-scale statement data to be ordinal data, which led to our choice of a nonparametric test.

significant, weak, positive correlation between students' perceptions was revealed regarding how much help they needed with English writing and that regarding how often they sought for help with English writing (rs=0.174, n=388, p=0.001).

That is, the surveyed Chinese students tended to perceive themselves as good English writers when they had a clear concept of what good writing is. When they perceived English writing to be challenging, they also tended to perceive the need for English writing support. However, their writing-related help-seeking did not seem to match the level of their perceived need for English writing support; although the students were aware of their needs for English writing support, they did not necessarily act upon such needs to seek out help accordingly. In addition, they tended to perceive the helpfulness of two forms of English writing support concomitantly: one-on-one writing tutorials and discussing writing with a tutor; in other words, they found it beneficial to talk to a tutor about their writing one on one during tutorials, which was the exact type of English writing support offered by the writing center.

4.1.2 Zooming in on students' needs for English writing support and help-seeking

Three multiple-choice questions further examined students' needs for English writing support and their writing-related help-seeking behaviors. Figure 1 shows the surveyed students' responses (n=388) to the question, "What type(s) of English writing do you often need to do?" The results presented that school-related writing (e.g., class assignments, English presentations, theses, and dissertations) was regarded as most needed for students, along with writing for purposes of graduate school and job application, publication, competition, and personal communication. Among the 11 participants who ticked the "Other: Please specify" box, 10 reported that they needed to complete exam writing, such as CET-4 and CET-6[1], and the English writing section in the graduate school entrance examination, while one participant wrote "comments for social media".

1 CET-4 and CET-6 refer to the nationwide College English Test Band 4 and Band 6, respectively, which are well-recognized English proficiency tests for non-English-major college students in China implemented by the Department of Education in China.

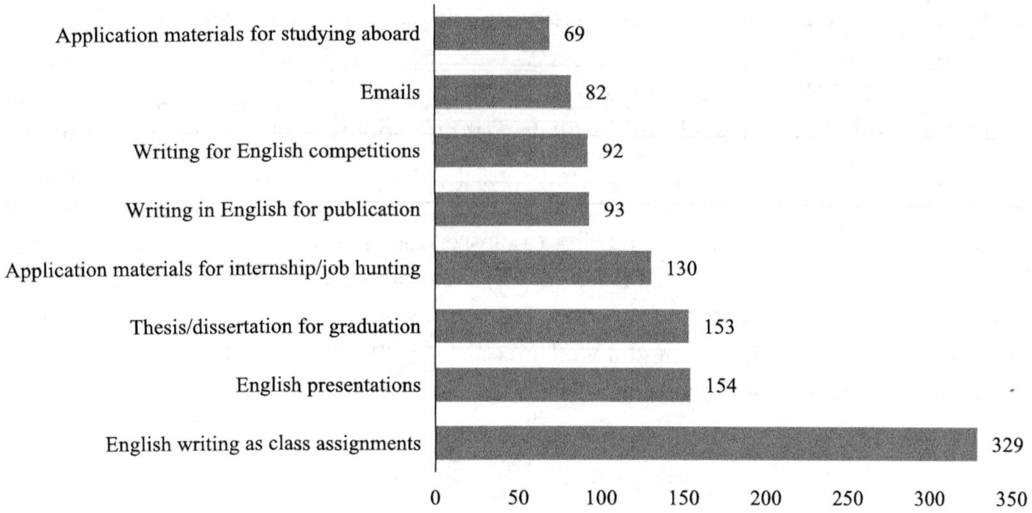

Figure 1. Types of English writing students needed to do

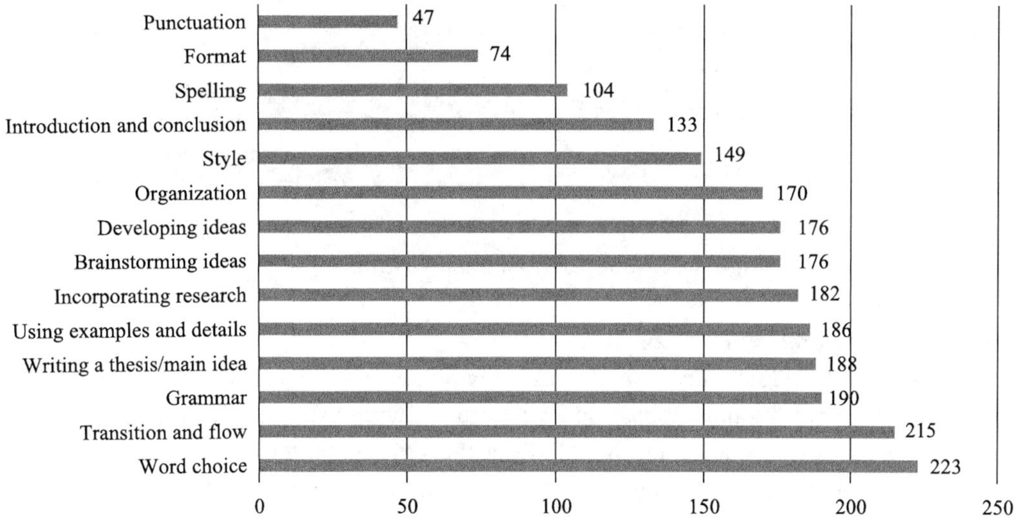

Figure 2. Areas of English writing in which students needed help

Next, Figure 2 shows the surveyed students' responses (n=388) to the question, "Which area(s) do you need help in with your English writing?" The results revealed that the most help was needed for local concerns, including word choice (n=223), transition and flow (n=215), and grammar (n=190), followed by higher-order concerns such as thesis (n=188), using examples and details (n=186), incorporating research (n=182), brainstorming ideas (n=176), developing ideas (n=176), organization (n=170), style (n=149), and introduction and conclusion (n=133). In comparison, less help was needed with mechanical issues, including spelling (n=104), format (n=74), and punctuation (n=47). In addition, two participants ticked the "Other: Please specify" box and reported needing help with "thinking in English" and "using advanced sentence structures and phrases skillfully."

In terms of help-seeking, Figure 3 shows the surveyed students' responses (n=388) to the question, "Do you seek out English writing support from any of the following sources?" The results indicated that English instructors (n=278) and classmates/friends (n=246) were reported as the main sources of help, followed by online automatic revising tools (n=130). They also reported turning to classes/tutors of for-profit language training institutes (n=77) and the writing center (n=68)[1]. Twenty-one students chose the "Other: Please specify" box and listed additional sources, such as Grammarly, Google Translator, dictionaries, reference books, and social media (e.g., WeChat, BiliBili.com), to teach themselves, while two participants reported not seeking help at all.

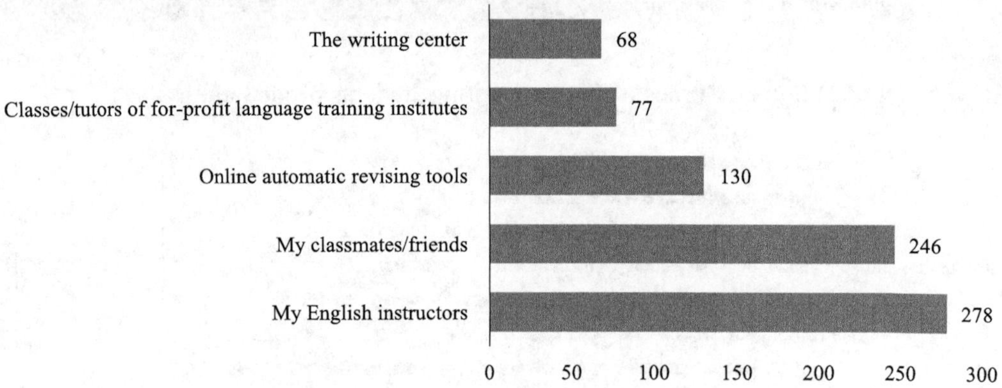

Figure 3. Sources of English writing support

4.2 Students' writing center usage

Among all the 388 survey respondents, only 69 students reported having heard about the writing center at the university, and 28 reported having used the writing center, while most of them reported not having heard about the writing center (n=319, 82%) or used it (n=360, 93%). That is, although the writing center was available to the entire student body, only a small portion of the survey respondents had knowledge about or utilized this campus resource.

1 Interestingly, although 68 survey respondents checked "the writing center" as one of their sources of English writing support, only 28 survey respondents reported having used the writing center in a following section of the survey (see the next subsection "Students' Writing Center Usage"). This suggests that some students might regard the writing center as a potential source of English writing support but had not actually used it.

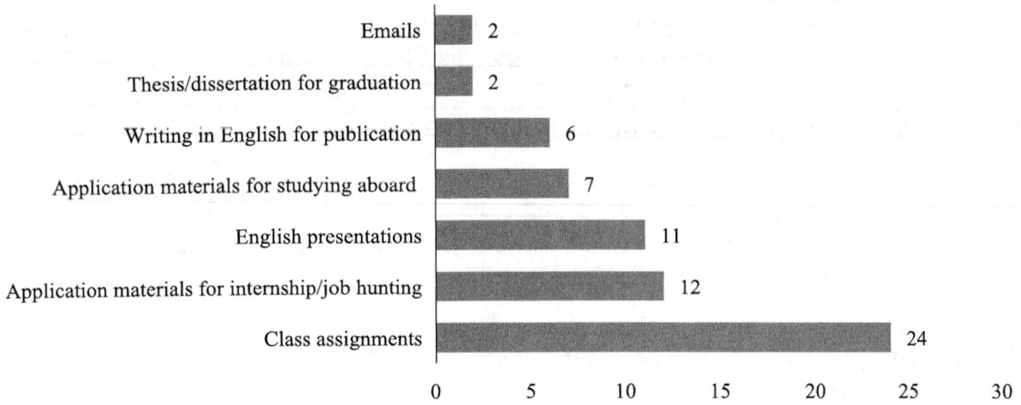

Figure 4. Types of English writing students brought into the writing center

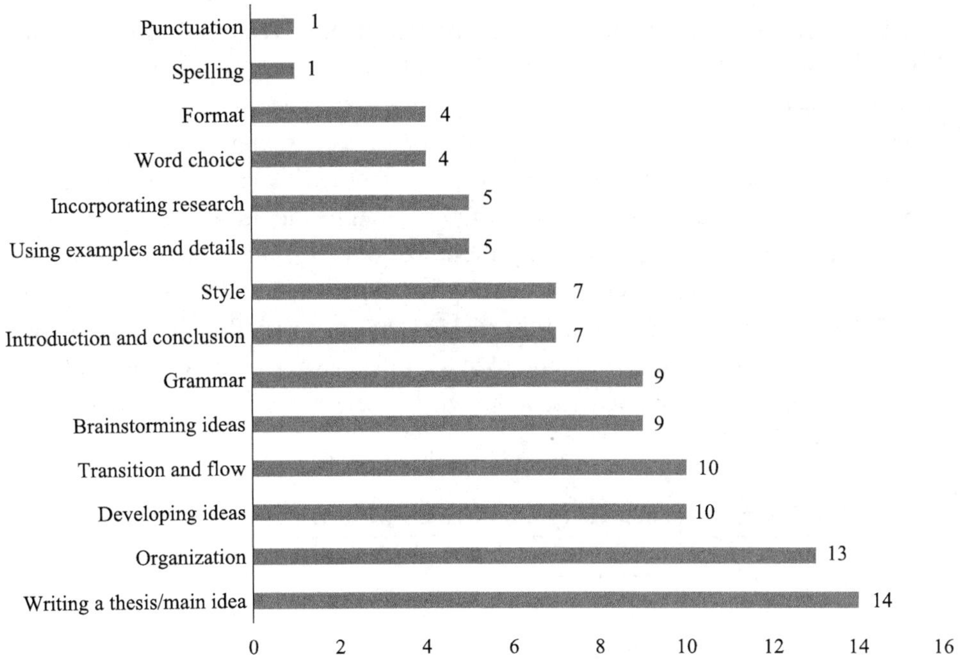

Figure 5. Areas of English writing discussed during writing center tutorials

For those who reported having used the writing center, an additional set of multiple-choice questions, Likert scale statements, and open-ended questions were given to generate an understanding of their experiences and perceptions regarding gaining help from the writing center. Figure 4 demonstrates the types of writing that students brought into the writing center for help, with class assignments (n=24), job/internship applications (n=12), and English presentations (n=11) as the most frequent types, which were generally consistent with the types of English writing that students needed to do (see Figure 1). Students also reported gaining help from the writing center to work on study-abroad application materials (n=7), writing for publication (n=6), graduation thesis/dissertation (n=2), and emails (n=2).

Likewise, Figure 5 demonstrates the areas of English writing discussed during writing center tutorials, with a few global concerns — such as thesis (n=14), organization (n=13), and developing ideas (n=10) — as well as a local concern including transition and flow (n=10), ranking as the most frequently discussed issues at the writing center. Thus, whereas students identified local issues (such as word choice, transition and flow, and grammar) as what they needed the most help with, they also discussed global issues (except for transition and flow, which were both identified as an area that the students needed the most help with and were actually addressed during writing center tutorials) during the tutorials.

4.3 Students' perceptions of their writing center experiences

We draw on three sources of data to present students' perceptions of their writing center experiences: (1) numerical and qualitative data were analyzed to outline writing center users' overall perceptions, (2) post-tutorial retrospective interview data were drawn upon to describe four student writers' perceptions of their recorded tutorials, and (3) snapshots of the recorded tutorials were referred to as supplementary materials to help substantiate students' reflection on their writing center experiences.

4.3.1 Survey Data: Students' Overall Perceptions of Writing Center Experiences

As Table 4 shows, the 28 survey respondents who had experience using the writing center reported feeling satisfied with writing center tutorials in general (M=6.36) and recognized the helpfulness of discussing their work with a tutor (M=6.43). Likewise, they reported receiving useful answers to their writing problems (M=6.29) and revising their writing accordingly after tutorials (M=6.36). The only area that was rated relatively low was the participants' perceived comfort with discussing their writing with a tutor (M=5.32). Overall, the students who used the writing center perceived their writing center experiences positively.

Table 4. Writing center users' experiences with writing center tutorials

Area	Mean	Std. Dev.
Satisfaction with tutorials	6.36	0.911
Comfort: Discussing writing with a tutor	5.32	2.074
Discussing with a tutor helps	6.43	0.836
Obtained helpful support	6.29	0.810
Revised after tutorials	6.36	0.870

The writing center users were also asked an open-ended question regarding whether they would recommend the writing center to others. All of those who responded (n=20) indicated that they would recommend the writing center to others, mainly for two reasons: the effective and professional tutorials and the patient, nice, and responsible tutors. They were asked another question regarding the benefits and/or limitations of the writing center tutorial approach during a designated tutorial session. Those who responded (n=17) mentioned benefits such as direct and accurate communication between students and tutors, tutors guiding students to find solutions, efficiency, and specific and concrete explanations with examples. On the other hand, they also identified limitations, such as ineffective communication in English, a lack of systematic instruction, time constraint, and forgetting details after tutorials.

4.3.2 Interview and Tutorial Data: Four Student Writers' Experiences

Next, we focus on four student writers' perceptions of their writing center tutorials based on retrospective interviews and tutorial recording data. As Table 5 demonstrates, the four recorded tutorials focused on various types of writing, including a class writing assignment, manuscript submission for publication purposes, and a personal statement intended for a master's degree program. All four student writers emailed their writing to the writing center prior to the tutorials, and their in-person tutorials focused on how to revise their work. Despite the idiosyncrasies of these tutorials, their focus of discussion seemed to share one theme in common: the tutorials all concerned "connection making," that is, synthesis writing. The tutors and students discussed the lack of connections between S1's arguments and examples, S2's lack of synthetic discussion of her findings in relation to relevant scholarship in her conclusion section, S3's inadequate synthesis of literature in her literature review section, and S4's lack of specific examples to establish a unique connection/match between herself as an applicant and her target university in her personal statement. This focus on connection making aligned with the survey finding that, although students reported needing help with both local and global concerns, what was discussed and addressed at the writing center tended to be global concerns.

Table 5. Description of writing center tutorials

Tutor (T)/ Student Writer (S)	Tutorial Duration (minutes)	Type of Writing	Agenda	Tutorial Focus
T1-S1	28	Essay for Management Skills (class assignment)	Revising	Connecting examples with values; using quotations
T1-S2	18	Manuscript for journal submission	Revising	Highlighting and expanding implications
T1, T2-S3	19	Manuscript for journal submission	Revising	Building connections among sources in the literature review
T1, S4	18	Personal statement for application to a U.K. graduate school	Revising	Adjusting order of information; appealing to the target university

Overall, all four student writers perceived their recorded tutorials as effective by rating them as five out of five during the retrospective interviews. Specifically, their reflection highlighted two benefits of individualized writing center tutorials: (1) writing center tutorials as a dialogic space for learning and (2) acquiring transferable writing knowledge.

First, all four student writers expressed their appreciation for the dialogic space that the tutors created during writing center tutorials with back-and-forth, question-and-answer exchanges. For instance, S1 stated that he enjoyed "the Socratic characteristic" of the writing tutorial because T1 guided him to explore and expand his thinking by asking questions (Interview with S1, Sept. 28, 2020). Similarly, S2 stated that discussing her manuscript in person with T1 helped her discover new issues, inspired her to revise, provided her with opportunities to understand the tutor's meanings directly, and allowed her to raise questions (Interview with S2, Sept. 30, 2020). For example, S2 referred to her following exchange with T1 during Tutorial 2 to illustrate how she managed to resolve her confusion and achieve learning:

S2: It, it's, in the introduction, and (.) interview

T1: [mm

S2: [Interview, ah, literature review, uh, about the pedagogy and the (.) positive and negative emotions (.) It's uh, just (.) just a small part.

T1: uh-huh mm

S2: So I think, if I really to (.) change it, should, I think I should, maybe I should change the

T1: The whole thing?

S2: The whole thing.

T1: I think you just need to make a mention (.) of the implications.

S2: Okay.

(Recorded Tutorial 2, Sept. 26, 2020)

S2, a doctoral student working on a manuscript intended for publication, misunderstood T1's earlier suggestion of expanding the conclusion section and thought that she would need to revise her paper extensively. Then, by raising her concern in the form of a solution ("maybe I should change the whole thing") and by obtaining a direct and clear answer from T1 ("I think you just need to make a mention of the implications"), S2 managed to resolve her confusion and realized that expanding her conclusion required a discussion of her research implications in her conclusion section rather than "revising the whole thing."

The student writers also highlighted the value of tutors' explanations as an effective way to help them learn about the why's behind writing issues. For example, S3 referred to the following explanation offered by T2 as effective because it helped her understand why her literature review looked like a list and needed to be revised (Interview with S3, Oct. 21, 2020):

T2: 你没有在观点之间产生联系，就是产生一种互动。就是说你两个观点 (.) 嗯或者几个观点之间，你要找出一些不同或者相同，或者是 (.) 产生一些新的 (.) 嗯，就是综合一点的想法。[There's no connection between different points of view, to produce interactions. That is to say, among the two or a few points of view that you discuss, you need to find some differences or similarities, or to produce some new, um, more integrated ideas.][1]

(Recorded Tutorial 3, Oct. 20, 2020)

S3 valued the tutors' explanations because her understanding of the why's behind her writing issues would enable her to make judgments under similar circumstances, as she illustrated in the interview as follows:

For instance, when I discussed the purpose of something in a sentence, I put it at the end, while T1 suggested moving the purpose part to the beginning of the sentence. But when I encountered a similar problem in the second half of my paper [which T1 did not annotate for me], I felt unsure whether I needed to revise it in a similar way because I wasn't sure if that particular revision suggested by T1 applies to just that one sentence or sentences of a certain type. But talking with the tutor about it during the tutorial helped me understand why she suggested the revision.

(Interview with S3, Oct. 21, 2020)[2]

S4 also stated that discussing writing with a tutor not only helped her see what to revise, but also why to revise it in certain ways; in other words, talking about it enabled her to see "the logic chain in which her [T1's] suggested revisions came into being" (Interview with S4, Nov. 24, 2020). Therefore, for student writers, the tutors created a dialogic space during writing center tutorials with back-and-forth exchanges and helpful explanations, which offered opportunities for in-depth learning. This benefit also appeared in the survey data (see 4.3.1).

Second, three student writers explicitly discussed how they acquired transferrable writing knowledge from writing center tutorials. For instance, S3 not only identified her main takeaway from Tutorial 3 (using noun phrases to make connections between sources in the literature review), but also clearly articulated her intention to transfer the lesson learned into future writing: "For instance, if I start a new paper, I'd have the awareness of making connections across sources in the literature review, and I'd write my first draft

1 English translation of T2's Chinese utterances were offered by researchers in square brackets.

2 Students' interviews were conducted mainly in Chinese, their L1. English translations were offered by the researchers.

with such awareness" (Interview with S3, Oct. 21, 2020). The emerging awareness and skills of synthesizing literature were crucial to S3, a novice scholar who strived to publish in English-medium international journals.

Similarly, S4, who was in the final year of her undergraduate study, identified important writing concepts that she learned from working on her personal statement and intended to transfer them into other types of writing. S4 referred to the following exchange as an example of transferrable writing knowledge that she learned from T1, that is, audience awareness:

> T1: And number two, immediately (.) start talking about Glasgow. (4s) A lot of students (.) will write one personal statement (.) and they will change it (.) only a tiny bit for every application, (.) okay? Universities don't like that. University of Glasgow (.) wants to feel like you ((patting on the table)) wrote this for them.
>
> S4: Okay.
>
> T1: Okay? Not that you wrote a personal statement and you changed it a little bit each time, (.) okay?
>
> S4: Okay.
>
> T1: Which is what we all do, (.) okay? But we've got to give them the feeling (.) that we didn't, so you need to start talking seriously (.) and extensively about Glasgow (.) as soon as possible. (.) Okay?
>
> (Recorded Tutorial 4, Nov. 18, 2020)

During her retrospective interview, S4 stated that T1's suggestions about focusing more and sooner on her target university in her personal statement were very helpful because they helped her improve her audience awareness:

> "She [T1] was actually cultivating a certain way of thinking in me, when I write personal statements, I need to focus on the thoughts of those receiving the personal statements and what they hoped to read. This is more important; it feels like 'Give a man a fish and you feed him for a day. Teach a man to fish and you feed him for a lifetime.'"
>
> (Interview with S4, Nov. 24, 2020)

S4's compelling quote demonstrated her clear awareness of the transferability of such knowledge. Therefore, the dialogic space enabled by writing center tutorials can be utilized as a conducive place for delivering transferrable writing knowledge and skills that student writers can carry into future writing tasks.

5. Discussion and Implications

5.1 Key results

Based on the survey results, four recorded tutorials, and four post-tutorial retrospective interviews with student writers, the present study revealed three main findings regarding Chinese students' needs for English writing support and their writing center usage and experiences, as follows:

(1) The surveyed Chinese students perceived strong needs for English writing support for various types of writing and identified both local and global issues as areas in need of help; however, their writing-related help-seeking did not seem to match their lack of confidence in English writing and the challenges that they perceived.

(2) Only a small portion of the surveyed Chinese students reported having heard about or used the English writing center on campus, and the tutorials tended to focus more on global issues than on local ones.

(3) The survey respondents with experience visiting the writing center generally perceived their writing center experiences to be highly satisfactory in helping them improve their writing. Similarly, the four focal student writers expressed their appreciation for writing center tutorials during the retrospective interviews, highlighting how individualized writing center tutorials provided them with a dialogic space for learning and helped them acquire transferable writing knowledge.

5.2 Chinese college students' writing-related challenges and unmet needs

The results of the present study affirmed the challenges and lack of English writing support faced by Chinese college students (Fu & Matoush 2012; Jiang et al. 2023; Sang 2017). As the survey results demonstrated, most Chinese college students did not generally perceive themselves as good English writers and did not seem to have a clear concept about what good writing is. This aligns with Sang's (2017) finding that many Chinese students struggle with English writing, especially in applying the writing knowledge and skills that they have learned to actual writing. Although many Chinese student writers perceived English writing as being highly challenging and needed writing support for various types of writing tasks, they acknowledged not seeking enough support to improve their writing. Meanwhile, when they sought out support, their main source of help was English instructors and classmates/friends. However, English writing education in China is constrained by contextual factors, such as oversized classes, inadequate class time, and the lack of timely and detailed feedback on student writing (Zhang 2006). Thus, with instructors being perceived as the main source of English writing support, it is very likely that Chinese students are not receiving sufficient help, especially individualized writing support. This lack of writing support demands timely changes and innovation, especially in that "writing instructions in the Chinese university-based English programs have yet to meet the demand for students' L2 writing development because a significant proportion of Chinese EFL students still experienced ineffective writing pedagogies in their curricula" (Jiang et al. 2023: 51). Therefore, Chinese students' low English writing self-efficacy and their expressed needs for writing support called for additional and more individualized writing support, thus accentuating writing center tutorials as a promising approach to addressing Chinese students' unmet needs.

5.3 Addressing Chinese college students' needs with the writing center approach

Specifically, our study demonstrated how writing centers can be utilized to support Chinese student writers by helping them acquire transferable writing knowledge in a dialogic space enabled by individualized tutorials. To begin with, our focal participants' appreciation for the dialogic negotiation of meaning during writing tutorials echoed Kwan's (2022: 391) finding that a Chinese tutee enjoyed "the give-and-take of formative feedback on writing" that she received from writing center tutors. The back-and-forth exchanges, especially through the use of questions and explanations, afforded students rich learning opportunities.

Meanwhile, our focal student writers' positive perceptions and explicit discussion of writing transfer reflected the emerging constructive metacognition proposed by Gorzelsky et al. (2016: 226), that is, "reflection across writing tasks and contexts, using writing and rhetorical concepts to explain choices and evaluations and to construct a writerly identity". In the fields of composition studies and writing center research, failure to transfer learned writing knowledge to other writing contexts has been perceived as a prevailing problem for student writers (e.g., Anson & Moore 2016; Driscoll 2015). Our interview data revealed multiple instances where student writers explicitly discussed their reflections on transferable writing knowledge that they had learned from writing center tutorials, such as the awareness of making connections for synthesis writing and audience awareness. Student writers' emerging awareness could be further developed to cultivate constructive metacognition and foster lasting and effective writing transfer, which also reflects the writing center's classic tenet of "producing better writers" (North 1984). With data showing Chinese students' lack of confidence as English writers and their inability to tell what good writing is like, the promotion of writing transfer during tutorials is especially meaningful and important to help Chinese students become more confident and resourceful writers with increasing writerly metacognition.

5.4 Implications

Based on our results, we offer implications for supporting Chinese college students with writing center tutorials. First, to reach more students — especially those who are unfamiliar with writing center services — writing centers should increase their visibility on campus and ensure that their services cater to students' perceived needs, including both global and local writing issues. Particularly for newly established writing centers in EFL contexts, it is critical to ground their service provision in the surveyed needs of local students and faculty rather than transplanting North American writing center models as rigid prototypes. Second, the dialogic space that is enabled by individualized tutorials, which can serve as a promising and flexible resource to address college student writers' needs in a tailored manner, should be capitalized upon. Specifically, students' writerly development can be supported by purposefully teaching key writing concepts to them, engaging them in inquiry-based exchanges, and offering detailed explanations so as to facilitate their writing transfer and foster their metacognitive development.

6. Conclusion

Drawing on quantitative and qualitative analyses of surveys, recorded tutorials, and interview data, the present study made one of thc first empirical endeavors to examine Chinese writing center praxis in light of local students' needs and perceptions, suggesting that writing centers are a promising approach to supplement the traditional classroom English writing instruction and provide EFL students with effective individualized writing support. Meanwhile, the current study is limited in its scope and methodology in that it surveyed students' writing-related needs from only one Chinese university and investigated only four student writers' writing tutorial experiences. As such, future research is needed to extend and expand this line of inquiry. Some potential directions include investigating effective tutoring strategies to help Chinese student writers work on specific genres (e.g., writing for publication, exam writing, and job/graduate school application materials), tutors' perceptions of tutorial effectiveness, tutor-student interaction during tutorials, and post-tutorial revisions and their relationship with writing transfer. It is hoped that further research will focus on the potential and promising outlook of writing center in the Chinese context and beyond.

References

Anson, C. M. & J. Moore. 2016. *Critical Transitions: Writing and the Question of Transfer* [M]. Colorado: The WAC Clearinghouse.

Barnawi, O. Z. (ed.). 2018. *Writing Centers in the Higher Education Landscape of the Arabian Gulf* [C]. London: Palgrave Macmillan.

Bond, C. 2019. "I need help on many things please": A case study analysis of first-generation college students' use of the writing center [J]. *Writing Center Journal* 37(2): 161-194.

Chen, F. & X. Wang. 2023. "Oops! I can't express this in English!": Managing epistemic challenges by Chinese EFL peer tutors in writing tutorials [J]. *Text & Talk* 43(1): 1-20.

Denny, H., J. Nordlof & L. Salem. 2018. "Tell me exactly what it was that I was doing that was so bad": Understanding the needs and expectations of working-class students in writing centers [J]. *Writing Center Journal* 37(1): 67-100.

Driscoll, D. L. 2015. Building connections and transferring knowledge: The benefits of a peer tutoring course beyond the writing center [J]. *Writing Center Journal* 35(1): 153-181.

Fu, D. & M. Matoush. 2012. Teacher's perceptions of English language writing instruction in China [A]. In C. Bazerman, C. Dean, J. Early, K. Lunsford, S. Null, P. Rogers & A. Stansell (eds.). *International Advances in Writing Research: Cultures, Places, Measures* [C]. Colorado: The WAC Clearinghouse. 23-39.

Gao, J. & F. Du. (高洁、杜方圆). 2022. The functioning and development of English writing center in the Chinese higher education context: Fudan University as a case (英文写作中心在中国大学中的设置运行与发展前景——以复旦大学为例) [J]. *Chinese Journal of Second Language Writing* (《二语写作》)5: 70-80.

Gilewicz, M. & T. Thonus. 2003. Close vertical transcription in writing center training and research [J]. *The Writing Center Journal* 24(1): 25-49.

Gorzelsky, G., D. L. Driscoll, J. Paszek, E. Jones & C. Hayes. 2016. Cultivating constructive metacognition: A new taxonomy for writing studies [A]. In C. M. Anson & J. L. Moore (eds.). *Critical Transitions: Writing and the Question of Transfer* [C]. Colorado: The WAC Clearinghouse. 215-246.

He, J. (何佳佳). 2018. Exploring L2 writing model in the writing center context – An empirical study under the perspective of dynamic systems theory (动态系统理论视域下高校英语写作中心个性化写作辅导模式研究) [J]. *Technology Enhanced Foreign Language Education* (《外语电化教学》) 180: 10-17.

He, J. (何佳佳). 2019. An empirical study of academic english writing tutoring model based on the peerceptiv peer assessment system (基于Peerceptiv在线同伴互评系统的学术英语写作个性化辅导模式研究) [J]. *Technology Enhanced Foreign Language Education* (《外语电化教学》) 186: 25-33.

He, J. (何佳佳). 2021. American English writing center model and its implications (美国高校英语写作中心运营模式及其启示) [J]. *Chinese Journal of Second Language Writing* (《二语写作》) 2: 71-82.

Hayward, K. 1994. Writing centers: The Hong Kong experience [J]. *The Writing Lab Newsletter* 18 (8): 10-11.

Jiang, L., S. Yu, N. Zhou & Y. Xu. 2023. English writing instruction in Chinese students' experience: A survey study [J]. *RELC Journal* 54(1): 37-54.

Kwan, Y. H. 2022. What do Chinese learners of English want from a university writing centre? A Chinese tertiary student's views on writing centre peer tutoring [J]. *Studies in Self-Access Learning Journal* 13(3): 389-394.

Lee, A. S. 2014. A transcultural framework proposal for international writing centers [A]. In E. Doman (ed.). *Insight into EFL Teaching and Issues in Asia* [C]. Cambridge: Cambridge Scholars Publishing. 129-143.

Lerner, N. 2014. Writing center pedagogy [A]. In G. Tate, A. R. Taggart, K. Schick & H. B. Hessler (eds.). *A Guide to Composition Pedagogies* [C]. Oxford: Oxford University Press. 301-316.

McKinley, J. 2010. English language writing centres in Japanese universities: What do students really need? [J]. *Studies in Self-Access Learning Journal* 1(1): 17-31.

Moussu, L. 2013. Let's talk! ESL students' needs and writing centre philosophy [J]. *TESL Canada Journal* 30 (2): 55-68.

North, S. M. 1984. The idea of a writing center [J]. *College English* 46(5): 433-446.

Okuda, T. 2017. The Writing Center as a Global Pedagogy: A Case Study of a Japanese University Seeking Internationalization [D]. Ph.D. dissertation. Vancouver: The University of British Columbia.

Raymond, L. & Z. Quinn. 2012. What a writer wants: Assessing fulfillment of student goals in writing center tutoring sessions [J]. *Writing Center Journal* 32(1): 64-77.

Saldana, J. 2009. *The Coding Manual for Qualitative Researchers* [M]. Los Angeles: SAGE.

Sang, Y. 2017. Investigating the "issues" in Chinese students' English writing and their "reasons": Revisiting the recent evidence in Chinese academia [J]. *International Journal of Higher Education* 6(3): 1-11.

Severino, C., D. Egan & S. Prim. 2020. International undergraduates' perceptions of their second language writing development and their implications for writing center tutors [J]. *Writing Center Journal* 38(1-2): 165-200.

Song, L. 2018. Joining the momentum of writing center establishment in China [OL]. https://www.wlnjournal.org/blog/2018/02/joining-the-momentum-of-writing-center-establishment-in-china-lingshan-song/ (accessed 10/15/2023).

Tan, B. H., L. Emerson & C. White. 2017. Reforming ESL writing instruction in tertiary education: The writing center approach [J]. *The English Teacher* XXXV: 1-14.

Thompson, I., A. Whyte, D. Shannon, A. Muse, K. Miller, M. Chappell & A. Whigham. 2009. Examining our lore: A survey of students' and tutors' satisfaction with writing center conference [J]. *Writing Center Journal* 29(1): 78-105.

Williams, J. D. & S. Takaku. 2011. Help seeking, self-efficacy, and writing performance among college students [J]. *Journal of Writing Research* 3(1): 1-18.

Winder, R., S. S. Kathpalia & S. L. Koo. 2016. Writing centre tutoring sessions: Addressing students' concerns [J]. *Educational Studies* 42(4): 1-17.

Zhang, J. 2019. Innovating English literacy instruction: A Chinese writing center model [A]. In B. Reynolds & M. Teng (eds.). *English Literacy Instruction for Chinese Speakers* [C]. London: Palgrave Macmillan. 229-243.

Zhang, J. 2021. Talking about Writing in China: How do Writing Centers Serve Chinese Students' Needs? [D]. Ph.D. dissertation. Indiana: Indiana University of Pennsylvania.

Zhang, J. & C. Liu. 2023. An investigation into the missions and practices of glocal writing centers in the Chinese context: ERPP and EAP-EGP hybrid approaches [J]. *Journal of English for Academic Purpose* 65: 101290.

Zhang, X. (张雪梅). 2006. Inquiry into the current state of college English writing pedagogy (大学英语写作教学现状之调查) [J]. *Foreign Language World* (《外语界》) 5: 28-32.

About the Authors

Jing ZHANG, 张婧, is a lecturer at the Department of Foreign Languages and Literature, College of Liberal Arts, Shantou University. Her research interests are international writing center praxis, individualized writing support, and multilingual and translanguaging writing. Email: zhangj@stu.edu.cn

Fan FANG, 方帆 (corresponding author), is a professor at the Department of Foreign Languages and Literature, College of Liberal Arts, Shantou University. His research interests are Applied Linguistics, Sociolinguistics, and Teacher Education. Email: ffang@stu.edu.cn

Appendix A: Survey

Block #1: Likert Scale Statements: Self-perceptions as a Writer (1=Strongly Disagree, 2=Disagree, 3=Somewhat Disagree, 4=Neither Agree nor Disagree, 5= Somewhat Agree, 6=Agree, 7=Strongly Agree)

1. I perceive myself as a good writer of English.
2. I have a concept of what good writing looks like in English.
3. I find English writing to be challenging.
4. I need help with my English writing.
5. One-on-one writing tutorials would help me with my English writing.
6. Discussing my English writing with a trained writing tutor would help me to improve my writing.
7. I often seek out help with my English writing.

Block #2: Multiple Choice: Self-perceived Needs for English Writing Support

1. Which types of English writing do you need to do? Please check as many as apply to you.

a. English writing as class assignments
b. Application materials for internship/job hunting
c. Application materials for studying abroad (e.g., exchange programs, graduate school)
d. English presentations
e. Thesis/dissertation for graduation
f. Publishing in English
g. Emails
h. Writing for English competitions
i. Others (please specify: ____________)

2. Which areas do you need help in with your English writing? Please check as many as apply to you.

a. Brainstorming for ideas
b. Developing ideas
c. Writing a thesis/main idea
d. Using examples and details
e. Introduction and conclusions
f. Incorporating research
g. Organization
h. Transitions and flow
i. Grammar
j. Spelling
k. Punctuation
l. Word choice

m. Style
n. Format
o. Others (please specify: ____________)

3. Do you seek out English writing support from any of the following sources? Please check as many as apply to you.

a. My English instructors
b. My classmates/friends
c. The Writing Center at [Name of University]
d. Paid classes/tutors of commercial language training institutes
e. Online automatic tools (e.g., pigai.org)
f. Others (please specify: ____________)

Block #3: Yes/No: Knowledge about the Writing Center at [Name of University]

1. I have heard about the Writing Center at [Name of University].
2. I have used the Writing Center at [Name of University].
a. No → Block 4a → Block #7→ Demographic Questions.
b. Yes → Block #4b → Block #5 → Block #6 → Block #7→ Demographic Questions.

Block #4: Multiple Choices (For Writing Center Users)

1. Which types of English writing did you bring to the writing center? Please check as many as apply to you.

a. English writing as class assignments
b. Application materials for internship/job hunting
c. Application materials for studying abroad (e.g., exchange programs, graduate school)
d. English presentations
e. Thesis/dissertation for graduation
f. Publishing in English
g. Emails
h. Writing for English competitions
i. Others (please specify: ____________)

2. Which area(s) did you and the writing center tutor work on? Please check as many as apply to you.

a. Brainstorming for ideas
b. Developing ideas
c. Writing a thesis/main idea
d. Using examples and details
e. Introduction and conclusions
f. Incorporating research
g. Organization
h. Transitions and flow

i. Grammar
j. Spelling
k. Punctuation
l. Word choice
m. Style
n. Format
o. Others (please identify: ____________)

Block #5: Likert Scale: Perceptions of Writing Center Experiences (For Writing Center Users) (1=Strongly Disagree, 2=Disagree, 3=Somewhat Disagree, 4=Neither Agree nor Disagree, 5= Somewhat Agree, 6=Agree, 7=Strongly Agree)

1. I felt satisfied with the tutorials provided by the writing center.
2. I felt comfortable with discussing my English writing with a tutor.
3. Discussing my writing with a tutor helped me to improve my writing.
4. My concerns about my writing were often addressed during the writing center tutorials.
5. I usually revised my writing based on what my tutor and I discussed during the tutorials.

Block #6: Open-ended Question: Perceptions of Writing Center Approach (For Writing Center Users)

1. Would you recommend the writing center to others? Why or why not?
2. As you have experienced, one of the prominent tutoring features of the Writing Center at [Name of University] is "talking," i.e., during 25-minute tutorials, a tutor provides you with English writing support by discussing your writing with you, e.g., asking you questions and guiding you to find solutions to address your concerns. What do you think about this approach, i.e., *talking about writing to improve writing*? Do you see any benefits and/or limitations with this approach?

Block #7: Demographic Questions (For All)

1. What gender do you identify with?
a. Male
b. Female
c. Prefer not to specify.
2. What is your class standing?
a. Freshman
b. Sophomore
c. Junior
d. Senior
e. Graduate student
f. Others (please specify: ____________)

3. What is your department and major?
4. How many years have you studied English?
a. 3-6 years
b. 7-10 years
c. More than 10 years
d. Others (please specify: ____________)

Appendix B: Close Vertical Transcription

Transcription Conventions

Pause:	(.) Short pause (1-2 seconds) (5s) Timed pause (2+seconds)
Filled pause:	**um, hmm**
Overlap:	Beginning shown by a right-facing bracket ([) placed vertically. Overlaps between participant contributions are marked using brackets aligned directly above one another. Overlaps continue until one interlocutor completes his/her utterance.
Backchannel:	**uh-huh, yeach, o.k., (all) right** Contributions made by other participants while the first speaker maintains the floor. Backchannels are written in lower-case (o.k.) to distinguish them from minimal responses.
Minimal response:	**Uh-huh** (= yes), **Uh-uh** (= no), **Yeah, O.K., (All) Right** Brief responses made by participants when they have the floor.
Paralinguistic:	Nonverbal features (( )) Additional observation–laugh, cough, sigh, etc. ^^ Finger snaps >> Hand striking a surface
Analytic:	*** Indecipherable or doubtful hearing => Turns focused for analysis

(Gilewicz & Thonus 2003: 29-30)

Appendix C: Interview Protocol

1. What is your major? What year are you in? What types of English writing do you need to complete and how much?

2. What types of English writing support do you often utilize or lack?

3. Why did you bring this piece of writing to the writing center? What were your challenges or concerns with this piece?

4. How was your tutorial experience? To rate the success of this tutorial on a scale of 5, with 5 being the most successful, how would you rate your tutorial? Why?

5. Please point to any effective or interesting utterances/exchanges in the transcript and cxplain why you consider them effective or interesting.

6. Did the writing center tutorial help you improve this paper? Did it improve your English writing abilities and your confidence in English writing?

7. As you have experienced it, the writing center provides English writing support for students with individualized writing tutorials. What do you think of this method?

职场英语写作课中协作学习对缓解写作焦虑的效果研究*

杨　晋

南京大学

摘要：写作焦虑一直受到二语习得界关注。研究认为协作写作有助于缓解写作焦虑，但目前研究仅限于通用英语写作，且以二人结对写作为主，对协作学习在外语学习中的具体作用研究存在争论，尤其是该模式对不同层次学生的影响差异有待进一步研究。本文把协作学习引入职场英语写作的课堂教学中，通过前测和后测以及访谈收集了实验组和对照组的外语写作焦虑和外语写作水平变化的数据。数据分析说明，协作写作营造了一个互帮互助的氛围，为学习者提供情感支持，学生之间互动增加，共同完成写作任务。访谈发现，不仅低水平学生从协作写作中受益，提高了写作水平，缓解了写作焦虑，中等水平学生和高水平学生也认同协作学习的作用。本研究结果对协作学习模式在写作教学中如何降低写作焦虑具有一定启示。

关键词：写作焦虑；协作写作；职场英语写作

DOI: 10.20081/j.cnki.cjslw.2023.07.008

1. 引言

英语课堂中，学生大都以个体的方式进行文章写作和修改。由于受到词汇量有限、语言规则运用技能不高等因素的影响，学习者在写作过程中容易对写作任务产生焦虑情绪，进而影响写作质量和水平，导致学习者表现出种种回避、不作为的行为。以往学者从各个角度研究了应对写作焦虑的方法，比如课堂教学角度（焦丽霞等 2017）、情感策略角度（郭燕、秦晓晴 2010）和多轮续写角度（张朦 2021）等。

除了以上角度，还有人提出，写作过程不能仅仅看成是个人独立进行的行为，因为写作是一个创新和思考的过程，那么这个过程能不能集合多个人的创新和思考，以使写作结果更加完善呢？如教师设计写作题目，介绍写作技巧，学生组成小组，共同参与写作任务，学习者交换思想，相互学习，相互帮助，不断完善写作环节，完成写作任务，也就是协作学习过程（Fathman & Whalley 1990）。

国内外教育界对协作写作进行了一些研究，发现协作写作与独立写作相比，能帮助学习者发现并修改语言错误，学习者在协作写作中使用的语言更准确、更复

* 本文系江苏省教育厅2017年度高校哲学社会科学研究项目（外语专题）（项目编号：2017SJA040）的阶段性研究成果；江苏省教育科学“十三五”规划项目“商务论文写作翻转课堂焦虑感及情感策略研究”的阶段性研究成果。

杂、更流利（Belcher & Lantolf 1998；Fathman & Whalley 1990；Flowers & Vassar 2008；Kroll & Duvvury 2003；Vygotsky & Rotherham 2007）。国内学者如徐锦芬和聂睿（2015）也研究了协作写作，他们肯定了协作写作的正面作用。但目前还不完全清楚协作写作是否适用于所有类型的二语写作任务，是否适用于所有水平的二语学习者，且以往研究仅限于通用英语写作，协作方式仅限于二人配对（徐锦芬、聂睿 2015；朱茜、徐锦芬 2019），至今还没有研究涉及协作写作对缓解写作焦虑的影响，有必要从这个角度进行更多的实证研究。

本研究在某大学英语系“职场英语写作”课中进行，旨在调查小组协作学习模式对缓解写作焦虑和提高写作水平的作用，以期对写作教学有所启示。本文研究对象（职场英语写作）不同于通用型英语写作，除了对语言形式的要求以外，还有诸如备忘录、手册、简历、文案和订单等要求，更加注重语言风格和组织，对学生的要求更高。传统的单兵作战的写作模式，要求学生独立完成，交给老师批改，容易使学生对写作产生恐惧心理，显然对提高写作水平不利。因此，英语教师面临的挑战是如何创建一个轻松的写作课堂帮助学生降低写作焦虑，在写作过程中持有正面的情绪状态，提高写作水平。

2. 文献综述

2.1 写作焦虑及其应对策略研究

就写作焦虑而言，大多数的前人研究结果都指向焦虑对学习者情感和写作成绩的抑制性效应（如Kirmizi & Kirmizi 2015；Liu 2014）。Madden et al.（2011）认为，作为产出性过程，外语写作涉及复杂的心理过程，高焦虑感将导致负面情感，降低写作质量，打击学习者的积极性。关于焦虑感的来源，Cheng（2004）认为高焦虑感一部分来自外部因素，比如，教师的负面评价、太过关注别人的评价以及对自身写作能力的信心不足等。然而，并非所有的焦虑都对外语学习有害。早在20世纪70年代，Scovel（1978：139）就提出焦虑可分为“促进性焦虑和抑制性焦虑”。他认为，前者激励学习者从情感上为新的任务做好准备，并“征服”新的学习任务，使他们向目标靠近；后者则使学习者逃避新的学习任务。Horwitz（2010）认为只有当学习任务比较简单的时候，焦虑感才会比较低，也就是说，他认为没有必要对焦虑感进行分类，但是Andrade和Williams（2009）认为焦虑的强度是两种焦虑感区分的关键。无论如何，低焦虑能起到促进性效果，而高焦虑因其扰乱学习者的注意力，分散精力，起到的是抑制效果。

国内学者针对写作焦虑的负面影响，展开了多方面的实证研究。谭梦玲（2013）调查了独立学院非英语专业学生写作焦虑，发现学生在写作中呈现中等程度的焦虑，被试的写作焦虑和写作成绩显著相关，其中课堂教学焦虑与写作成绩相关度最高，构思焦虑第二。关于如何应对写作焦虑，有研究发现，翻转课堂教学模式可以帮助学生缓解写作焦虑（焦丽霞等 2017）。还有研究者建议使用情感策略来应对写作焦虑（郭燕、秦晓晴 2010）。张朦（2021）发现学习者多轮续写后焦虑水平与成绩前后差异显著，语言水平与写作焦虑呈负相关，语言水平高的学习者更能适应多轮续写教学模式，续写过程中的语言输出有助于调节写作焦虑，最终提升语言水平与语言能力。

2.2 合作学习、协作学习及其效果研究

2.2.1 合作学习的教学效果研究

协作学习的教育理念发展之前，合作学习一直是教育界关注的重点。合作学习是发源于美国的教学理念，它以小组共同学习为主要方式，利用教学中各种动态因素的互动来促进学生学习，指导学生完成共同的学习目标，团队成绩作为学生成绩的考核标准。合作学习的教学促进性作用得到很多实证研究的支持（Johnson & Johnson 2005；Millis 2010；Storch 2013）。Johnson和Johnson（2005）的早期研究发现，合作学习能让学习者获得知识和处理问题的策略，促进学习者的心理健康。Kagan（1994）注意到，合作学习能减少焦虑，为学习者提供更多机会产出语言。国内不少学者发现，合作学习提高学生的写作水平、写作动机和兴趣（张晓兰 2006），促进学生的课堂参与度（卢植 2004），显著降低英语写作焦虑（刘丽敏 2010；吴育红 2011）。因此，学生对合作学习持积极态度并给予正向评价（卢植 2004；吴育红、顾卫星 2011）。

也有学者关注合作学习的不足之处。有人认为，合作学习模式让优生受益更多；但在优生和弱生组成的小组中，优生的成绩反而会有所降低；中等生和弱生受益最大（蒋波、谭顶良 2011）。合作学习可能对弱生的效果更好，但是对水平较高的学生帮助不大，而且有可能打击他们的积极性。还有人指出，由于小组成员的异质特征导致小组成员意见不一致，同伴之间互相怀疑评价效度，从而不愿意合作；同时，低水平学生在文章撰写、修改过程中得到的帮助较多，而优生从同伴那里得到的有价值信息和帮助少，写作提高的速度反而不如弱生。

2.2.2 合作学习和协作学习的区别

有学者指出，合作学习在课堂操作中出现不同结果，可能跟研究者没有区分合作学习和协作学习有关（朱茜、徐锦芬 2019）。协作学习与合作学习相似，但又不同。在合作学习中任务是垂直划分的（即成员或多或少同时在项目的不同环节工作），而在协作学习中，任务是横向划分的（即成员或多或少地在一起按项目的不同方面顺序工作）（Chandra 2015；Dillenbourg 1999），协作学习是基于这样一种观点，即知识是一种社会结构。协作活动通常基于三个原则：

1）学习者是教学的主要焦点；

2）互动和“做”是最重要的；

3）小组合作是一种重要的学习方式。

协作学习可以在对等（peer-to-peer）或更大的群体中进行。同伴指导是协作学习的类型，包括学生成对或小组讨论概念，或找到解决问题。这通常发生在向学生介绍

课程材料后的课堂上，通过课前阅读或视频和/或通过讲师讲座实现。许多导师发现，通过同伴指导，学生们可以通过解决、误解和澄清误解互相教学（Chandra 2015）。

徐锦芬和聂睿（2015）基于CiteSpace 检索了2004到2015年近11年的国际二语写作研究，发现合作写作的小组以二人结对比较多见，由于仅仅是二人互动，在结对写作过程中，两位学生仅仅接收到一个人的反馈，文章修改次数仅限于一次到二次修改，有限的写作练习次数也许并不能带来写作水平的提高，因此，有些研究结果得出合作写作并不能帮助学生提高写作水平的结论（朱茜、徐锦芬 2019）。朱茜指出，其中原因之一是不少研究没有区分协作学习和合作学习的概念，实验结果可能不一致。合作学习和协作学习的共同点是都以小组为基本形式组织学习，都有团体目标和预设任务，都重视通过团体中的积极互赖、促进性互动以及个体责任形成合作性学习环境。而协作和合作的区别在于为了完成全部任务，成员间的劳动分工程度的不同（Dillenbourg 1999）。"协调"指的是一种协调性的、同步活动，成员共同工作，以完成全部学习任务，他们之间没有固定分工，相互间的角色也经常转换。而在"合作"模式下，成员之间的模式比较明确，他们往往将任务分解，每个个体完成子任务，最后将各自的任务组合起来形成最终产品。合作学习的开放性不高，主要适合基础性知识的学习，协作学习开放性强，适合非基础性（即需要更多推理和质疑能力）知识和批判性思维能力的培养。合作学习关注学习结果，关注成员是否完成目标；协作学习关注过程，关注学习者口头和书面的互动（朱茜、徐锦芬 2019）。

纵观国内外研究可以发现，协作学习在外语学习中的作用还需要具体研究，尤其是协作学习模式对不同学生的影响差异需要进一步考察。本研究采用了协作写作的方法，试图考察其对缓解写作焦虑的作用，本研究拟回答以下三个问题：

1）协作写作是否能缓解写作焦虑感?

2）如果焦虑感得到缓解，学习者的写作成绩能否提高?

3）不同水平的学生对协作写作的反馈如何?

3. 研究方法

3.1 研究对象

本研究于2021年秋季期间在一所普通高校英语系的"职场英语写作"课程上进行。研究对象是英语系三年级学生。实验班和对照班各有30名学生。

3.2 研究过程

研究者于2021年9月至2022年1月进行了协作写作实验。实验班同学组成六个五人小组（根据上学期写作成绩，五名学生中有一名高水平学生，三名中等水平学生，一名低水平学生）。为了保证协作学习的效果，研究者制定了学习目标，即风险共同承担，回报共同分享。如果每个成员的写作成绩能达到10分，那么整个小组里的成员才能得到10分，这部分分数占课程总分的70%。

本研究的课堂操作共分三个阶段进行。首先，在写前阶段，教师要求受试者阅读和观看跟课程内容相关的视频和讲义，然后要求学生在课堂上汇报所阅读和观看的材料。其次，要求学生按照以下四个步骤开始写作（如表1所示）：写作前计划、第一稿、第二稿（修改稿）、第三稿和第四稿（终稿）。这几个步骤要求全体成员共同承担任务，整个写作过程中，成员需要采用解释和协商等学习技能，最终老师给出的分数是整个小组的得分，而非某个成员的得分。每个成员负责五个步骤的一个。职场英语写作一共有六个写作任务，因此每个小组成员至少都能负责五个步骤中的任何一个。对照班的写作任务与实验班一致，写作任务采用传统方式完成。

表1　小组协作写作翻转教学模式框架

写作步骤	学生行为	教师行为
写作前计划	全体成员讨论写作任务的风格、内容和语言结构，第一位成员记录全组的讨论。	布置学生阅读相关写作讲义，布置写作任务，讲解作文要求。
第一稿	第二位成员写出第一稿。	讲解作文修改要求。
第二稿	全体成员讨论修改第二稿（该稿需要特别注意语言的准确性），第三位成员记录全组的讨论内容。	展示范文，指导学生修改方法。
第三稿	第四位成员写出第三稿。	教师反馈（抽查写作情况）。
第四稿	第五位成员根据全组讨论结果写出终稿。	教师示范批改。
（终稿）	全体成员总结反思协作写作过程。	教师评价作文，给出分数。

3.3 研究工具

1）调查问卷

本研究采用了SLWAI（Second Language Writing Anxiety Inventory，简称SLWAI）（Cheng 2004）测量实验对象的焦虑情况。该量表包括焦虑的三个方面的维度：认知、身体和行为。该工具分别测量实验前后的焦虑水平。得分采用李克特量表的形式进行，每个选项有五个选择，分别代表对某个观点的五种态度（1代表强烈同意，5代表强烈不同意）。所有句子都是正面措辞，比如，"I usually feel comfortable and at ease when writing in English"，如果受试者选1，则认为该生的焦虑程度不高，如果受试者选5，则被认为焦虑程度很高。问卷共包括27个项目，如学生得分越高，写作焦虑感越强。问卷填好以后，研究者又随机抽选了一批学生做深度访谈。

2）写作测试

第二个数据收集工具是写作测试。实验对象共参加了两次测试（实验前后），测试的内容为某次大学英语四级作文，题目为"写作很重要"，为了计分方便，总分换算为100。由于实验过程长达四个多月，练习效应可以忽略不计。阅卷老师根据四个标准（语言准确性、内容、长度和组织结构等）对实验班和对照班的学生作文进行评分。

3）访谈

从实验班选出英语水平高、中、低的三名学生进行半结构化访谈。访谈内容主要是受试者对协作写作学习模式的反馈。所有访谈在2021年1月实验完成后的一周内进行。

所有问卷数据和写作测试数据采用SPSS 20.0分析。访谈数据转化成文字，以待深入分析。为了保护调查对象的隐私，隐去问卷和访谈中的人名。

4. 数据分析和讨论

两个班的变化和组内的变化通过独立样本双侧t检验和双关联样本t检验。p值小于0.05被认为统计上具有显著性。

研究问题一：协作学习是否能显著缓解写作焦虑感?

为了减少其他因素的干扰，在实验前后，实验班和对照班均进行了独立样本双侧t检验。统计结果表明，实验前，对照班的写作焦虑和实验班没有显著不同（对照班平均得分=90.4，标准差9.1；实验班平均得分=91.2，标准差8.4）。实验班采用协作学习的模式，对照班采用传统模式，实验后两班之间的焦虑感水平出现了显著差异（p=0.001<0.05)。

表2　英语写作焦虑水平的平均值和独立样本双侧t检验结果

	班别	人数	平均值	标准差	t	df	Sig(2-tailed)
实验前焦虑水平	实验班	30	90.4	9.01	1.03	128	0.321
	对照班	30	91.2	8.34	1.03	137	0.321
实验后焦虑水平	实验班	30	90.1	15.09	-3.3	107.23	0.001**
	对照班	30	92.2	10.38	-3.3	110.43	0.001**

注：*p<0.05; **p<0.01.

表3的数据说明实验班的焦虑水平在实验后显著减少，而对照班却没有显著变化。

表3　写作焦虑的配对样本双侧t检验结果

		组内差异						
配对样本 1	实验班前测	10.88	标准差	95% 置信区间值		t	df	Sig (2-tailed)
	实验班后测		11.37	上限	下限	6.43	59	0.005*
配对样本 2	对照班前测	1.35	4.29	7.31	13.61	1.65	59	0.088
	对照班后测			0.18	2.59			

注：*p<0.05; **p<0.01.

研究问题二：如果学习者的焦虑感得到缓解，他们的写作成绩是否能提高?

如表4所示，实验前，实验班的写作测试平均分数为75.04，对照班的测试分数为74.98。两班作文水平相似，$p=0.95>0.05$。

表4 实验前后两班写作得分的比较

	组别	人数	平均值	标准差	*t*	*df*	Sig(2-tailed)
实验前写作得分	实验班	30	75.04	9.12	-0.06	118	0.95
	对照班	30	74.98	8.77	-0.06	117.28	0.95
实验后写作得分	实验班	30	81.34	6.52	4.48	118	0.008**
	对照班	30	79.56	8.09	4.48	114.46	0.32

注：$^*p<0.05$; $^{**}p<0.01$.

实验后，两班的作文水平出现了显著差异（$p=0.008<0.05$）（如表4所示）。

表4数据表明，实验组在实验前后的显著变化（$p=0.008<0.05$），而对照组前后的变化并不显著（$p=0.32>0.05$），证明小组协作学习已经有效地提高了学生的写作水平。

研究问题三：不同水平的学生对协作写作的反馈如何？

由于实验班人数的限制，该部分的结果主要采用的是访谈数据（数据于2022年1月收集）。

1）协作写作对写作焦虑感的作用

以上结果显示，小组协作写作模式显著减轻了学习者的写作焦虑水平（$p=0.005<0.05$，见表3）。这样的结果可用社会互依理论来解释。根据这个理论，小组成员为了一个共同的目标而工作，成员之间相互依靠，互相提供动力，共同解决问题，齐心协力完成任务的氛围降低了成员的焦虑水平，该结果也和前人研究结论一致（卢植 2004）。

①低水平学生

协作写作中的“风险分享原则”提升了小组成员的安全感，水平较低的同学（弱生）不会因为语言水平低而在写作时忐忑不安。这类受试者提到最多的关于协作学习的优点是这种学习方式让他们处在一个相对放松、不用担心出丑的学习环境。访谈对象A这样说道：

> 我高中阶段的英语基础不是很扎实，上了大学以后，觉得写作课的压力比较大，尽管我很努力，但是作文还是不行。我常常很苦恼。但是现在觉得安心多了，因为老师给的是全组的分，我不会觉得丢面子，无论我写得怎么样，我的小组同伴都会给我即时反馈，帮助我改正错误。

从以上访谈数据来看，小组内“风险分担原则”帮助学习者（特别是低水平学生）降低了写作过程中的焦虑感水平，这也和蒋波和谭顶良（2011）研究结果一致。

其次，协作写作模式提供了互相支持、互相帮助的学习模式，学生不用担心自己在同学眼里的形象，焦虑感中“关注别人的评价的焦虑”得到缓解，正如访谈对象B所言：

> 我的基础不太好，但不敢向老师求助，其他同学们都在忙着自己的作文，不会有时间和精力帮助我，我如果老是提问，别人可能会认为我挺差的。现在大家共同讨论问题，我可以很自然地向小组成员提问，问题很快就解决了。每次我有疑问向大家求助的时候，我给人的印象是我很认真地为全组的成绩做好我分内的事情。

对弱生来说，独立写作缺少督促，容易懈怠；而协作写作模式下，每个小组成员都必须为集体的分数做贡献，无形中对差生的学习态度起了督促作用。访谈对象C是这样说的：

> 我知道自己的写作水平不太好可能跟我的学习态度有关，现在通过协作学习，优秀的同学组织我们进行对作文讨论，监督我们的写作进度，还会设定讨论时间给我们答疑，我觉得这样的方式挺好。

②中等水平学生和高水平学生

前人文献中指出，协作学习对低水平学习者的效果比较明显，对中等生和优生的作用不大（Andrade & Williams 2009），但在我们的研究中，发现中等水平和高水平学生也能从协作作写作受益。一位中等水平访谈对象D是这么说的：

> 在以前的写作课里，我总是独立完成写作任务，我觉得我的写作水平总是不上不下，句型总是限于简单句，表达法有限，达不到地道的水平。通过同学互相反馈，查看其他同学的修改，一下子就能看出自己的不足。但是我也有优点，我总能想出不少新奇的观点，这让老师不至于给我难看的分数，我还是很想提高写作。协作写作的模式下，我的优点得到我们组成员的肯定，他们鼓励我表达自己的观点，因为我的观点将帮助全组取得好成绩。

高水平学生受益的表现不仅体现在作文水平上，而且他们作为指导者、启发者和促进者的角色得到很大程度的发挥。访谈对象E（高水平学生）是这样说的：

> 我写作能力还可以，但我不太想被人说“这个人爱表现，爱炫耀”。后来老师组织小组合作协作写作，要求我担任小助教，我觉得在帮助别人的同时，自己也受益不少。在修改作文时，我虽然是终稿写作者，但在写作过

程中，我积极贡献观点，并认真阅读其他同学完成的版本，提出自己的修改意见并和其他组员讨论，也由此发现其他同学的优势，比如有的人擅长收集资料和信息，有的同学有一些实习经验，我们在写作“用户手册”的时候，他提供的信息起了很大作用。我觉得多讨论有好处，大家思想碰撞，使作文质量有突破。

总的来说，本研究中协作写作的教学方式让不同水平的学生感到受益。首先，小组得分取决于个人得分的原则，促使全体成员相互鼓励，相互支持。对于低水平学生来说，小组内互帮互助、互相监督的气氛，让他们有了安全感，增强了写作的信心。中等水平学生和高水平学生也能从协作学习中得到帮助。在小组讨论和修改文章时，他们需要不断澄清观点和事实，说服同组成员，这样的解释和协商行为让优生获得成就感。他们不仅积极参与教师组织的课堂活动，而且对协作写作的具体操作提出改良方案，最重要的是，他们从班级的领先者变成了具有团队精神的引领者。团队合作改变了传统单兵模式下的学习者孤立无援的行为，互相帮助和个人贡献成为小组团队成员生存的必要条件。

2）小组协作学习对写作水平的影响

由于小组协作学习模式的采用和写作焦虑的缓解，学生的写作水平有了显著进步（见表4），以下几点值得思考。首先，协作写作让每个学生得到更多的练习机会，每个同学都有机会就某个题目写出作文，其他同学帮助修改，自己的文章至少被修改四次。其次，每个学生可以从阅读、讨论和修改中了解自己作文中的弱点，有更多机会注意自己语言输出中的一些常见的语法错误，组内成员互相帮助，指出一些学生自己不易发现的错误时，该学生对错误用法的印象会特别深刻。第三，由于小组共同讨论、共同修改作文，学生的作文长度逐渐增加，由原来的150词能扩展到300词左右。

协作写作模式下实验组的写作焦虑显著缓解（见表2、表3），在一定程度上解释了学习者愿意在完成作文时付出更多努力，以及写作水平随之提高的原因。其一，在协作写作状态下，写作焦虑从抑制性变成了促进性。根据Andrade和Williams（2009）提出的原则，焦虑强度决定了焦虑的类型，低焦虑的状态具有促进性功能。本研究中，写作焦虑显著减少，让学习者对完成写作任务充满希望，而不是对写作任务持负面态度或者干脆放弃。这种情感上的转变在理论上可以得到Krashen情感过滤假设的支撑。Krashen（1982，2003）认为学习者的语言输入会受到情感因素的过滤。在上述讨论中，我们看到，当写作焦虑在协作写作过程中被缓解了，情感过滤器的通道增宽，语言输入能更好地被吸收，学习者的写作水平就能提高。

实验班里最大的变化之一是学习者开始认真对待小组成员的反馈，而不是像对照班的某些同学对建议置之一边。原因是这些同学开始享受写作过程，并愿意学习更多知识。访谈对象F是这样说的：

> 我以前很怕看老师的评语，因为这些评语总在提醒自己有多差。即使这次我改正了一些错误，下次作文里又会犯新的错误。有的时候，还会犯同样的错误。但是现在我很急切地希望得到组员们的反馈，因为我们之前已经讨论了内容、语法和其他一些作文中的细节，真的很想知道讨论结果有没有效。有时候，我们争论没有得出结论时，还会去找老师问清楚。这种主动性跟之前的不情不愿很不一样。奇怪的是，这种参与的过程竟然让我能很容易地记住写作知识。

此外，当学习者低层次的焦虑缓解了以后，学习者更有精力学习高层次的知识（比如元认知知识和技能）。从采访数据可以看出，小组成员之间互相交流，互相解释和讨论作文中的观点，准确表达语言等元认知知识。中高级水平的学生通过表达观点和澄清观点也提高了写作能力。而对照班经过一个学期的学习，写作水平并无明显进步，说明对不同层次的学生需要采取适当的教学对策。

5. 结语

本文报告了开展小组协作写作的实验过程，证明了协作学习模式在显著降低学生写作焦虑水平、提高写作能力上的可行性和有效性。但本研究仍有不足之处。首先，此实证研究是基于应用文写作的一个初步尝试，协作写作缓解写作焦虑的研究仍然欠缺，还有很大改进空间。比如，本研究采用了SLWAI（Second Language Writing Anxiety Inventory）（二语写作焦虑量表）作为测量学生写作焦虑的工具，但在实验和教学操作中发现，该量表无法区分不同学习水平的学习者的焦虑状态，研究者必须依靠实验后访谈更深入了解学习者的具体表现和应对策略。

其次，本次实证研究获得不少协作写作教学经验教训，研究者向教师提出以下建议：

1）课程准备：教师除了课前充分备课以外，在协作学习开始前需要给学生一定的时间了解小组成员的语言水平、学习风格、个性等信息，以便在分组时做出比较适当的选择。

2）灵活分组：前人研究比较强调协作学习小组的异质性。然而，研究发现，受东方人际关系崇尚和谐的理念影响，一些学生会选择和朋友或室友分在一个组。但是从访谈数据来看，学生还是倾向于跟水平高的同学分在一组。因此教师必须仔细观察学生的需求，及时调整。

3）不断调整协作模式：本研究过程中发现，虽然教师精心设计了协作写作的程序，但仍有同学反映写作过程稍嫌烦琐，可以适当简化进程，比如，可以等所有同学完成写作后，老师再给出反馈，这样同学们有更多机会考虑如何修改。

4）及时调整教师的角色：协作学习模式下的写作教学，教师应逐渐从主导角色退下来，应让学生相信协作写作是正规而有用的教学方式，教师应当制定非常具体的写作步骤，要参与组员的讨论，保证小组讨论能够有效率。

最后，将来的研究课题可以围绕协作写作的多样性，比如鼓励组内竞争来提高小组士气或者采用改进得分的方法来更客观跟进小组每个阶段的进步情况。还可以把小组协作学习模式应用到其他课型上，综合考察协作学习在外语教学中的作用。

参考文献

Andrade, M. & K. Williams. 2009. Foreign language learning anxiety in Japanese EFL university classes: Physical, emotional, expressive and verbal reactions [J]. *Sophia Junior College Faculty Journal* 29: 1-24.

Belcher, D. & J. P. Lantolf. 1998. Collaborative language learning: The role of 磋商 in the development of second language writing skills [A]. In W. Aitchison & J. Aitchison (eds.). *Second Language Writing: Research Insights for the Classroom* [C]. Cambridge: Cambridge University Press. 124-147.

Chandra, R. 2015. Collaborative learning for educational achievement [J]. *International Journal of Research & Method in Education* 5(3): 2320-7388.

Cheng, Y. 2004. A measure of second language writing anxiety: Scale development and preliminary validation [J]. *Journal of Second Language Writing* 13(4): 313-335.

Dillenbourg, P. 1999. *Collaborative Learning: Cognitive and Computational Approaches. Advances in Learning and Instruction Series* [M]. New York: Elsevier Science.

Fathman, A. & E. Whalley. 1990. Teacher response to student writing: Focus on form versus content [A]. In B. Kroll (ed.). *Second Language Writing: Research Insights for the Classroom* [C]. Cambridge: Cambridge University Press. 178-190.

Flowers, J. & R. Vassar. 2008. Collaborative writing: Multiple perspectives on the writing process [A]. In J. Flowerdew (ed.). *Theories and Methods in Second Language Writing Research* [C]. Mahwah, NJ: Lawrence Erlbaum Associates. 57-78.

Horwitz, E. K. 2010. Foreign and second language anxiety [J]. *Language Teaching* 43(2): 154-167.

Horwitz, E. K., M. B. Horwitz & J. Cope. 1986. Foreign language classroom anxiety [J]. *The Modern Language Journal* 70: 125-132.

Johnson, D. W. & R. T. Johnson. 2005. New development in social interdependence theory [J]. *Generic, Social and General Psychological Monograph* 131(4): 285-358.

Kagan S. 1994. *Cooperative Learning* [M]. San Clemente, CA: Kagan Publishing.

Kirmizi, Q. & G. Z. Kirmizi. 2015. An investigation of L2 learners' writing self-efficacy, writing anxiety and its causes at higher education in Turkey [J]. *International Journal of Higher Education* 4(2): 57-66.

Krashen, S. D. 1982. *Principles and Practice in Second Language Acquisition* [M]. Oxford: Pergamon.

Krashen, S. D. 2003. *Explorations in Language Acquisition and Use* [M]. Portsmouth, NH: Heinemann.

Kroll, B. & N. Duvvury. 2003. Collaborative writing: Multiple perspectives on the writing process [A]. In J. Flowerdew (ed.). *Theories and Methods in Second Language Writing Research* [C]. Mahwah, NJ: Lawrence Erlbaum Associates. 13-34.

Liu, D. 2014. *Research on the Psychology and Language of ESL Writing* [M]. Beijing: China University of Geosciences Press.

Madden, N. A., R. E. Slavon & M. Logan. 2011. Effects of cooperative writing with embedded multimedia: A randomized experiment [J]. *Effective Education* 3(1): 1-9.

Millis, B. 2010. *Cooperative Learning in Higher Education: Across the Disciplines, Across the Academy* [M]. Sterling, VA: Stylus Publishing LLC.

Scovel, T. 1978. The effect of affect on foreign language learning: A review of the anxiety research [J]. *Language Learning* 28(1): 129-142.

Storch, N. 2013. *Collaborative Writing in L2 Classrooms* [M]. Bristol: Multilingual Matters.

Vygotsky, L. S. & A. J. Rotherham. 2007. Collaborative language learning: What can we learn from research on collaboration in second language writing [A]. In J. Flowerdew (ed.). *Theories and Methods in Second Language Writing Research* [C]. Mahwah, NJ: Lawrence Erlbaum Associates. 57-78.

郭燕、秦晓晴，2010，中国非英语专业大学生的外语写作焦虑测试报告及其对写作教学的启示 [J]，《外语界》（2）：54-62+82。

蒋波、谭顶良，2011，学优生、中等生和学困生：合作学习对谁更有效 [J]，《教育理论与实践》（2）：43-45。

焦丽霞、任春蕾、吕翠俊，2017，基于iclass平台的"翻转课堂"模式在大学英语写作教学中的可行性研究 [J]，《北京邮电大学学报：社会科学版》（1）：87-93.

刘丽敏，2010，高职英语写作教学合作学习法可行性研究 [J]，《中国职业技术教育》（14）：72-75。

卢植，2004，合作式英文写作作用效度的实验分析 [J]，《暨南学报（哲学社会科学版）》（2）：104-108。

谭梦玲，2013，独立学院非英语专业大学生写作焦虑的实证研究 [J]，《牡丹江教育学院学报》（4）：121-122。

吴育红、顾卫星，2011，合作学习降低非英语专业大学生英语写作焦虑的实证研究 [J]，《外语与外语教学》（6）：51-55。

徐锦芬、聂睿，2015，基于CiteSpace的国际二语写作研究动态可视化分析（2004—2014）[J]，《外语电化教学》（4）：3-9。

张朦，2021，"多轮续写"对写作焦虑和写作成绩的影响 [J]，《上海理工大学学报》（3）：256-262。

张晓兰，2006，合作学习在英语专业写作教学中运用的实验研究 [J]，《外国语文》（3）：137-140。

朱茜、徐锦芬，2019，协作写作对学习者二语发展影响的实证研究 [J]，《外语教学理论与实践》（3）：26-33+98.

作者简介：

杨晋，南京大学大学外语部副教授，博士。主要研究领域：应用语言学研究。电子邮箱：shigulu@nju.edu.cn

数字技术赋能二语写作——兼评《二语写作中的技术运用：撰写、翻译、教学与数据驱动学习的进展》

杜　宇

山东大学

摘要：当今信息时代背景下，二语写作与前沿技术的结合日趋紧密，其有效性亟待检验。《二语写作中的技术运用：撰写、翻译、教学与数据驱动学习的进展》一书通过多维研究视角对这一前沿话题进行了探讨，内容涵盖机器翻译、在线反馈及多模态写作等不同方面，通过范围综述、个案研究、语料库研究等方法，重点讨论了当前二语写作领域中主流技术手段的应用及其效果。相关研究表明，技术手段在二语写作教学中的应用有利于学习者语言能力的提升，对其思辨能力及体裁知识的培养也具有积极影响。对研究者而言，相关技术手段的使用可有效拓宽研究视野与思路。该书对于技术手段在写作教学与研究中的应用具有重要的启示意义。

关键词：二语写作；技术手段；写作教学与研究

DOI: 10.20081/j.cnki.cjslw.2023.07.009

1. 引言

当前背景下，数字技术手段同人文学科的融合不断加深，其发展也为外语学科内涵的深化与视角的拓宽发挥了重要的引领作用（宁琦 2023）。二语写作涉及认知心理与社会文化因素交织的复杂过程，与技术手段结合的有效性亟待检验（Overstreet et al. 2023）。由Jingjing Qin和Paul Stapleton合编的《二语写作中的技术运用：撰写、翻译、教学与数据驱动学习的进展》（*Technology in Second Language Writing: Advances in Composing, Translation, Writing Pedagogy and Data-Driven Learning*）一书近日由Routledge出版社出版发行。该书立足写作与技术这一前沿话题，通过不同的研究视角与方法，关注不同背景下二语学习者的写作实践，进而展现二语写作与当代科学技术的结合成果与教学应用。该书对二语写作教学与研究的视角拓展与工具应用具有启示意义。

2. 研究视角

本书聚焦二语写作中的技术手段应用，是国际范围内的前沿研究集合，在研究视角的多样性与前沿性上具有显著优势，分别从机器翻译、在线反馈以及多模态写作等视角为当前数字时代的写作研究与教学提供了重要启示。

首先，本书从机器翻译视角出发，分析该工具在二语写作中的应用问题。当前，机器翻译应用于二语写作的研究愈发受到关注，学习者态度以及技术深入开发等问题亦成为相关研究的焦点（吴影、李朝 2022），这一热点话题重点体现在本书第二、三、四章。相关章节关注不同视角，采用量化、个案等研究方法深入探讨机器翻译工具对于二语写作质量的影响。例如，第二章主要探讨了谷歌翻译工具对中国非英语专业学习者写作的辅助作用。结果表明，借助译后文本修改作文，能够显著改善修改稿的词汇、语法和整体语篇质量，且受试对机器翻译工具的写作应用普遍持乐观态度。第三章关注谷歌翻译与其他辅助手段在以中文为母语的加泰罗尼亚语学习者写作中的应用情况。研究者通过对个案写作全过程的记录与分析，探讨了以谷歌翻译为代表的机器翻译工具在二语写作过程中的功能性与有效性。

其次，本书转向写作在线反馈视角，探讨数字工具在写作反馈中的重要作用。基于数字手段的在线写作反馈已成为二语写作反馈研究的主流，且未来发展前景广阔（屈琼等 2021）。其中，在线教师反馈兼具共时与历时的特点，其对学习者写作修改质量的有效性虽已有所证明，但仍值得进一步探究（Ene & Upton 2018）。本书第五章则进一步聚焦共时与历时在线写作反馈对二语写作质量的影响。作者将任务重复与两种在线反馈方式相结合，探究学习者的写作文本在复杂度、准确度、流利度以及议论文结构上是否存在差异。研究发现，接受两种不同在线反馈方式的学习者在文本的准确度与复杂度上存在显著差异。受益于良好的互动与写作任务的适度重复，接受共时反馈的学习者在写作文本的准确度与复杂度上具有更为良好的表现，且相关影响具有延时效应。同时，两组学习者的写作文本在流利度与议论文结构上虽有所不同，但在后测与延时后测的结果上均未表现出显著差异。

再次，本书也关注到了多模态与符号学理论视角下的二语写作的研究与教学。现代数字与科技手段的进步为多模态写作的发展提供现实基础（王乐等 2023）。且多模态写作环境对学习者批判性思维的塑造、身份意识的唤醒均存在积极影响（Li 2021）。第七章和第八章均涉及技术手段在多模态写作中的应用问题。第七章由四位研究者合作完成，研究以多模态与符号学理论为基础，采用多模态方式探讨学习者对平等主题视频的写作反应。研究者发现，学习者通过与多模态资源的互动过程，对于社会文化问题的主体身份意识有所提升，且其批判性思维能力也得以激发。第八章则聚焦于二语写作中在线社交媒体的对话作用。研究者通过对俄语学习者在线社交媒体写作过程的会话分析，发现在与俄语母语者的在线合作写作活动中，初级学习者的二语写作能力与信心均得到明显提升，而社交媒体写作具有多模态与在线交互等特点，有利于母语者为二语初学者的写作提供有效的鹰架支持。

除以上视角外，本书其他章节还从维基写作、语料库应用、数字写作识别等维度展现当前写作与技术的融合成果。其中，第六章展现了中国香港理工大学维基写作教学项目的研究成果。研究聚焦于医学专业的“学科英语”（English-in-the-Disciplines）写作教学，采用过程体裁教学法，通过撰写维基百科词条等学科英语写作任务，探究相关任务设计对医学专业学生学科英语及学术英语写作能力的影响。

研究者发现非英语专业学习者的基础语言表达能力有所提升，在学科专业知识掌握及自主学习能力培养等方面均取得积极成效。第十一章则从学习者数字写作的识别过程入手，重点关注了键盘跟踪工具在二语写作课堂中的实际应用问题。本章节首先对键盘跟踪工具的分析过程及结果进行展示，同时选取两个教师应用此类工具的场景，进一步讨论其在提升学生数字写作能力、元认知意识和论证能力发展中的作用。

3. 研究方法

本书除研究视角的前沿多样性之外，同时采用了诸如范围综述、个案研究以及语料库研究等不同方法，讨论科技手段与二语写作的结合成效，为研究者开展写作研究与教学提供更多可行路径。

首先，书中所选用的范围综述法为二语写作领域的新兴方法。相较于系统综述的方法，范围综述法尤为适用于文献相对较少的新兴领域，因其能够涵盖研究设计与方法相差较大的相关研究，从而更能揭示该领域存在的空白（Arksey & O'Malley 2005）。该方法多用于医学、工程学等领域，近年来虽已有少数学者将该方法移植于二语研究（如Tullock & Ortega 2017；李成陈、陆筱俊 2022；徐锦芬、杨嘉琪 2023），但其在二语写作与教学中的应用仍有待进一步开展。该书第四章则借助范围综述方法，从研究话题入手全面综述了机器翻译工具用于二语写作的研究成果，从而将该话题内基数较少、但研究设计差异较大的相关研究进行了梳理。指出当前二语写作教学中机器翻译手段运用不足，并展望了未来发展趋势。

其次，本书诸多章节采用个案研究法对写作过程进行深度分析。个案研究法以其描写的生动性、清晰性、社会文化性等特点（Duff 2020），在二语写作与教学领域方兴未艾（如Chen & Lee 2022；王菲 2019）。本书诸多章节，如第三章、第七章、第八章，均采用个案研究法，对受试运用机器翻译工具、应对平等主题视频以及社交媒体互动的写作过程进行记录。深度描写了三组二语学习者文本产出过程的内容细节，从而辅助论证写作成果的产生原因。其中，第三章中研究者通过关注单一受试的二语邮件写作全过程，揭露该受试写作中使用相关机器翻译工具的类型、次数以及技巧等信息，从而清晰呈现二语学习者在写作过程中同机器翻译工具互动的复杂过程，进一步阐明其使用相关工具的原因、方法及成效。

此外，语料库研究法的写作研究与教学应用也在本书中有所涉及。信息技术的进步推动语料库在二语写作领域广泛应用（陈夜雨、项歆妮 2015），且以其为基础的数据驱动学习也已广泛应用于写作教学中（Chen & Flowerdew 2018）。本书第九章探讨了语料库工具在不同母语背景的学习者写作研究与教学中的实际应用，进一步丰富了语料库与数据驱动学习的研究成果。三位研究者通过自建学习者语料库，探究身处伊拉克、美国的英语二语学习者与母语作者在议论文写作中直接和间接标记语的使用情况。研究者通过对语料库结果进行量化与文本分析，将母语与二语作者的相关标记语使用差异进行展示，进一步讨论了产生以上差异的社会文化因素，并介绍了利用语料库索引行功能引导学习者进行二语写作、将数据驱动学习融入写作教学中的实际应用。

4. 教学重点

本书通过选用前沿视角与方法，对当前数字技术与二语写作的融合应用进行概述，与此同时，将关注写作过程、培养思辨能力以及增强体裁意识等重点教学理念也渗透于章节内容之中。

第一，本书内容侧重对写作过程的关注。相较于侧重写作结果的传统二语写作教学模式（邓鹂鸣、肖亮 2020），该书所涵盖的诸多研究对于学习者的写作过程更加关注。本书第三章、第七章、第八章及第十一章均重点关注了二语学习者的写作过程。得益于键盘跟踪工具与在线社交媒体平台等数字技术工具的应用，相关章节研究者对个案受试的写作过程细节进行了深度描写。其中，第八章将对话理论与二语写作过程教学相结合，全面、清晰地揭露了在线社交媒体写作过程的对话细节，从而构建出相关应用模型，并为中高级学习者数字写作教学提供了可行建议。

第二，本书内容强调对二语学习者思辨能力的培养。近年来，二语写作教学在发展基础语言能力之外，更加关注学习者思辨能力的培养与提升（如Pu 2022；邱瑾 2023），本书亦将该教学理念纳入各章节内容之中。例如，在第六章中，医学专业的英语学习者通过完成维基写作任务环节，不仅在语言能力上有所提升，在学科内容知识以及写作修辞意识方面也取得积极成效。在第七章中，受试在完成多模态写作任务后，逐渐形成社会问题意识以及批判性思维，这反映出由数字技术支撑的多模态写作教学培养与发展二语学习者思辨能力的可行性。

第三，本书内容仍关注学习者体裁意识的加强。体裁理论应用于写作教学的相关研究发展迅速，且当前跨学科与数字化的趋势有利于二语写作体裁教学与研究的进一步开展（邓鹂鸣、肖亮 2020）。本书第六章的维基写作任务是专门用途英语学派体裁教学法的应用表现。教师通过布置学科英语写作任务，使非英语专业二语学习者逐渐熟悉所在体裁，并通过对本领域内专业、修辞知识的掌握，为进一步“由外及内进入语篇群体核心”（孙厌舒、王俊菊 2015：46）创造条件，从而体现出该教学方法对学习者或新手研究者步入所在专业领域的助力作用。

5. 结语

除前言外，该书共汇集十个章节，从不同视角与方法关注了当今先进技术手段在二语写作教学实践中的应用。各章节的作者从机器翻译、在线反馈、维基写作、社交媒体、键盘跟踪等多个研究视角入手，深入探究技术手段在写作反馈、自动评价、远程协作等方面的可行性与有效性，采用了测试、问卷、个案、观察、语料库以及范围综述等多种研究方法，为读者展现了技术与二语写作结合的更多可能性，并为不同语言与学科背景下学习者的写作教学提供了更为前沿多样的教学理念与应用路径。

当然，该书亦存在不足之处。首先，虽然该书聚焦新兴技术在二语写作中的应用，但未能将人工智能视角纳入并进行系统介绍。当前有关人工智能与大数据等技术手段已在语言教学中得到广泛运用（李灵丽等 2023），对写作领域的影响也势必存在，未来可对此更加关注。此外，本书主要从实践视角入手探讨技术手段与二语写作教学与研究的融合，除少数章节（如第七章与第八章）涉及理论基础或分析框架外，理论探讨和升华相对不足，在一定程度上影响了本书的理论贡献。

但瑕不掩瑜，《二语写作中的技术运用：撰写、翻译、教学与数据驱动学习的进展》一书以其视角、方法以及教学理念的前沿性与丰富性等特点，能够进一步拓宽二语写作领域研究者的研究视野，将该书中所介绍的二语写作与先进技术相融合的经验推广应用到二语写作教学一线与研究实践当中，将有利于推动当今数智化时代背景下的二语写作教学改革与创新，实现二语写作在研究视野和研究方法上的突破。

参考文献

Arksey, H. & L. O'Malley. 2005. Scoping studies: Towards a methodological framework [J]. *International Journal of Social Research Methodology* 8(1): 19-32.

Chen, M. & J. Flowerdew. 2018. A critical review of research and practice in data-driven learning (DDL) in the academic writing classroom [J]. *International Journal of Corpus Linguistics* 23(3): 335-369.

Chen, X. & I. Lee. 2022. Conflicts in peer interaction of collaborative writing – A case study in an EFL context [J]. *Journal of Second Language Writing* 58. doi: org/10.1016/j.jslw.2022.100910.

Duff, P. A. 2020. Case study research: Making language learning complexities visible [A]. In J. McKinley & H. Rose (eds.). *The Routledge Handbook of Research Methods in Applied Linguistics* [C]. Abingdon & New York: Routledge. 144-153.

Ene, E. & T. A. Upton. 2018. Synchronous and asynchronous teacher electronic feedback and learner uptake in ESL composition [J]. *Journal of Second Language Writing* 41: 1-13.

Li, M. 2021. *Researching and Teaching Second Language Writing in the Digital Age* [M]. Cham: Palgrave Macmillan.

Overstreet, M., D. Akhmedjanova & S. Vaccino-Salvadore. 2023. Brain-bound vs. extended: Contrasting approaches to second-language research writing in digital environments [J]. *Journal of Second Language Writing* 61: 101019.

Pu, S. 2022. *Critical Thinking in Academic Writing: A Cultural Approach* [M]. Abingdon & New York: Routledge.

Qin, J. & P. Stapleton (eds.). 2023. *Technology in Second Language Writing: Advances in Composing, Translation, Writing Pedagogy and Pata-Driven Learning* [C]. New York: Routledge.

Tullock, B. & L. Ortega. 2017. Fluency and multilingualism in study abroad: Lessons from a scoping review [J]. *System* 71: 7-21.

陈夜雨、项歆妮，2015，基于语料库的学术英语写作教学研究 [J]，《现代教育技术》（12）：84-89。

邓鹂鸣、肖亮，2020，《体裁与二语写作研究》[M]。北京：外语教学与研究出版社。
李成陈、陆筱俊，2022，外语学习中的无聊情绪研究：基于范围综述的方法[J]，《外语教学》(6)：70-76。
李灵丽、唐平平、林晓娟、左璜，2023，基于人工智能的语言教育研究：国际进展与前瞻[J]，《外语界》(2)：45-53。
宁琦，2023，数字人文赋能外语学科的思考与探索[J]，《外语界》(1)：12-17。
邱瑾，2023，探索学生英语写作和思辨能力协调发展的行动研究："苏格拉底圈"的应用[J]，《外语教育研究前沿》(1)：45-52+94。
屈琼、刘媛媛、兰宁艺，2021，国内二语写作反馈研究现状与趋势的可视化分析[J]，《外语电化教学》(3)：37-43+6。
孙厌舒、王俊菊，2015，二语写作体裁教学研究的回顾与反思[J]，《解放军外国语学院学报》(1)：44-50。
王菲，2019，学术写作课堂同伴互动低效的原因分析——基于四名中外博士生视角的个案研究[J]，《外语与外语教学》(2)：92-99+149-150。
王乐、王晓涔、张宇驰，2023，国际多模态二语写作研究及其发展趋势[J]，《外语界》(4)：49-55。
吴影、李朝，2022，机器翻译对二语写作的影响研究：焦点与趋势[J]，《上海翻译》(4)：35-39。
徐锦芬、杨嘉琪，2023，技术赋能外语合作学习研究的范围综述[J]，《外语电化教学》(2)：42-48+111。

作者简介：

杜宇，山东大学外国语学院研究生。研究方向：二语写作、外语教育。电子邮箱：duyuleo6@foxmail.com

注释文献

国内出版的二语写作书目及内容简介（2023）

1. 张洪芹，2023，《二语写作教学的多维研究》[M]。北京：中国财富出版社。

内容简介：对于我国二语学习者来说，英语是过渡语，介于母语与目标语之间。因此，英语写作更困难一些，英语写作教学需要教师投入更多的时间与精力。本书从英汉对比视角、互文视角、认知视角三种视角研究二语写作教学，拟建构适合我国语境的二语写作教学的文化思维理论与实践模式，为我国二语写作教学提供可行、高效的实践模式与框。

2. 王仁雷，2023，《中国学生法语写作偏误检测与教学对策（法文版）》[M]。上海：上海交通大学出版社。

内容简介：本书采用定量和定性研究方法，探究了法语学习者的写作偏误和写作能力，并提出了相应教学建议。本书共分五章：第一章对偏误分析相关基础理论进行全面阐释，包括偏误概念、偏误评判标准、偏误分类、偏误分析发展历程和偏误分析步骤；第二章对研究设计进行详细分析，涉及研究问题、研究目标、研究背景、语料收集和分析；第三章从语用、篇章、句子、次句及词汇五个层面深入分析学习者法语书面作文中的偏误，旨在了解其对于法语写作知识的掌握和技能的应用；第四章基于教学"铁三角"，即知识、学生和教师，尝试说明学习者法语写作偏误的可能性来源；第五章从体裁意识、文本运作、语言工具等方面提出教学对策，以提高中国学习者的法语写作能力及促进法语写作教学发展。

3. 邹德平，2023，《初中英语写作教学理论与实践》[M]。济南：山东大学出版社。

内容简介：本书的前六章注重对初中英语写作教学理论的介绍。第一章介绍了当前初中英语写作课教学现状，针对目前现状，提出了本书的研究目的与意义，进而对相关的初中英语写作教学理论进行了阐释并对《义务教育英语课程标准（2022年版）》关于初中英语写作部分进行了解读。第二章介绍了主流的初中英语写作教学法。基于教学方法，对初中英语写作课堂进行了教学设计。第三章主要介绍基于英语学科核心素养的写作课堂教学设计。第四章主要介绍基于写作体裁的课堂教学设计。第五章主要介绍基于教材的写作课堂教学设计。第六章主要介绍基于写作类型的课堂教学设计。《义务教育英语课程标准（2022年版）》明确提出要进行"教—学—评"一体化设计，因此第七章介绍了初中英语写作课的教学评价，主要有终结性评价、过程性评价、表现性评价、多元化评价。基于前七章的理论介绍，本书的后两章注重初中英语写作教学的实践层面。第八章结合真实的初中英语课堂，从写作话题入手，针对不同年级设计写作教案。第九章以思维导图的方式呈现写作课堂教学步骤，继而对学生的写作内容进行自评、同伴互评和教师点评，最终进行佳作共赏。

4. 徐方，2023，《工作记忆与二语学习》[M]。青岛：中国海洋大学出版社。

内容简介：本著作首先阐述了短时记忆与外语学习的关系，然后分别对短时记忆在国内二语习得中的研究、二语习得视域下句子理解中的工作记忆研究、神经机制下工作记忆和二语句子理解研究、工作记忆容量差异对二语句法歧义加工的影响进行综述。同时，本著作分别实证研究了语块理论与外语词汇记忆的关系和短时记忆、外语听力理解与输入假设的关系，并对工作记忆容量与二语句子加工中的生命性和世界知识的关系进行ERP实证研究，证明了工作记忆在二语学习中的重要作用。大量证据表明工作记忆与读写能力和计算能力这些必不可少的学习有关。二语学习尤其与工作记忆密切相关。

5. 汲传波，2023，《汉语二语者书面语体习得研究》[M]。北京：北京大学出版社。

内容简介：该研究主要采用语料库对比的方法，利用BCC语料库中的微博语料和科技语料对学界现有语体特征标记研究成果进行验证，归纳出了一批能够有效区分正式语体和非正式语体的特征标记。在此基础上，通过对比外国留学生和汉语母语者书面语语料库，发现外国留学生书面语总体上存在口语化有余、典雅度不足的问题。然后通过对不同水平、不同国别留学生汉语书面语体习得情况进行比较，发现留学生汉语书面语体的习得总体上在口语化程度与典雅度上呈对应关系，但也存在部分“语体习得不匹配现象”。这些观点对面向国际中文教育的语体教学与习得研究有重要的参考价值。

6. 吴唯，2023，《中英隐喻对比及对外汉语词汇教学研究》[M]。北京：中国纺织出版社。

内容简介：英汉语言中都有着丰富的隐喻词汇，隐喻词汇的差异体现了中西文化的差异。语言学习者在汉语学习过程中会频繁地接触到大量反映隐喻式思维方式的语言表达。因此作者认为从认知的角度研究隐喻对二语习得，尤其是汉语学习的影响和作用，是非常有益和必要的。《中英隐喻对比及对外汉语词汇教学研究》首先从中英文化差异和隐喻认知关系的角度，选取动物隐喻、植物隐喻、火隐喻、水隐喻等特殊样本对英汉隐喻词汇进行了对比分析，探讨了不同语言文化中不同隐喻表达的生成机制和差异成因。其次分析了对外汉语教学与隐喻能力培养的关系。汉语隐喻词汇习得是词汇学习乃至语言学习的难点，学习者必须优选限度地利用自己的知识因式和体验去理解隐喻词汇表达的内涵。

国内发表的二语写作论文目录及摘要（2023）

1. **文秋芳**，2023，**构建大学外语教材编写理论体系**[J]，**《外国语》**（06）：2-11。

摘要：本文报告了在实践基础上凝练的大学外语教材编写理论体系。该体系包括五个要素：1）国家与社会要求；2）外语教材文化范畴；3）外语教与学的理论；4）外语学习者成长特点；5）编写管理规范。“国家与社会要求”是外语教材编写的指南针。“外语教材文化范畴”是落实“国家与社会要求”“外语教与学的理论”和“外语学习者成长特点”的内容载体。“外语教与学的理论”是设计教材语言实践活动类型、内容和顺序的依据。“外语学习者成长特点”是选择教材内容和设置育人目标的理据之一。“编写管理规范”是落实前面四个要素的必要保障。每个要素有自身特点，但又互相关联。从初始操作程序上看，它们有先后顺序，但在编写过程中，这五个要素须协同发挥作用，才能保证外语教材编写的高质量。

2. **徐锦芬**，2023，**外语教材建设：教师专业发展新途径**[J]，**《外国语》**（06）：12-19。

摘要：外语教材建设与教师专业发展是高等外语教育教学改革能否成功的关键。外语教材建设不仅对学生而言有着重要的实现人才培养目标的功能，而且对教师的专业发展也具有积极的促进作用。本文首先阐释了外语教材建设的内涵，指出外语教材建设具有价值引领、理论引领、专家引领和技术引领等四大主要特征，然后从提升外语教师的专业知识、专业能力、道德情操及情感认同感等方面讨论了外语教材建设对教师专业发展的促进作用。最后建议未来给广大外语教师提供更多教材二次开发的培训。

3. **束定芳**，2023，**教育生态理论视角下的中国外语教材理论体系构建**[J]，**《外国语》**（06）：20-32。

摘要：外语教育是个生态系统。教材开发与编写是外语教育过程中重要的一环。教材是实现学科教学目标的载体与途径。在中国教育体系中，教材不仅仅体现课程方案、课程标准的要求，承载学生学习学科课程的内容，充当教师落实课程要求、贯彻“立德树人”教育方针的依据和蓝本，更是学生学习学科知识、提升核心素养的最重要的支撑与资源。因此，教材理论研究，不仅仅要研究教材的性质与特征、教材编写的指导思想、理论和实践依据，还应研究教材编写的组织实施过程以及教材使用的情况。所有这一切，都需要在充分研究外语教育生态系统特征的基础上才能进行。教材理论体系既应该包括宏观角度对教育生态系统中各参与者和重要因素间的相互关系的研究，还应该包括中观角度教材编写、评估和使用的依据和标准，以及微观角度教材的构成、内容、呈现方式等。

4. **刘艳、廖小根、倪传斌，2023，混合教学情境下对比续写的协同效应**[J],**《外语电化教学》**(04)：38-45+118。

摘要：文章构建了强化互动的对比续写混合教学模型，并考察了该模型对英语专业学习者二语写作的协同效应。结果表明：1）在语言形式层，与传统的“话题—讨论—写作—评价”模式相比，对比续写对学习者词汇多样性、词汇复杂度、句法复杂度均有显著协同效应；对句法准确度的协同效应不显著。这表明不同语言层面的协同敏感度不同，由此引发不同程度的促学效应。2）在语言修辞层，对比续写对学习者语篇中引用、排比、例证、过渡、呼应、比较和对比等修辞指标均有显著的协同效应。文章借助三元循环协同模型阐释对比续写的动态协同机制。

5. **曾罡、李贝贝、冯志伟，2023，在线同伴互评模式对英语写作同伴评语的影响研究**[J],**《外语电化教学》**(04)：54-59+120。

摘要：本研究旨在探究在线文本和语音两种同伴互评模式对英语写作同伴评语的影响及学习者对两种互评模式的态度。48名英语专业学生两人一组，利用腾讯会议的语音模式和微信平台的文本模式完成两个写作任务的互评活动。在线同伴评语按照定位问题、解释说明、提供解决方案、给予建议、称赞等五种类型进行编码、归类和分析。结果显示，文本模式的互评更多地指出问题和错误，而语音模式的互评则更倾向于给出建议、提供解决方案及称赞。学习者对在线同伴互评总体持积极态度，但相比语音模式，更喜欢文本模式，并且认为文本模式更能促进写作。该研究有助于加深对在线同伴互评的理解，为提升同伴互评的有效性、促进学生写作能力的发展提供新思路。

6. **姜晖、岳纪维，2023，学术博客评论中异议话语的共同体关系管理**[J],**《外语教学》**(04)：49-55。

摘要：学术语境下的异议话语研究多关注面子威胁和礼貌，鲜有从人际语用角度研究异议话语的关系管理。本文基于Spencer-Oatey的和谐关系管理模式，分析科学网学术博客评论中的异议话语，探讨不同形式的异议话语如何实现共同体关系管理。研究发现，评论者基于对面子、身份和社交权的关照或者忽视，采用缓和与非缓和性异议话语，并结合网络表情包、链接、语码转换等非语言形式，建构和解构学术共同体关系。本研究不仅从理论上拓宽了异议话语的研究视角，而且为数字学术语境下异议话语研究提供了人际语用研究路径。

7. **李燕、姜峰，2023，中外学者英语学术语篇词块使用的共性与特性**[J],**《外语教学》**(05)：41-46。

摘要：词块是语言地道性的重要标志，亦是连贯语篇的基石，具有明显的语域、体裁和学科特征。本研究采用语料库驱动方法，对比分析应用语言学领域中外学者国际期刊论文中四词词块的使用特征。结果表明，中国学者比英语母语学者更依赖于使用词块来构建学术语篇，基本遵循以of-短语为主的学术写作惯例。结构上，中国学者偏重于小句类词块，而英语母语学者更倾向于短语类词块。功能上，中国学者侧重文本导向词块，以推理、因果和对比标记功能最为突出，而英语母语学者更倾向于研究导向功能，尤其是描述功能词块的使用。研究还发现中国学者学术文本呈现出大量特有词块，这与中西文化差异、英汉两种不同语言以及学术传统有着密切的关系。研究发现对中国英语学习者的词块习得和学术英语写作教学有一定参考价值。

8. **高莉**，2023，**英语学术语篇视角的主观性探析**[J]，**《外语教学》**(06)：37-42。

摘要：人类有从不同视角观察问题的能力，任何语篇都是作者从特定视角对事件识解的结果，体现其主观性。此识解过程包括三个层面的认知互动：所描述事件的知识内容层面、附加在知识内容上的说话人自我表达层面以及说话人与听话人的认知协作层面。英语学术语篇中，论文作者选取特定视角表达学术观点、交流研究成果，其视角主观性可以区分为常态主观性、显性主观性和隐性主观性，这为理解英语学术语篇背后的认知机制提供了统一阐释。

9. **杨姗姗、束定芳、王蓓蕾**，2023，**高校外语教师教育者在教材编写中的专业发展研究**[J]，**《外语教学》**(06)：49-55。

摘要：本文采用个案研究法探析7名高校外语教师教育者在教材编写项目中的专业发展情况及其影响因素。通过半结构化访谈、教师反思和文本资料采集数据，采用文本分析法进行数据分析。研究发现，外语教师教育者的专业发展体现在理论自觉、实践自觉、共同体自觉和身份自觉四个主要方面。影响因素包括个体、项目机制、学术机构和宏观因素四个层面。最后，基于研究结果提炼出高校教师教育者有效专业发展项目框架图。本研究对于教师教育和培训项目设计具有一定的启示意义。

10. **屠国元、李志奇**，2023，**论译者的写作过程**[J]，**《外语教学》**(06)：71-78。

摘要：本文试从翻译学角度描述译者写作过程的特殊性、一般性与创造性。译者的写作过程是翻译的输出环节。就笔译而言，它是笔头作文；口译而言，是口头作文，且均为命题作文，是决定翻译结果优劣的重要环节之一。译者的写作是双语转换时的目的语写作，其过程具有原语写作的一般性，因为译者是通过对原文本的解读，用目的语表述原文所蕴涵的意义，其过程同样要遣词造句与布局谋篇；译者的写作过程有其特殊性，其原因是译者的写作过程受到更多因素的制约，包括原文本、译者的阅读质量、译者的写作能力、目的语文本的语境等。译者的写作过程有其创造性，因为译者是脱离了原文本的个体存在，有其主体性和能动性。

11. 苗佳、姚委委，2023，书面纠错反馈对英语写作语法准确度影响的元分析研究 [J]，《外语教学理论与实践》(04)：50-61。

摘要：本文探索了书面纠错反馈对英语写作语法准确度影响的总体效应和调节效应，研究结果表明书面纠错反馈对英语写作语法准确度有显著中等程度的正向影响。同时，书面纠错反馈对英语写作语法准确度的促进作用受到学习者的教育层次、反馈类型、反馈范围、反馈时机以及反馈来源等调节变量的影响。基于研究结果，就书面纠错反馈对英语写作语法准确度的影响及其发生作用机理进行了思考，为英语写作教学的有效设计与实施提供借鉴和参考。

12. 张慧、林正军、董晓明，2023，生态语言学观照下气候变化新闻语篇中的态度资源研究 [J]，《外语教学理论与实践》(05)：44-54。

摘要：本研究基于生态语言学视角，结合气候变化论域下的生态哲学观，借助对美国气候变化新闻语篇中态度资源的考察，探赜其呈现出的生态理念与生态价值取向，以此鼓励有益性话语，改善模糊性话语，抵制破坏性话语。研究发现：气候变化新闻语篇中态度资源的三个子类使用频次的排序依次为判断资源、鉴赏资源和情感资源；气候变化新闻语篇中的态度资源分别呈现出有益性生态取向、模糊性生态取向和破坏性生态取向。本文通过探析美国气候变化新闻语篇中的态度资源，检视出“美国至上”“经济优先”等有违生态和谐的理念。

13. 杨凯、王俊菊，2023，国际传播视域下的二语写作能力培养 [J]，《外语教育研究前沿》(03)：41-46+94-95。

摘要：百年未有之大变局下亟须加强国际传播能力建设。本文立足新时代语境，梳理国际传播的新需求，分析外语教育的新使命，探索二语写作的新功能，思考二语写作能力培养的新思路。笔者认为，为了实现讲好中国故事，传播好中国声音，展示真实、立体、全面的中国的对外传播目标，外语人要具备能讲、善讲中国故事的国际传播能力，二语写作也要承担起讲述中国故事、传播中国文化、提升我国国际传播效果的社会政治功能。当下，二语写作要面向国家战略需求培养人才，在培养目标、课程体系、教学内容、教学评价、教材编写等方面均需加强。

14. 武尊民、梁燕婷、王子倩，2023，高校英语对话式日志写作的教育教学意义探究 [J]，《外语教育研究前沿》(03)：47-55+95。

摘要：对话式日志写作是一种自由写作形式，是写作课程或语言学习课程常用的教学活动。近几十年来，国内外学界对对话式日志写作做了不少研究，并发现持续的写作训练对不同年龄的学生，以及对英语为母语或外语的学生都具有积极作用。笔者在教学实践中发现，对话式日志写作不仅有助于提升学生的英语写作能力，还具有独特的教育功能。本研究通过分析学生写作，探究学生在对话式日志写作中展现的思想活动及思维能力的发展。对话式日志写作能促进师生互动。教师反馈在促进学生英语写作能力发展的同时，发挥教书育人、教育立德树人的重要作用。

15. **张琳涛、杨鲁新，2023，高中英语教师写作评价素养现状的个案研究**[J],**《外语教育研究前沿》**(03)：64-72+96。

摘要：本研究采用质性个案研究方法，通过收集多种数据，基于Lam (2019) 和Xu & Brown (2016) 提出的分析框架，对两位高中英语教师的写作评价素养现状进行了深入探究。研究发现，教师写作评价素养呈现复杂性与情境性特征。丰富的写作评价实践性知识帮助教师获得了较高的自我效能，树立了以评促学的评价观念，使教师对写作构念有了较为正确的认识。受制于学生人数、考试频次等特定情境因素，教师的评价情绪较为负面。在实践方面，两位教师主导了评价实践，但都努力利用评分标准、学生范文等评价资源来促进学生的元评价认知发展，积极践行以评促学理念。本研究对外语/二语教师写作评价培训的设计与开展具有重要启示。

16. **于书林、朱文蕾、张海霞、梁承刚，2023，二语写作话语视角下高校英语写作课程建设和教学**[J],**《外语界》**(04)：42-48+90。

摘要：现有二语写作研究主要关注写作文本特点、学生写作能力发展、写作教学方法、写作反馈与评价等方向，鲜有研究从宏观角度探讨二语写作课程设计与开发。本文以Ivaniĉ的写作话语框架为理论基础，探讨了技巧性话语、创意话语、过程性话语、体裁话语、社会实践话语、社会政治话语六类写作话语及其教学观，并通过对二语写作课程话语实证研究的分析，结合我国高校英语写作课程现状从写作课程建设、写作教学、写作课程和教学研究三方面提出相应建议。

17. **王乐、王晓涔、张宇驰，2023，国际多模态二语写作研究及其发展趋势**[J],**《外语界》**(04)：49-55。

摘要：多模态二语写作是国际写作研究的前沿领域，对赋能二语学习者数字素养发展具有重要作用，但尚未引发我国学界充分讨论。本文在界定多模态二语写作内涵与特征的基础上，从研究论题和研究方法评述相关研究。分析发现，多模态二语写作研究涵盖写作教学的实践探索、写作过程的影响因素、写作文本的语类特征、写作产品的评价方法等论题。研究方法主要包括个案研究法、准实验法、问卷调查法和访谈法，定性研究占主流。文章进而展望了多模态二语写作研究的发展趋势。

18. **刘永厚、龚子晴，2023，研究问题的类型与逻辑——基于学术新手与专家英语学术论文的对比研究**[J],**《外语界》**(05)：31-39。

摘要：研究问题是确立研究目标和设计研究框架的基本依据，具有重要研究价值。本研究以应用语言学领域的450篇英语论文为语料，自建学术新手与专家语料库，对比分析了两类群体研究问题类型与逻辑的异同。研究结果显示：1）学术新手与专家语料中，研究问题类型的频次均按“描述性问题>关联性问题>对比性问题>解释性问题>规范性问题”顺序排列；2）专家在研究问题的层级合理性上显著优于学术新手，学术新手的研究问题构建能力随着学习阶段推进逐步提升；3）符合层级逻辑的研究问题包含同阶平行、依序递进和平行递进三种组合模式。

19. **林正军、黄丹**，2023，**“续论”的互文性框架及其教学应用**[J]，**《外语界》**(05)：49-55+72。

摘要：“续论”认为语言通过“续”学会，“续”促进了语言理解和产出的互动，达到高效促学的效果。本文构建了“续论”的互文性框架，认为“续论”教学的有效性源于语篇互文性的多重互文关系，包括语篇实例与语境知识的互文、续写语段与给出语段的互文、续写语段内部的互文、语篇实例与相应目的语语篇的互文以及目的语语篇与母语语篇的互文等。这些互文关系促成了续任务中的多重互动，确保了“续论”教学的有效性。基于“续论”互文性框架的教学应充分利用互文关系，加强给出语段的理解和学习，提高续写语段产出的质量，减少母语对续作产出的负面影响。

20. **周杰、王俊菊**，2023，**续论促学效应及其调节变量的元分析**[J]，**《现代外语》**(04)：490-501。

摘要：续论的促学效果已为大量研究所证实，但其总体效应却缺乏统计验证。本文运用元分析方法整合续论相关实证研究，验证其整体促学效应和调节变量的调节作用。结果表明，续论的整体促学效应量达到中等水平，主要调节变量按效应大小依次为目标语言、任务类型、体裁类别、外语水平和外语能力。上述发现证实了续论促学机制的有效性，对续论促学效应的进一步优化具有启发作用。

21. **郑咏滟、李慧娴**，2023，**复杂动态系统理论视角下二语写作发展的变异性研究**[J]，**《现代外语》**(05)：650-663。

摘要：本研究基于复杂动态系统理论，采用两种变异度计算指标，对39名中级水平英语学习者一年间的写作数据进行回归分析和聚类分析，旨在探究写作发展中的变异度与写作水平提升度间的关系，从而揭示二语写作水平动态发展的内在模式。结果显示，在初始水平相同的情况下，差数标准差这一变异度指标可以显著正向预测写作水平的提升度。以初始水平、变异度和写作水平提升度为变量的聚类分析揭示了四种书面语发展模式，在高度相似的子集内部也验证了“变异预示发展”的规律。上述发现丰富了复杂动态系统理论的变异性研究。此外，本文基于研究结果，探讨了如何透过表面上繁复芜杂的发展波动数据揭示发展模式，从“遍历合集”的角度为探究个体路径和群体模式的波动搭建了接口，回答了发展过程中的遍历性问题。

22. **李绍鹏、于涵静、胡越竹、葛现茹，2023，二语水平和隐喻类型对二语写作隐喻产出过程的影响[J]，《现代外语》(05)：664-675。**

摘要：本研究考察二语水平和隐喻类型对二语写作隐喻产出过程的影响。利用键盘记录软件Inputlog 8.0收集学习者写作活动的在线数据，结合刺激性回忆与访谈，对隐喻产出过程中的停顿行为进行分析。结果显示：1）不同水平学习者在二语写作隐喻产出过程中的停顿行为存在差异，高水平组在停顿频次和时长上均显著高于低水平组；2）不同隐喻类型对停顿行为产生不同影响，相较于传统隐喻，学习者产出新奇隐喻时的停顿时间更长，频次更高；3）二语水平和隐喻类型对隐喻产出过程的影响存在显著的交互效应，高水平组产出新奇隐喻的停顿时长高于传统隐喻，低水平组在两类隐喻产出的停顿时长上不存在显著差异。研究结果对二语写作教学具有启示意义。

23. **何莲珍、姜子芸，2023，考生工作记忆对综合写作测试表现的影响[J]，《现代外语》(06)：817-828。**

摘要：本研究聚焦读听写结合的综合写作任务，探究考生工作记忆对其综合写作测试表现的影响，包括文本特征和写作得分两个方面。研究以64名考生为对象，以听力广度、运算广度和阅读广度任务为工作记忆容量指标，以托福考试总分为二语水平指标，提取考生作文的文本特征，包括词汇复杂度、句法复杂度、准确度、流利度和源文本使用，并通过三位评分员的整体评分得出考生的综合写作得分。结果表明：1）考生的工作记忆容量与词汇复杂度、准确度和源文本使用显著相关，与句法复杂度和流利度的相关性不显著；2）考生的工作记忆容量对写作得分没有显著的直接影响，但通过二语水平有显著的间接影响。研究结果深化了我们对综合写作测试构念的理解，为综合写作测试分数的解释和使用提供了效度证据。

24. **吴佳健、熊建国、郭丽琳、何静、梁雨倩，2023，《中国日报》拐卖儿童新闻话语表征的历时研究——基于立场名词的及物性分析[J]，《解放军外国语学院学报》(04)：77-85。**

摘要：通过自建拐卖儿童历时新闻语料库（2001—2022），本研究对立场名词的小句环境进行了及物性分析，探究了拐卖儿童“涉事者”的话语表征和表征变化。研究发现，话语表征形式体现意义选择、立场表达、社会现实和读者影响，又受其制约。如“政府话语”中，新闻作者倾向于用物质、言语过程及事件和方式名词建构“中国政府打拐”语义，体现政府保护人民的决心和作者对打拐的支持，引导读者关注拐卖儿童问题。此外，相比2001—2008年，2009—2022年作者更多地使用物质过程和事件名词建构“中国政府打拐”语义，其动因是其间拐卖儿童问题仍然严重，政府因此开展更多的行动，媒体和群众则给予更多的关注。

25. 杨颖莉、靳光洒，2023，任务复杂度、构思方式及语言学能对二语写作产出的影响 [J]，《解放军外国语学院学报》(04)：110-118+161。

摘要：任务复杂度和构思方式是影响二语写作表现的重要因素。本研究以英语专业大学生为研究对象，探究任务复杂度、构思方式及语言学能对二语写作表现的影响。结果显示，任务复杂度与构思方式对限时二语写作的词汇复杂度有显著交互效应。此外，在完成复杂度较低的任务时，在线构思组语法推断测试分数与词汇复杂度呈显著负相关；词汇语法构思组语法推断测试分数与准确度呈显著负相关。在完成复杂度较高的任务时，在线构思组语法推断测试与写作准确度呈显著正相关，词汇语法构思组语音辨别测试和语法推断测试与词汇复杂度呈显著正相关。

26. 燕浩、张艺、赵琪、段绪，2023，自主学习能力影响学术英语阅读与写作——来自眼动的证据 [J]，《解放军外国语学院学报》(06)：96-103+127。

摘要：本研究采用眼动技术探讨自主学习能力对中国理工科大学生学术英语阅读与写作能力的影响。结果发现：高自主学习能力者阅读/写作能力显著高于低自主学习能力者，其阅读时的总注视次数、总注视时间、重读时间显著少于低自主学习能力者；写作时其平均眼跳幅度高，而回视次数、总注视次数低于低自主学习能力者。阅读显著正向预测写作，高自主学习能力负向调节阅读对写作的影响。研究表明自主学习能力越高，学生认知加工效率越高，更善于内化并运用文献阅读信息创造性地完成学术写作。

English Abstracts

Digital Multimodal Composing in a Second Language Context: A Scoping Review of Research .... (1)

Emily Di ZHANG, Shanghai Jiao Tong University, China
Chunhong LIU, Simon Fraser University, Canada
Shulin YU, University of Macau, China

Abstract: Given that digital multimodal composing (DMC) has received increasing attention from researchers and teaching practitioners in second language (L2) learning contexts, this study employed the scoping review method and explored the overall landscape of the current scholarship on L2 DMC. Following a constant comparison approach, three themes emerged from the literature: (1) the "learning" of DMC; (2) the "teaching" of DMC; (3) the "assessing" of DMC. Discussion on the thematical and methodological issues in the current DMC research was presented, and directions for future research were discussed. This review could deepen our understanding of L2 DMC by sketching out what and how current research has found about DMC, and it also illustrates the learning and teaching affordances embedded in DMC practices.

Keywords: digital multimodal composing; scoping review; educational technology; research synthesis; writing instruction

Conversations Around Translingual Practice in EAL Writing Education .... (18)

Li ZHANG, Yushan Middle School
Yachao SUN, Duke Kunshan University
Ruiyun SUN, Northeast Forestry University

Abstract: This review explores the increasingly popular concept of translingual practice within English as an Additional Language (EAL) writing education. While translingual practice has been advocated for promoting linguistic and cultural diversity and encouraging writer agency, it also raises concerns related to theoretical understandings, ideological acceptance, and pedagogical implications. Confusion between translingual and L2 writing, resistance to dominant language norms, and potential negative impacts on students' academic success have all been highlighted as key issues. Through a critical examination of these benefits and concerns, this review emphasizes the need for further refinement of translingual pedagogies and more empirical research on their effectiveness. Recognizing these issues can contribute to a more inclusive and equitable approach to writing instruction that values the linguistic and cultural diversity of all students.

Keywords: translingual practices; EAL; writing education; benefits; concerns

Pingping HU, Zhejiang Normal University
Yuqin WANG, Zhejiang Normal University

Abstract: This paper employs CiteSpace to carry out a bibliometric analysis of L2 writing anxiety studies published in domestic journals in the CNKI database from 2013 to 2022 and draw relevant scientific knowledge maps of L2 writing anxiety studies. The results show that the number of L2 writing anxiety studies published in domestic journals in the past ten years has shown an M-shaped fluctuation trend, and there is much room for development; the research institutions of the core literature are mostly normal universities; the core research areas mainly include writing instruction, writing competence, writing performance, teacher feedback, anxiety expressions, etc. Future studies should attach more importance to creating a core academic community, expanding the scope of research objects, and enriching research content.

Keywords: L2 writing anxiety; feedback method; writing instruction; visualized analysis; bibliometric analysis

Xi YANG, Changzhi University

Abstract: Second language writing research is an important research content of foreign language teaching with clear research fields and research methods. Recently, writing teaching research has gradually formed a complete professional network from the original relatively discrete state, among which teaching strategies of second language writing research is one of the most essential research topics. Combined with the application of "dual-line" teaching in the epidemic era and the emergence of a large number of English writing aid software boosted by big data and artificial intelligence, it is of great significance for the field to study the choice and effectiveness of teachers' teaching strategies under the background of "mixed teaching". This study conducted a one-semester action study in the writing class of sophomore English majors in an independent college in Taiyuan, taking the Postmethod pedagogy as the theoretical framework to explore the development and change of teachers' teaching strategies under the background of "mixed teaching". It was found that using the macro-strategy of the Postmethod theoretical framework to empower teachers to integrate and adapt writing teaching strategies has a significant effect on improving students' writing levels. Among them, the cases of the higher writing level develop their writing performance steadily, and the cases of lower writing levels make the most significant progress. Through thematic analysis, the research concludes with factors influencing students' writing levels: individual differences, environmental factors, and task factors for future study and second language writing.

Keywords: English writing; teaching strategies; action research; postmethod pedagogy

Chinese-English Academic Writing Practice from a Biliteracy-Informed Genre Perspective .... (61)

Ningyang CHEN, Soochow University

Abstract: The competition of talents in the new era compels us to think of ways to cultivate in students the ability to function in both native and foreign languages, as well as the ability to participate in national and international knowledge construction with sufficient understanding of the local and the global modus operandi. To balance the current efforts to aid the use of English as an international academic lingua franca, there is a pressing need to direct attention to the largely dismissed research and teaching of the development of Chinese as a native language for academic purposes. From a biliteracy-informed genre perspective, this article explores the bilingual academic writing practice of L1 Chinese L2 English novice authors, including scenarios of practice, genre knowledge, and the application thereof. Results show that novice authors are expected to deal with a variety of scenarios and genres, among which L1 Chinese plays a significant part. The authors' genre knowledge is found to be less comprehensive and systematic than is required. Their L1 academic writing practice features imitation and a mixture of genre features, whereas their L2 academic writing practice involves comparison and borrowing. Based on reflections on current practice, the article also discusses genre-based pedagogical practices for developing local students' bilingual academic writing skills. These practices are intended to improve students' academic biliteracy in preparation for their effective participation in national and international knowledge construction.

Keywords: a biliteracy-informed genre perspective; genre knowledge; academic writing; Chinese; English

Construction and Effectiveness Verification on the Teaching Model for Critical Academic English Writing .... (72)

Qiong WU, Fujian Normal University

Abstract: *The College English Teaching Guide (2020 Edition)* assigns significant importance to the teaching of academic English. At present, many domestic universities are implementing reforms in college English education, incorporating academic English into their college English teaching systems. This study, grounded in the cognition of conventionality, sociality, contextuality, dynamism, and openness of academic English, undertakes critical academic English writing teaching for doctoral students from the perspective of cultivating critical thinking abilities. It involves three rounds of empirical research to verify the effectiveness of this teaching model in enhancing doctoral students' academic English writing skills. The research reveals that (1) employing critical skills to reflect upon, investigate, evaluate, and question the conventional features of academic English, (2) using critical standards to assess academic discourse, (3) engaging in critical thinking disposition to carry out social practice academic writing, (4) prioritizing the construction of social practice significance, the development of authors' academic identities, and the enhancement of learners' critical thinking abilities as primary objectives in college English teaching for doctoral students, can not only effectively alter students' traditional perceptions of English learning, but also strengthen students' logical thinking and academic expression abilities, thereby cultivating students' academic English literacy, and build their personal academic identity.

Keywords: academic English; critical thinking ability; teaching for critical academic English writing

Jing ZHANG, Shantou University
Fan FANG, Shantou University

Abstract: English writing centers have gained scholarly attention in China in recent years as a promising means to supplement traditional English writing instruction. To address the lack of empirical research on Chinese writing center praxis, this study collected 388 sets of survey responses, four writing center tutorial recordings, and four post-tutorial retrospective student interviews at a Chinese Normal university with the aim of examining Chinese college students' writing center usage and perceptions in light of their self-perceived needs for English writing support and writing-related help-seeking behaviors. Our study revealed the following: (1) The surveyed Chinese students perceived strong needs for English writing support for various types of writing, yet their writing-related help-seeking did not match their expressed needs. (2) Only a small portion of students reported having heard about or used the writing center, and tutorials tended to focus more on global issues than local issues. (3) Students perceived their writing center experiences as being positive, highlighting individualized tutorials as a dialogic space that helped them acquire transferrable writing knowledge. Pedagogical and research implications are offered for those who hope to provide students with individualized writing support in Chinese higher education and to contribute the Chinese voice to the international writing center community.

Keywords: writing centers; student needs on writing; writing support; writing tutorial

Jin YANG, Nanjing University

Abstract: Writing anxiety has long been a concern in the field of second language acquisition. Previous research suggests that collaborative writing can help alleviate writing anxiety, but they have been limited to general English writing and primarily focus on pair-based collaboration. The specific role of collaborative learning in foreign language learning, especially its impact on students of different proficiency levels, remains debated and requires further investigation. This study introduced collaborative learning into classroom instruction for workplace English writing. Pre- and post-tests, as well as interviews, were conducted to collect data on foreign language writing anxiety and proficiency changes in both the experimental and control groups. Data analysis revealed that collaborative writing created a supportive atmosphere, providing emotional support for learners and increasing interaction among learners to complete writing tasks together. Interviews revealed that not only weaker students benefited from collaborative writing by improving their writing proficiency and reducing writing anxiety, but average and high-achieving students also acknowledged the effectiveness of collaborative learning. The findings of this study provide insights into how the collaborative learning model can help reduce writing anxiety in writing instruction.

Keywords: writing anxiety; collaborative writing; workplace English writing

Yu DU, Shandong University

Abstract: In the context of the information age, second language (L2) writing is increasingly integrated with cutting-edge technology, and its effectiveness needs to be urgently tested. *Technology in Second Language Writing: Advances in Composing, Translation, Writing Pedagogy and Data-Driven Learning* explores this cutting-edge topic through multiple research perspectives, covering different aspects like machine translation, online feedback, and multimodal writing. It focuses on the application together with the effectiveness of the current mainstream technological tools in the field of L2 writing by methods including scoping review, case studies, and corpus studies. Relevant studies demonstrate that the application of technological tools in the teaching of L2 writing is conducive to the enhancement of learners' language competence, and it also has a positive impact on the development of their critical thinking skills and genre knowledge. For researchers, the use of technological tools can effectively broaden research horizons and ideas. This volume provides important implications for the application of technological tools in writing teaching and research.

Keywords: second language writing; technological tools; writing teaching and research

征稿启事

《二语写作》是国内第一本关于二语写作教学与研究的学术集刊。由中国英汉语比较研究会写作教学与研究专业委员会主办，山东大学二语写作教学与研究中心承办，外语教学与研究出版社出版，编辑部设在山东大学外国语学院。本刊已被中国知网（CNKI）数据库收录。

一、办刊宗旨

《二语写作》重点探讨二语写作理论、写作修辞、写作教学、写作教师教育、写作测试、ESP/EAP写作、机辅写作、技术与写作等相关领域的研究问题。本刊接受中、英文稿件，欢迎不同语境下的研究成果，除英语外，亦刊登非英语和对外汉语等领域的二语写作研究成果。本刊倡导理论创新，关注研究方法，强调学术的高度、深度和厚度，尤其注重跨学科视角下的研究与探讨，旨在为我国二语写作研究学者、教师和研究生提供学术交流的平台，推动我国二语写作教学与研究的发展。

二、重点栏目

本刊设有"理论视角""写作研究""写作教学""写作测评""跨学科研究""研究述评""新秀论坛""学术动态""新作评介"等重点栏目，真诚欢迎国内外专家、学者和广大外语教师及研究者赐稿，稿件语言中英文均可。

三、稿件要求与投稿说明

1. 来稿应具有科学性、原创性，论点鲜明、论据充分、数据准确、逻辑严谨、文字通顺、图表规范。每篇论文以8000字左右为宜，最多不超过1万字，中英文均可。

2. 来稿请详细注明作者简介、作者单位、地址、邮编、联系电话及电子邮箱。稿件不涉及保密问题，署名无争议，稿件一律文责自负，本刊有权对来稿做文字修改。

3. 本刊恕不退稿，请作者自留底稿，切勿一稿多投。

4. 请不要把稿件邮寄给个人，以免影响审稿和发表。

5.《二语写作》实行同行专家匿名审稿制度。审稿周期为三个月。三个月后，若没有收到编辑部反馈，作者可自行处理。

6.《二语写作》不收版面费。稿件发表后，赠送作者当期样刊两本。

四、投稿方式

投稿邮箱：writing-journal@sdu.edu.cn

五、联系方式

地址：山东省济南市洪家楼5号山东大学外国语学院《二语写作》编辑部

邮编：250100

电话：0531-88375183

Chinese Journal of Second Language Writing Guide for Authors

The *Chinese Journal of Second Language Writing* is devoted to publishing reports of research and discussions that contribute to understanding of issues in second and foreign language writing and writing instruction. Areas of interest include L2 writing instruction, L2 writer development, features of L2 written texts, L2 writing processes, L2 writing teacher education and professional development, feedback and assessment, ESP/EAP writing, technology and writing, and any other topics closely relevant to L2 writing instruction and research. Review articles are considered for publication if they deal with critical issues in second and foreign language writing. Manuscripts should take care to emphasize the pedagogical implications of the work.

Before submitting your manuscript, make sure that your submission adheres to the author guidelines and follows the formatting instruction. Please pay particular attention to the reference section, the formatting of headings, tables, figures, and author's biography.

Formatting and references

1. Length

Manuscripts should be 8,000 to 10,000 words in English or Chinese, including references, tables, figures, notes, and appendices.

2. Headings

- *CJSLW* uses only three header levels. Format them as follows:

1. First Level Heading (Size 12, Boldface, First Letter Caps)

1.1 Second level heading (Size 10, Boldface)

1.1.1 Third level heading (Size 10, Italics)

3. Tables

- Please submit tables as editable text and not as images.
- Tables should be numbered consecutively with single numbers, e.g. Table 1, Table 2, Table 3 ...

4. Figures

- Figures should be numbered consecutively with single numbers, e.g. Figure 1, Figure 2, Figure 3 ...
- Both tables and figures should be referenced in text and be placed next to the relevant text.

5. Keywords

Up to 5 key words are required upon submission. Only abbreviations firmly established in the field should be included.

6. Acknowledgements

Please submit the acknowledgements after your paper is accepted.

7. Funding sources

Authors are required to identify who provided financial support for the conduct of the research and/or preparation of the article. List funding sources in the following way:

Funding: This work was supported by Grant Name [grant number].

8. Author biography

This part includes author's full name, title, affiliation, research interest(s) and email address. Please clearly indicate who is the corresponding author if there are more than one author.

9. References

List your references by following the format shown in the examples.

Examples:

Atkinson, D. 2002. Toward a sociocognitive approach to second language acquisition [J]. *The Modern Language Journal* 86(4): 525-545.

Creswell, J. W. 2013. *Qualitative Inquiry and Research Design: Choosing Among Five Approaches* [M]. Thousand Oaks, CA: SAGE.

Friedlander, A. 1990. Composing in English: Effects of a first language on writing in English as a second language [A]. In B. Kroll (ed.). *Second Language Writing: Research Insights for the Classroom* [C]. Cambridge: Cambridge University Press. 109-125.

Jiang, Y. 2000. The Tao of verbal communication: An Elementary textbook on pragmatics and discourse analysis [OL]. http://www.polyu.edu.hk/~cbs/jy/teach.htm (accessed 30/04/2006).

Whalen, K. & N. Ménard. 1995. L1 and L2 writers' strategic and linguistic knowledge: A model of multiple-level discourse processing [J]. *Language Learning* 45(3): 381-418.

Robertson, M., M. Line, S. Jones & S. Thomas. 2000. International students, learning environments and perceptions: A case study using the Delphi technique [J]. *Higher Education Research & Development* 19(1): 89-102.

Authors are requested to submit their papers electronically by using the *Chinese Journal of Second Language Writing* online submission web site (https://eyxz.cbpt.cnki.net).

If you have further questions, please contact: writing-journal@sdu.edu.cn.